Everett L. Freed
1601 Pennsylvania St. Unit H-08
Albuquerque, NM 87110

River of Lost Souls
(A HISTORICAL NOVEL)

by

Everett Freed

Bloomington, IN Milton Keynes, UK

authorHOUSE®

AuthorHouse™
1663 Liberty Drive, Suite 200
Bloomington, IN 47403
www.authorhouse.com
Phone: 1-800-839-8640

AuthorHouse™ UK Ltd.
500 Avebury Boulevard
Central Milton Keynes, MK9 2BE
www.authorhouse.co.uk
Phone: 08001974150

First published by AuthorHouse 7/24/2006

ISBN: 0-7596-2533-6 (e)
ISBN: 0-7596-2534-4 (sc)

Printed in the United States of America
Bloomington, Indiana

This book is printed on acid-free paper.

PROLOGUE

(April 1921, Grand Junction, Colorado)

Monroe Morgan picked his way through a rain-slick alley in south Grand Junction. He was on his way to a whorehouse on Pitkin Avenue with a half-gallon jug of booze under his arm. He operated his whiskey distillery in the basement of Grand Junction's Vinegar Works. He'd been Superintendent there before Prohibition. Now, with prohibition in full swing, his still was making money hand-over-fist.

In the dark alley, he strained to see the rain soaked earth beneath his feet. His heavy hobnailed boots slipped into—and out of—deep wagon ruts. He tripped over fist-sized rocks and smiled at himself for doing so.

However, fear of breaking the glass vinegar jug under his arm, made him think he'd try another route next time. But, in the meantime, he'd look for landmarks—a unique streetlight, a special tree, or a peculiar bush—just in case he did decide to come this way again.

Off in the distance, he heard a woman scream. A man's guttural yell followed the woman's wail. Hushed, he listened. Must be some happy couple having a spat, he thought. Halting, lingering and listening, he considered his own thumping heart.

Taking a new grip on the valuable container, he stepped out of the alley into the street and glanced in both directions for signs of life. A black cat crossed his path half a block ahead. Streetlights hung from wires that attached themselves to tall intersection poles. Silence everywhere.

He turned west toward the railroad tracks while scanning the nearest house for a street number. Finally he glimpsed number 518. Every house on either side of the street had a screened-in porch.

The same woman screamed again. Her anguish jarred him. He twisted around. Sonuvabitch! They're up ahead. Not far, either.

He weighed the possibility of a policeman being on the scene. That wouldn't be good. But then, the idea was far fetched.

Monroe noticed that the houses all sat back about twenty-five feet from the sidewalk and there were no fences. As he checked the streetlight at the intersection, he glanced into the night sky beyond the light, and saw a full moon rising. His breath faded into the cold air. A loud cracking sound snapped his gaze back in the direction of the noise. He saw a house with every light lit. An unforgiving, nasal-bellow boomed from a man's throat. "You'll do exactly as I tell you!"

"But Sam! Why can't I go to the movies by myself?" Monroe considered the woman's question and it didn't seem out of line.

Sam's low-pitched voice sneered. "So, my little Greaser wants to vamoose by herself does she?" The voice lowered to a growl. "You'll do what you're told, you bitch. You're lucky to be living with a white man." Concern moved Monroe closer. He stopped in front of the house.

Sam continued. "On second thought, Bonnie dear, I'll give you an outing you won't forget."

Monroe heard a loud tromping on hardwood. He peered through the open window. A big sandy-haired fellow strode across the room. The woman was probably hidden in a corner. Monroe turned away, starting to move on, but a high-pitched shriek interrupted him. "Don't touch me, you bastard. If it weren't for Harold, I'd have left you long ago."

Looking back, Monroe saw a struggling redhead being carried to the front door. She thrashed the air, groaned, and wriggled. Tried to scratch the man's face. The door wouldn't open.

"Don't put me outside, Sam! I can't leave Harold!"

Sam tossed Bonnie's small body into the air, grabbed her around the waist as she came down, and pinned her tight against his chest. "Oh, you'll go all right, Mrs. Bonnie Isgar. You'll go into the night—alone."

Sam's left hand unlocked the door. He bumped Bonnie's head, arms and legs against the jam as he forced her onto the porch. Juggling her to the screen door, he hurled her into the yard. She stumbled across the stoop, lost her footing, and tumbled onto the cement walkway leading away from the house. Huddling at the bottom of the steps, Bonnie moaned.

Monroe saw Sam staring in his direction—obviously surprised to find a stranger in his yard. Suddenly, Sam turned back into the house and slammed the door. A lock clicked.

Monroe watched Bonnie struggle to her knees, then sink back on her heels. He set his package near a small tree, turned toward the stricken woman, hesitated and wondered whether he should take a hand. Thinking she might be hurt, Monroe walked toward her.

After a few hesitant steps, he stooped to grasp her arm. She recoiled, hissing like a wildcat. "Get away from me, you bastard!"

Monroe jumped back.

"Oh! I thought you were … him." She ducked her head toward the house, sobbed, and then looked up.

The light from the moon and the house flooded over Bonnie. Monroe saw a lovely face, twisted with pain, smeared with dirt, and wet with tears. Her tangled dark hair glowed with red-highlights and contrasted with milk-white skin. Torn clothes sagged. He peered closer. She was … very special.

"Who are you?" she gasped."

He extended an open hand. "I'm sorry. I didn't mean to frighten you. I only wanted to help."

"No man scares me—least of all, him. If I was bigger, he wouldn't throw me around, either." She pulled her disheveled clothing about her body, bowed her head, and cried like a lost child in a thorny thicket. Monroe removed his jacket and cautiously placed the coat over her shoulders.

One by one, every light in the house went out. Only the corner streetlight and the moon remained. A breeze swirled and a baby cried.

Monroe stepped to the tree and lifted his bundle. "Do you have family ... friends?"

"No."

Monroe hesitated, and then asked, "Where does a woman go when her husband throws her out?"

Bonnie looked lost. "I don't know. I went to the church last time."

"St. Joseph's?"

"Yes."

He helped her to her feet. The moon revealed her eyes. Neither guile nor design appeared in those limpid pools. He gazed while moments passed. Her eyes stared back. Finally he said: "Goodnight."

"Goodnight," she said, quietly handing him his jacket.

Monroe forced himself to turn away. Drifting down the street, he heard Bonnie shout, "Sam, please let me in. Harold is crying."

"Go away. Go wherever you want. My son stays here with me," Sam returned.

On his way to the next corner, Monroe stopped and turned around. He hesitated. Listened. Nothing.

Long before Monroe reached the whorehouse on Pitkin Avenue, he felt his gut grab like it had never grabbed before. He felt lost ... lonesome. "You fool!" he said, aloud. "Don't get involved. Move on down the road."

A wise old owl on the tree branch above his head, said, "To who? To who?"

CHAPTER ONE

September 1922, Durango, Colorado

When Monroe's sleeping body jerked awake, he realized a bedbug was sucking blood from his chest. He refused to open his eyes. Acknowledging pain wasn't part of his disposition, and after three nights in this bedbug-infested house, he'd learned to expect bites. This kind of irritation was child's play compared to what he'd endured recently, so he remained still. He'd concentrate on other things, he thought—like starting another day. First though, he'd evaluate the world around him. That brought him to Bonnie and her son in the bed with him. If he had to petition God for something, he wanted Bonnie to have <u>their</u> baby today. That, of course, wasn't his main goal in life. Not even close. Although, all his hopes, all his ambitions, had to do with Bonnie. She was more precious than anything else in his miserable world. She was his only happiness.

Nowadays, he started everything with caution. This urge for prudence hadn't always ruled his life. Indeed, before he met Bonnie, he'd often slept carelessly until noon, or later, if he chose. His early years had been worry-free. He often thought that being an only child with affluent parents had made him "slightly spoiled." But he'd never worried about that, either.

He had taken life pretty much as it came, trusting in his own abilities to arrange a proper outcome for whatever happened. But the last year had changed all that. Extreme caution was his watchword now.

For the moment, however, he'd simply listen to the sounds around him, smell the air, get a sense of how he felt physically, and begin to plan the day.

Laying on his right side, his body in a fetal position, Monroe became aware of Bonnie's back spooned warm and tight into the curvature of his own torso. His right arm cradled her head in a way that allowed her long, wavy hair to flood the pillow and spill onto his face. His left arm stretched downward across her breast and lay lightly on her stomach, large with child. Suddenly, the baby moved. Monroe's eyelids fluttered and opened—almost. His breathing halted entirely. He contemplated the life at his fingertips while his own restricted breath began to move in and out again. Would the baby be born today?

Outside the one-room house, Monroe heard the wind, full of rain, smash itself against the north wall, drenching the window and squeaking the old boards. How much pounding could this dilapidated shack take? Then, rhythmically, like thousands of tiny fingers extending from a giant's palm, the rain pelted the old walls. He could hear a huge cottonwood tree digging its branches into the small tack room, which sat between the house and the barbed-wire corral. The corral, between the house and the Animas River, held his mules and his saddle horse.

This was no ordinary rain—too late in the year to be seasonal, and much too heavy to be normal. The deluge had been falling for more than a week, on and off. The Animas River had reached flood stage two days ago. He had no idea how high the river's crest might be today—certainly higher than yesterday.

Monroe remembered that the worst flood in Durango's history occurred in 1911. That had been named the "100 years flood." It destroyed bridges, roads, houses and fields, all up and down Animas Valley. Of course, the "city fathers" hadn't done anything to keep the river from doing the same thing again.

Suddenly, In the Good Old Summer Time began to hum its way through his mind. Though Monroe dreaded the idea

2

of winter, he supposed it wasn't the worst thing that could happen. He made no effort to stop the song. He simply turned to thoughts about how difficult the coming winter months could be: to how much trouble might be added to their lives as a result of bad weather. Winter sure as hell wouldn't make things easier.

Bonnie Isgar, the exciting young woman beside him, nudged closer. Probably making room for Harold, her eighteen-month-old son. Almost on cue, Harold wriggled restlessly. Probably hungry. Poor little devil. The running and hiding they'd been doing wasn't Harold's fault. But it was his father who'd been doing the chasing. Harold couldn't help being born to an abusive father, like Sam Isgar.

Monroe's mind turned to his precious Bonita Jean Gunn, Bonnie's maiden name. Her Spanish mother called her Bonita, and her Scottish father called her Bonnie.

It was a lucky thing that Bonnie, a Catholic, had married Sam Isgar, a Protestant, before a Justice of the Peace in Grand Junction, because now a divorce would come easier. At least, the Church wouldn't stand in the way.

Sam had never concerned himself with Harold, or Bonnie, for that matter—until she left him. Now, Monroe believed, Sam had people all over the state looking for, as Sam put it, "his beloved son and his two-timing wife."

Though Monroe continued to keep his eyes closed, he became aware of lightning so bright it lit the one room shanty and penetrated his eyelids. Thunder rocked buildings across town until church bells swung in their steeples and issued mournful tones that floated like weary specters beneath the clouds and above the earth, never stopping, just fading away. Storm sounds scattered violence up and down the valley, bumping into mountainsides and sliding away into the dark distances. Finally, silence settled within the tiny house.

Monroe Morgan kissed the soft skin behind Bonnie's left ear, and eased his body from beneath the warm covers.

He pulled his long-john-covered-frame to a sitting position on the side of the bed, braced himself, and set his bare feet on the cold floor. Sliding his hand between the buttons down his chest, he crushed the bedbug as he pulled it from its feeding place. He squeezed the pest extra hard and tossed it to the floor. Squinting into the darkness, he noticed that daylight was filtering into the room. No real surprise. Rising early was something he'd been doing for several months.

Two steps from the bed, he tested the old Majestic stove by placing his right hand on the boiler. Finding it warm, he moved his hand closer to the iron lids that covered the firebox. He believed there were enough live coals to ignite kindling. So, he put two pieces of wood and four chunks of fresh coal into the firebox. The resulting fire would amply heat the small room. He blew a long, but steady, breeze under the fresh wood. The wood lit.

Lightning tore the morning darkness aside. Instantly, crashing thunder ripped the sky above the house. Monroe reached for his matches, turned to the kerosene lamp and lit it. Bonnie mumbled something indistinguishable. Little Harold seemed to be asking about the "fire." Everybody was awake!

"What'd you say, Honey?"

"These bedbugs are driving me crazy!" Bonnie sat up in bed, legs akimbo and threw the bedclothes from Harold's young body. She pulled his nightshirt over his head and inspected his diapered physique. "They're in this old mattress, maybe in the floor cracks, and the walls ... under the wall paper."

Monroe felt her pain. "I poured kerosene in the floor cracks yesterday."

"I know. Give me another diaper, will you?"

Monroe rummaged through a laundry basket on the floor. As he handed Bonnie the soft cloth, he reflected on the curious fact that Bonnie was wide-awake and sitting up. She wasn't known for early rising. Maybe she knew something he didn't about the length of her term.

"Are you all right?" he asked, as he noticed the soft whiteness of her skin that contrasted with the warm richness of her hair. Mesmerized, he turned to retrieve his pants from the back of a chair.

"I feel fine." Bonnie laid a damp diaper at the foot of the bed. She folded the exchanged cloth into a triangle. As if to punctuate her "fine" statement, she began to hum aloud—the same tune that haunted him. He loved to hear her sing.

Monroe slipped into his black wool trousers and grabbed a white dress shirt. "Know something funny?" He flung the shirt over his shoulders and tried to glimpse his reflection in his shaving-mirror.

Bonnie looked up expectantly. Monroe said, "I've had 'the good old summertime' running through my head all morning. Think we're both looking for warmer weather?"

Bonnie slid out of bed. "We've got a lot to do before summer arrives, and we'll have a swell time doing it if this rain doesn't stop." She yanked her tiny, bare feet back from the cold floor, then, replaced both feet determinedly and raised her five-foot-three-inch form to a vertical position. She stripped her long flannel nightgown over her head revealing her body, splendid and shapely in motherhood.

Monroe's gaze never wavered. He marveled at her graceful, rhythmical movements. He'd searched all his life for this wonderful woman, and hadn't even realized he was looking for her. Again, he remembered that fateful night in Grand Junction, at moonrise, while on his rounds delivering booze. She had been literally thrown from her house onto the sidewalk in front of him. Then, when he'd tried to help with her struggles, he'd fallen head over heels in love with

5

her. But miracle of miracles, she had fallen in love as well. And now, every day, every night, and every moment in between, they fell deeper in love.

Overwhelmed, Monroe moved closer to her. He touched her bare shoulders and pulled her nearer. "Have you any idea how much I love you?"

"Just a smidgen less than I love you, I think." Bonnie smiled and leaned her warm body against his hairy chest.

"I doubt it, Bonita. I loved you first, you know."

"Only because the pain in my knees distracted me. Of course, I couldn't see your face, either. The moon had risen behind you, and my eyes were full of tears. I'll always begrudge you that moment, Roe." Her eyes sparkled in the pale light. Her dark-auburn hair accented the pink eagerness of her oval face.

They gazed into each other's eyes, each smiling happily. Content to be in each other's arms. Confident that their love would stand the test of time. They kissed, softly, gently. Their cares seemed to recede as the day dawned.

Gently, Monroe stepped back, pretending extreme seriousness, and said, "I've got to go to the outhouse." With quick gestures to the pot under the bed, he said, "You can use the thunder-mug!" The urgency of the moment gave him no relief as he shoved his feet into his overshoes, slipped his yellow slicker over his head, and buckled his belt while heading for the door.

Bonnie's cheerful voice reached him as he banged the door. "Don't fall in the mud."

* * *

When Monroe returned, steam rattled the teakettle's lid. Bonnie continued to dress.

Monroe picked up his straightedge razor, strapped it, and checked his appearance in the round mirror he'd hung beside the stove. Warmth filled the room. After brushing his hair straight back, he parted it in the middle. Then with every lock in place, he shined his high-topped shoes, placed a pink sleeve-holder at each elbow and tucked the white shirt collar under, so he could shave.

"Fastidious, Roe. That's what you are. The word fits you to a tee." Bonnie's happy smile exuded appreciation.

"Is that all?" Monroe pressed.

Bonnie thought momentarily, then said, "No, not really. You are honest. Almost as honest as my father, and that's saying something. Now don't continue to fish."

Monroe grinned. "Oh, I get it. You want me to let everything go—my beard, my shoes, everything—and lie to you, is that right?"

Bonnie stepped close, placed a balled fist under his chin, and kissed him on the mouth. "Not on your life. I love you just the way you are."

Forty minutes later breakfast was over. Through the meal, Monroe hadn't noticed a change in Bonnie's demeanor, nor had he heard anything unusual as they conversed. But, while washing dishes and making the bed, Bonnie's actions alerted Monroe to a new agenda she seemed to be establishing. She had something on her mind. He waited for her to speak.

While he waited, he realized that Bonnie hadn't taken her usual sip of Grand Junction distilled brandy. She hadn't touched her pipe, or the brandy, before or since breakfast. It was important medicinal stuff, she'd said, and now, she wasn't making the slightest move in the direction of her pipe or a second cup of coffee.

Bonnie's movements seemed more fidgety. Then, abruptly, without a word, she fixed a bottle for Harold, set the dirty clothes bag and three packing boxes around Harold on the bed, reached for her hat, crammed it on her head, and began putting on her rubber boots.

"Where're you going?" Monroe wanted to know since he'd dedicated himself to caring for her. Now, no matter where she went or how long it took her to get there, he intended to support her and protect her all the way.

"I've got to go outside. This house is getting the best of me. I need some fresh air. Want to come?"

"Sure. I think it'd be neat to get some fresh air. Muddy, but neat." Monroe reached for his jacket. "It looks like the rain has stopped for a while. How about Harold?"

"He's got his bottle and his rattle. I've got him pinned in. We won't be too long."

Monroe moved quickly. "I'll put on my overshoes and bank the fire."

Thunder rumbled far up the valley as Bonnie moved toward the door. The tiny house on Roosa Avenue shuddered.

Monroe moved in front of Bonnie, threw open the door and led the way by jumping from the doorsill to the ground. He turned to take Bonnie's hand while she crossed the rotting step that made entrances and exits difficult.

The yard's surface was firm. It gently declined toward the river that rushed beyond the corral east of the house. The compacted black Mancos shale had spilled onto the property when they carved Roosa Avenue out of the hillside west of the house. The hill, covered with tight groves of scrub oak, banked steeply up to a large grassy meadow dotted with huge ponderosa pines. There, among the lush grass and the majestic trees, Durango buried its dead. They called the quiet slope, Greenmount Cemetery.

Monroe continued to reassure Bonnie that they weren't alone in Durango. "Mother will be here early, I think. About 10 or 10:30 this morning."

"She's wonderful, Roe. It's a long way for her to come, though. I hope I don't disappoint her."

"Only five miles. She enjoys her buggy ride, and she'd be the disappointed one if we didn't include her."

Bonnie smiled her appreciation. "Let's look in the tack room. I bet there aren't any bedbugs in there."

"It's crammed with stuff that doesn't belong to us. I was barely able to hang the mule harnesses and get my saddle inside. Not much room left over."

The steady footing quickly turned to slippery, old, blue mud. Monroe grabbed Bonnie's arm. "Hang on to me."

Glancing into the corral behind the tack room, Monroe observed his two black mules, Jack and Jinni. They seemed to be mesmerized as they gazed at the swollen river. Chukaluks, Monroe's big sorrel stallion, sidestepped nervously and raised his white-splashed face as they approached. Chukaluks whinnied at the two people moving about his yard, but the mules ignored their human master and concentrated on the river. They may have been more concerned about the shrinking corral space, and the potential for the land to be usurped by the water.

The lowlands across the river seemed to be converting into a wide lake. A large tree, floating down from the north, had entangled its roots into the corral's barbed wire fence that dived into the water. The fence was threatening to come loose and go down the river with the debris.

"Roe, let's not bother. I know there's no room in there for me. We can't set things outside." Bonnie craned her neck as she evaluated the haystack beyond the tack room.

"What are you looking for?" Monroe's curiosity was reaching outer limits.

Bonnie turned quickly to the right, skirted the big freight wagon they'd driven all the way from Grand Junction, and strode toward the corral gate.

Monroe followed with arms outstretched, hoping he'd catch her if she slipped. The fence stopped her as she grasped a large post and allowed her body to lean heavily against it.

"Now what are you doing?"

"I'm looking for a place to have our baby. I won't stay in that house." Her eyes searched the corrals northwest corner. "It's dry under that lean-to—in the manger."

Surprised, Monroe jerked his head toward the manger. "Honey!"

From somewhere high in the western mountains, deep thunder rumbled, then rolled down the canyons and dissipated in the chill wind from the north. A train engine near the roundhouse gave one long toot that let everyone in Durango know the morning train to Silverton would soon be at the depot to take on passengers.

Monroe gazed at the lean-to. His stomach churned. He turned away. Why hadn't he found a house without bedbugs? Did he agree to rent the house, too quickly? He wondered if he'd been careless at this sensitive time. He gazed again at the manger. A long, wide manger, full of fresh timothy hay, nestled in a sheltered corner by the tack room and haystack—all dry.

"Honey, I don't know."

"I think so," she replied.

* * *

By the middle of the morning, the weather had taken a definite change for the better. The only weather-question in Monroe's mind was about how long it would stay clear. The dark storm clouds were gone. A brilliant sun warmed the hills, the trees, the town and the little white clapboard house on the bank of the Animas River. Great patches of azure sky appeared where scudding white clouds fluffed their edges, bumped gently into each other, rebounded, and floated away. The Rock Wrens and the Magpies obviously hadn't gone south, because they danced and chirped among the giant box elder trees, which lined the river on both sides.

These small, gay creatures acted as if they'd been given a new lease on life and a great celebration was in order. They were a symphony.

* * *

Later, at river's edge, Monroe, with a long two-by-four, tried to push free an entangled tree that threatened the fence on the corrals northern side. The struggle helped him calm himself. He was spending time trying to get used to the idea that Bonnie would move into the corral—specifically, the manger. And no sooner had his mind reconciled the manger-idea, than he began to wonder how he'd break the news to his mother.

So intense were his thoughts about the tree and the manger explaining, he missed his mother's arrival. The raging river had limited his hearing, and he hadn't been able to see Roosa Avenue from his position under the riverbank.

Long before he was ready for the meeting, he heard Bonnie's voice from the top of the bank. Glancing up, he saw Bonnie standing in the sun with his mother beside her. His mother held Harold in her arms. Both Bonnie and Anna smiled while Harold waved his arms trying to reach a tree branch, which swayed nearby.

"Hello, son."

"Hello, Mama. Let me give this thing a couple more shoves. It just may go on down the river."

Monroe wondered if Bonnie had told his mother about the manger. He knew Anna wouldn't accept the idea easily. But then, his mother wasn't like every other mother in Animas Valley, either. She'd been back and forth between Durango and Pittsburg, Kansas several times, always in a wagon. She knew about having babies in inconvenient spots because she'd had children born on those trips. All had died, though, except Monroe and three girls. He was hoping Anna wouldn't fuss about a grandson being born in a manger near downtown Durango. But, being deeply religious, she might see sacrilege in Bonnie's plans. God knew neither he nor Bonnie had planned to be a modern day Mary and Joseph. They weren't hypocrites, either. They could go to the hospital, but Monroe thought the hospital was too public and someone might report the fact to Sam Isgar.

Since Anna was smiling and happy, maybe Bonnie had broached the subject and resolved the whole situation. He couldn't tell by looking. Monroe purposely averted his eyes because he didn't want his mother to see his searching gaze.

Anna had already tried to persuade them to stay at her Cascade Ranch, but Monroe felt the ranch was the first place Isgar would look. Sam might have already assigned one of his Klan's people to spy on the place.

Anna hunched down and peered over the bank. "What are you trying to do?"

"I want to get this tree unhooked and move it on down the river before it tears the corral down and I lose my stock."

"Why hell, son," his mother shouted against the roar of the river. "You're goin' about it all wrong. You can't push it away from the fence with that danged two-by-four. The current's too strong."

Analyzing the sound of his mother's voice and considering the fact that she was talking about the offending tree, Monroe was able to determine that Bonnie and Anna had discussed the manger proposition. He also concluded that his mother had accepted the idea—at least tentatively. She might not like it, but she'd help, and there'd be nothing else said. Maybe.

"Ma," Monroe shouted in objection to her argument. Here he was twenty-nine-years old and his mother was still telling him what to do and how to do it. His dear father,

Henry Morgan, had often said, "Listen to your mother, Son." And now that his father was gone, he wanted to honor his father so he practiced listening to his mother.

Anna Morgan crouched atop the riverbank, waggled her head back and forth to get a better look at the problem.

"Why hell, son, if you want to get that tree away from the fence, you'll have to pull the log back up river and separate the two. Once you get 'em apart, you can get your two-by-four on the tree and push it around the end of the fence, then let the darn thing float on down the river."

"Ma. I thought I had it moving a minute ago."

"I can see you didn't. Those barbed wire marks on the roots tell me the tree hasn't moved much. I'd be surprised if you moved it at all. You sure won't clear the fence that way."

Monroe gave up. "Okay, Ma. What do you think I should do?"

"Get one of those mules out here. Bring a rope and a singletree. Lasso that branch sticking up over there, then wrap the rope around a tree and pull the whole thing back up river. You've got a rope haven't you?"

"Yes, Ma—and a chain, too, if I need it. I brought everything along in case I got stuck on the road from Grand Junction." Monroe wondered why he hadn't thought of his mother's idea in the first place. He climbed away from the river.

Standing on the riverbank, towering over his mother, Monroe glanced at the sun, made the time to be about eleven o'clock, and helped his mother to her feet. She was too thin, he thought. She had never been heavy, but she'd always stood tall and straight, making her look more slender than she was. Most people said she had a ramrod for a backbone. But when folks got beyond the stern face and the graying hair that had been tied in a tight knot at the back of her head, they invariably found a gentle lady with a heart that went out to everyone. "Have any problems coming in from the ranch, Mama?"

Anna cast a searching glance at her son. "Why, would I? Charlie harnessed old Blue and hitched him to the buggy. I just sailed down the valley like a golden leaf off an aspen tree."

"I thought the storm might've washed the roads out, here and there."

"Nope. The road's fine. Your father didn't build any roads to be washed out. Any way, I think the rain's over."

Bonnie stared at Monroe. "Who's Charlie?"

"He's my right arm," Anna said. She smiled and turned quickly to Monroe. "When Monroe isn't home."

"He's my best friend," Monroe said, gazing at his leather gloves. "I guess, we should explain a little. He's very unusual."

"Always has been," Anna said, her voice trailing off softly.

"People call him 'One-armed Charlie,'" Monroe said. "I should have told you about him before. A horse fell on him in a rodeo accident and he lost his left arm about four inches below the shoulder. The accident didn't stop him; he wouldn't allow that. He chops wood. Uses a shovel. Rides like the wind, fights, makes love, everything except eat with his left hand."

"But you say people call him 'One-armed Charlie,' why do they do that?" asked Bonnie, curiously.

"Because he's Indian, I guess. Navajo."

Bonnie's face lit. "Oh! How wonderful! I've never met an Indian."

"You'll meet him. He's something special, isn't he Mama?"

Anna nodded emphatically. "Very."

"Okay. Tell me why he's special."

Monroe hesitated, but he enjoyed Bonnie's curiosity. "Well, he's tall, for one thing, and most Indians aren't. He ties his black hair at the back of his neck with some red rag. All Indians have black hair and black eyes, but not many men wear their hair in a bun with a red cloth tying it down."

"Yes, yes. But how can he do all those things with one hand?"

"I don't know. Why don't you can ask him when you get to know him better?"

"What do you think, Mama? What intrigues you about Charlie?"

"Oh, the way he dresses, I guess. He generally wears a black, flat-brimmed Stetson with a leather thong under his chin. He wares dark-colored shirts, blue or black, with a light-brown leather vest. The vest has red and white beads sewn in different little patterns. Then he wears beaded ties, beautiful turquoise jewelry, bracelets, rings, and buckles. He's something."

"Sounds like his clothes cost a lot of money."

"Well, he has money. And his family sends him money. Also, he has what he earns," Monroe said. "He's never broke. His mother weaves special Navajo rugs for him. She beads his gloves and vests. Don't ever worry about Charlie, Honey. But, Mama, I wanted to ask you, why didn't you drive the Ford? It'll just sit and rust, if you don't drive it."

"You know I won't drive that darn thing. I don't like to crank it. I'm going to sell it, if you don't want it."

It had been five months since the death of Monroe's father. Monroe was proud to see his mother bearing the burden so gracefully. Hearing her talk about the car without crying meant Anna had made great progress since her dear Henry departed. Happy inside, Monroe put his arm around her slender shoulders, squeezing her against his chest. "I love you, Mama, and, if I haven't said it before: we appreciate what you're doing for us. Don't we, Honey."

"We really do."

"Why hell, son, it's nothing." Anna turned toward the street. "Now, Bonnie and I are going for a little walk up the road here. Not far. But, while you finish what you're doing and get started on the corral, we're going to talk about having a baby, tonight."

15

That was the first positive knowledge Monroe had had about the baby being born tonight. "Okay. I'll unharness Blue and put him in the corral."

Monroe gazed after the two most important women in his life and realized that coming to Durango had been a masterstroke. Counting his blessings, he turned toward the corral, and Bonnie, Anna and Harold picked their way toward Roosa Avenue.

* * *

Later that day, the sun cast long shadows in the corral. Monroe, without his jacket, but still wearing his white shirt, pink-satin sleeve-holders, and black derby hat, carried Harold toward the manger. Bonnie leaned against a stanchion that supported the shed's slanting roof. She seemed tired. He stepped over a pile of horse-manure and came to a stop while noticing a blaze of sunlight reflecting on Bonnie's auburn hair. Harold struggled to escape. Monroe let him down, but maintained a grip on the youngster's hand.

"Is the famous dancer and singer, Miss Bonnie Jean Gunn, going to be comfortable here?" Monroe gestured in the direction of the manger.

"I will," Bonnie said emphatically. "But from now on, dear sir, I'm just plain old Bonnie Morgan." Bonnie frowned and tilted her head upward. "I don't want to talk about any other names." She gazed across the river to the city. "It's so wonderful out here, Roe—with you, in the fresh air, listening to the river." Her hand gripped his arm. "I love this river. It makes music like the dance music in the Chautauqua. Being here is like dancing, singing, and playing the piano, all at the same time!" Bonnie's enthusiasm built with every word.

Anna busied herself arranging the bed on the fresh timothy hay that filled the manger. Bonnie leaned against Monroe as they moved closer to the manger.

"Why hell, Monroe!" Anna's strong voice boomed across the corral, "are you really going to let Bonnie have that baby in this manger?" Her rigorous gestures as she went about her bed making, disguised her sixty-seven-years of age, as did her strong physique.

As Monroe carefully stepped through the manure, which covered the ground, he glanced first at his mother and then at Bonnie. Bonnie hugged his right arm and Harold clung to his left. His mother's, handsome face reflected nothing but gentleness and forgiveness.

"Is there any reason we shouldn't have the baby here, Mother?" asked Monroe, glancing at the western sky and noting the fading daylight. He shifted Harold to his right hand when Bonnie leaned herself against the side of the manger. "The house is crawling with bedbugs," Bonnie pointed out.

"But, but … ." Anna sputtered.

Considerate, but still determined, Bonnie interjected from her position near Monroe's elbow: "As I said, I'd much rather be outside in the fresh air, Mother Morgan. It'll be a lot more comfortable." Then summoning a brighter tone, Bonnie said, "Besides, I want the city lights at my feet and the night around me. Not that old house."

"In a corral with horses and mules?" Anna persisted.

"I'll get their halters, Ma, and tie them to the opposite side of the corral," said Monroe.

Anna stood with hands on hips, facing up-river toward Animas City. Monroe saw his mother out-pointed but unconvinced. She appeared to evaluate the weather and the time of day, and then turned down-river toward the smelter. She sighed. "You better get your tying done, before dark. And while you're at it, rake a wide path through the corral … from the gate to the manger. I don't want to dodge road-apples all night. Clean-up around the manger, too." Anna walked toward the house.

17

Bonnie ignored the tension engendered by the exchange with Anna and turned her back to the low side of the elongated trough. "Let me try my bed. The timothy <u>smells so good,</u> Roe! So fresh and clean."

Bonnie's hands reached back testing the bed's resiliency. While smiling at Monroe, she heisted herself to the edge of the manger and tumbled backward. "You'll have to help me out." She laughed and aligned her body with the length of the structure.

Monroe pushed his hands into the feed by her head. "Think I should add some hay? Build it up?"

"Oh no, Roe. It's wonderful. See," she said pointing. "I'm almost even with the sideboards."

Harold began to cry, quiet little complaints, but with some urgency. Monroe placed Harold on his hip and jostled him in an effort to pacify the toddler.

"If a manger was good enough for Jesus, I guess our child will be all right." Monroe smiled down at Bonnie.

Anna came into the shelter, walked over to Monroe and took Harold into her arms. "I'll take him inside and give him something to keep him quiet. He hasn't had a nap, you know. Probably wants to lie down."

Anna, the matriarch of the Morgan family, was in charge again. No one wanted to change her, and no one doubted her authority. She seemed to understand that a woman having a baby gets her own way. "It's too early to put him down for the night, but what are the chances Sam Isgar will show up here tonight and raise hell?"

"Chances are slim, Mama. We're pretty sure he's in Grand Junction. We'd know if he weren't. He makes a pretty big splash wherever he goes."

Bonnie spoke, as though she hadn't heard the reference to her husband. "I know I'm making extra work for everyone, but if I'm going to have a baby, I might as well make myself as comfortable as possible."

Anna leaned over and kissed her forehead. "Why hell, don't give it another thought. You couldn't get me to stay in a bedbug-infested house, either. Just hope it's not too cold. We could get snow anytime." She started for the house, and then turned. "Everything else being equal: tomorrow I'll pour some kerosene around the house, in the floor cracks and other places. That'll help get rid of the bugs. They won't bother much tonight 'cause we won't be sleeping anyway. Come along, big boy." Anna left carrying Harold.

Monroe kissed Bonnie's forehead. "Bonita. You stay put. I'll put the finishing touches on your new room. I'll put Chukaluks and the mules on the other side of the corral, then I'll clean up around here."

Monroe felt a sudden need to hurry. The sun was sinking behind the mountains. Darkness would arrive soon. The new moon would be late, around eleven o'clock, he thought.

* * *

After securing the animals to the corral fence, Monroe raked a wide swath from the corral gate to the manger. He moved the manure away and sprinkled clean, fresh hay all around letting the hay odor take over. Approaching the manger, he noticed that Bonnie had covered herself with a blanket. "I may just sleep over there by the hay stack," he said.

From the corner of Monroe's eye, he noticed the first city lights flash bright across town. As he stared at the lights, a gentle breeze blew against his cheek. The crashing river, the sparkling lights, the burgeoning stars; all happening together as the eastern mountains faded into the darkening sky; mesmerized him. His mind slipped back to Grand Junction and that fateful night last May when Bonnie called and announced that their chance to run away had come. Sam

19

Isgar was away on business. With the news, Monroe had tied Chukaluks to the back of the wagon, hitched his mules, loaded Bonnie and Harold into the wagon and hurriedly left Grand Junction.

They had gone to Collbran first, because Monroe had thought this little out-of-the-way town might be overlooked by Sam's searching. It was during the trip to Collbran that Bonnie first mentioned Sam's affiliation with the Ku Klux Klan. That information had been a shock. It made Monroe realize that Sam had the Klan to help him search for his runaway wife. Thank God, the Klan hadn't spread its tentacles into Collbran and their life had been happy. However, neither Monroe nor Bonnie had planned on her pregnancy. Collbran wasn't a good place for a woman to have a baby, so they'd traveled to Delta.

The Klan was active in Delta. It was active in Montrose and Ouray, also. The Klan seemed to be everywhere. Monroe had began to wonder where they might go and remain undetected? Finally, he decided on Durango. At least, he could expect help from his mother and his friends.

Now, most everyone knew he was in Durango, but no one outside his family knew he had Bonnie and her son. Monroe and Bonnie wanted to keep it that way, if they could. Certainly, until Bonnie's divorce was final. One thing for sure, they couldn't run again until Bonnie and the babies were able to travel.

Bonnie touched his hand. "What are you thinking?" She gazed intently at Monroe as he stood beside her bed.

Monroe turned his full attention on Bonnie. "I'm thinking that I'm not sorry for any of the things we've done together." Leaning down, Monroe placed a long, lingering kiss full on her mouth.

"Why do you love me so much?" Bonnie asked.

Monroe thought for a second. "Because you're real … and you're muy bonita."

"Sure, I'm real." Then, giggling, "You'll have to explain the other."

"Well, Honey, have you ever noticed on a brilliant fall afternoon, how the sun shines through the golden aspen leaves?"

"Yes," answered Bonnie.

"It's so beautiful it's almost unreal, but it really is real, isn't it?"

"Yes," of course, said Bonnie.

"You're, like that. You're like sunlight through golden leaves."

"Oh, Roe," said she.

Monroe watched Bonnie slowly turn her face away and saw a tiny tear run across her nose. He stooped and kissed her ear.

Somewhere in a narrow-leafed cottonwood down by the river, a mourning dove cooed. Lights from the city shimmered in the night.

"Are you comfortable in your new bed?"

Bonnie scooted up in her bed. "I can't remember being more comfortable, or more happy. And it's all because of you. But, maybe I should get up and dress for tonight?" She made no move, however, to leave the manger and Monroe didn't urge her. They held hands gazing at the lights.

Finally, Bonnie asked, "Can you hear my soul singing?"

"I can hear the breeze in the trees along the river. I can hear the rivers roar. Is that your soul?" He smiled ducking low to kiss her nose.

"No, silly. That's just the wind and the water. My soul is something else. Something between us—you, me and God." She hesitated. "But considering the size of my sins, I'm surprised my soul can still sing." She raised herself to an elbow. "But, oh Roe, I'm so happy! I can't understand my happiness. By tomorrow, I'll have brought another child into a very scary world. I've broken Church sacraments and sinned against God."

21

Monroe gripped her hand. "We both want to continue our religious practices, but, it seems, living keeps getting in the way."

"I guess ours is a difficult religion, even in the best of times. We haven't made it easy for ourselves, either."

Monroe waved his hand at the night. "Don't think about it, Sweetheart. We'll make it right as soon as we can."

"I didn't intend too make a mess of things. I'm sincerely sorry for offending God." Bonnie spoke just loud enough to breach the whispering wind. "I haven't lost my faith. I believe in His forgiveness."

Monroe struggled to think of something to say—something that would make Bonnie feel better. He fell silent.

Soon, he began to think of the business at hand. "Not many women would want to have their baby in a corral that's perched on a flooded river bank."

"What does Animas mean, Roe?"

"The river used to be El Río de las Ánimas Perdidas. 'The River of Lost Souls.' That's what the early Spaniard's called it when they first came here. Now it's just plain Animas River ... soul river, I guess.'"

"River of Lost Souls," Bonnie repeated, staring at the city lights. "That could include us."

"I don't know. I hope not."

The mournful sound of a train whistle split the quiet valley. The sharp interruption signaled the arrival of the evening train from Silverton. Bonnie's hand gripped his fingers. He knew she had experienced a contraction. "That busy little stream starts high in the mountains to the north and cuts deep canyons all the way to the desert. Once there, it meets the San Juan River, and they flow together to the mighty Colorado. From that point, they all go hand-in-hand to the sea."

Monroe bent low, kissing Bonnie's forehead. "Are you all right?" he asked.

"Yes. I'm getting some pain in my back, though. You better get your lanterns lit and start picking a name."

"Okay. I'll tell Mother."

When Monroe headed for the house, Bonnie said: "Just a minute. You know what I wish?"

"No. What?"

"I wish you'd prop me up, get me a sip of brandy, and give me my pipe."

"That's right," said Monroe recalling the day, "you haven't smoked your pipe today, have you?"

"No. I didn't want to for some reason. But get it and we'll smoke together."

"Okay. Be right back." Monroe hurried to the house trying to think of what he might have left undone. Nothing came to mind. Plenty of firewood to heat the stove—Mama resting—hot water simmering—clean towels and string all laid out and waiting. He'd made his bed between the haystack and the manger. Bonnie couldn't make a sound he didn't hear.

He hurried back, lit both pipes and gave Bonnie hers. "Here's your brandy," he said.

Bonnie puffed a couple of times then sipped her drink. They sat quietly smoking as time passed. "The lanterns brighten the place a lot," she finally said, as she knocked her pipe against the manger. Burning ashes fell from the bowl.

Monroe watched the sparks fall to the ground and twisted them under his boot. The animals snorted, tugged at their ropes then lazily munched the hay that had been pitched near the fence. Not a breeze stirred.

* * *

Next morning at 3:35 A.M., the lusty cry of a nine-and-a-half pound boy rent the air along the Animas River near downtown Durango. The birth was trouble-free. Monroe had a name ready.

23

"I want to call him Wade, Wade Morgan."

Anna looked surprised. "Who for? Bonnie's family? There's no one in our family named Wade."

"You know ... Wade Templeton, Ma."

"Oh for God's sake!" Anna scoffed. "Not him. He's the town drunk."

"I know, Mama, but he's also the happiest man I know. And I want my son to be happy."

"Do you want him to be a drunk?"

"No, Ma. Just happy."

"Wade it is," Bonnie interjected with a tired but firm voice, "Wade Matthew Morgan."

Monroe glanced at Bonnie. "Why Matthew?"

"My father. Matthew Gunn."

* * *

Before the sun found its way into Animas Valley, Monroe knelt in the Catholic Church giving thanks for a healthy son and praying that he'd find work. Minutes later, he drove his wagon to the main office of Wood & Burnside where he saw a large crowd filing through the front door. Probably men seeking jobs in the transportation business, he thought. With plenty of room at the curb, Monroe parked his rig, climbed down and followed the last man in line.

Herbert Wood, a sloop-shouldered, balding man, with his left hand full of papers, approached the long counter that separated the waiting room from the office space behind the rail. Monroe had often seen Herbert around town. Even knew him slightly, due to the years his father, Henry Morgan, had done business with Wood & Burnside. Henry had been a staunch union man and had made several attempts to unionize the transportation business in Durango. All efforts failed.

24

Monroe believed Herbert Wood to be ten years his senior. But since Herbert had never played baseball, ridden in rodeos, or worked outside his father's business, Monroe didn't really know the man.

As Herbert's gaze passed from man to man, Monroe counted twenty-three applicants and realized that landing a job wouldn't be easy. "Now fellows, I wish I had jobs for all of you because I know most of you are good, steady workers, but the fact is, I only need one man with a team and a wagon that can haul at least one ton of coal. We're gonna' bring coal out of Porter in Wildcat Canyon and The City up Lightner Creek. We're laying in our supply for winter. How many of you have wagons? Raise your hands." Monroe put up his hand while he glanced around the room. A fellow he didn't know, on the far side of the room, lifted his arm. No other hands went up.

"Where's your outfit, Andy?" Herbert Wood asked the man who raised his hand.

"I can have it here by ten o'clock."

Herbert looked at Monroe. "Is that your rig outside?"

"Yes, sir."

"Then, I'm going to take you, Morgan. Stay here a minute. And the rest of you—thanks for coming—I'm sorry. Come back when we put out another call."

While the men filed out, Wood moved to a desk in the back, scribbled something on a note pad and came back to the counter.

"First name's Monroe, isn't it?" Herbert didn't wait for an answer. "I want you to go down to the yard, get an order from Wes Taggart there and try to make two loads today. Can you do that?"

"Yes, sir."

"How much does your wagon carry?"

"I can haul two tons pretty easy—three if I push it. I'll push it when the roads are good and the hills aren't too steep. Most of it'll be downhill from the mines along Lightner Creek."

"All right. We have a contract with Porter and The City. We'll pay three dollars a day plus two dollars for each ton of coal you bring in. Fair enough?"

"Yes, sir."

* * *

Monroe felt his heart pound as he drove to the coal yard. He thought he could surely haul four tons a day— make two trips. Eleven dollars a day, total. Not bad. He wondered how long the job would last. Well, he'd do his best, regardless. After all, he was a father now and he was lucky to find work.

Minute's later in the coal yard Monroe met Wes. He picked up his orders and drove toward the west gate. Looking southwest across the river, he noticed a long column of smoke clouding the sky. His jaw dropped. "My God!" he breathed. "That smoke's coming from our house."

Straining his eyes, he struggled to see. "Hell! It's the haystack! No. It's the dammed house!"

He wanted to whip the mules toward the gate, but the turn was too tight. He'd roll the wagon. His mind was a jumble. How could he get home quickest? Should he leave the team and run on foot? Was the Ninth Street Bridge still in place? He'd crossed it this morning but the river's crest was only a foot below the bridge girders. Where should he cross the river? The Ninth Street or the Main Avenue Bridge ... which? He turned the mules tight to the left and the wagon squealed unmercifully as he headed south to the Ninth Street Bridge. He reached his whip. Was Bonnie okay? Had they all gotten out? "Get up Jack!" The whip cracked over the mule's head and the wagon rolled faster.

Monroe jammed his foot near the brake, leaned forward, and strained to see the fire through the trees on both sides of the river. The mules galloped toward the bridge. The smoke floating up river made him nauseous. He thought he might vomit. Agonizing, he struggled to watch the road and the house. "Come on, mules!" he yelled and swung his whip.

CHAPTER TWO

(September 1922, Grand Junction, Colorado)

In Grand Junction, Colorado, Sam Isgar entered the new Klavern he'd built for the Klan. He'd been a clever, he thought, i.e., locating the Klan's meeting room above his Golden Pheasant Restaurant's kitchen and pantry. The place provided a private room for his Klan meetings, and since it was a part of his restaurant, it was convenient for him. In addition, the room's location satisfied his desire to increase his popularity and power in the organization. In fact, he was very proud of all he'd accomplished since, Paul Unger, his friend in Denver, had invited him to meet Dr. John Galen Locke, just a year ago. He hadn't known, at the time of the introduction, that Dr. Locke was Grand Dragon of the Colorado Ku Klux Klan. However, on that occasion, Sam learned that the Klan's ideas fit his philosophy like an expensive pair of gloves. He and Locke hit it off like long lost brothers. That very afternoon, he was made Kleagle for the entire Western Slope of Colorado. He was also given a commission on each membership sold, as well as a percentage of the dues paid.

Turning his attention to the new structure he called the Klan's Klavern, Sam was struck by the smell of new lumber and fresh paint. He concluded that the odor came from the white paint on the exterior of the building and the bare unpainted boards forming the interior.

Sam began to sweat. The room's corrugated-tin roof absorbed the sun's heat, intensified it, and baked everything inside. This twenty by twenty-six-foot oven, would receive men with grievances, prejudices and axes to grind. He would address their problems and take action to resolve their gripes. Up to now, the groups he'd been organizing on Colorado's Western Slope, had practiced initiations and conducted business discussions in church basements, hotels, parks, and various other spots in their various communities. This afternoon, however, the Mesa County, the Delta County, and the Montrose County groups would meet in a place they could call their own.

A heavy wooden door hinged in the west wall. The door opened to a platform atop a stairway that ran down the outside of the building to the alley below. The stairway provided the only entrance to the upstairs room.

One tiny window in each exposed wall and two operable skylights in the ceiling provided the only other openings. The skylights tried to ventilate the place, but they also provided an uncomfortable amount of sunlight on bright days. Each of the three windows peeked into the alley, i.e., one window east, one window west and the third north. Guards posted at these points could detect all comings and goings around the Klavern. Sam didn't think he needed to guard the south side, because he didn't think any sane person would climb over the steep restaurant roof. But to make sure, he sprinkled sharp pieces of broken glass over the entire roof. The hot sun had softened the roof-tar and the glass had become firmly embedded.

Sam wanted to be elected Titan of Mesa County. As Titan, he'd be the supreme ruler of his county. Then, shortly after accomplishing that hurdle, he expected to be an Exalted Titan over the entire Western Slope of Colorado. That political base could eventually lead to his becoming Governor of the State.

When curious people asked about the new construction at his restraunt, Sam passed the room off as a second storage space and a part-time office. In truth, only the secret papers and protocols of his burgeoning Klan had ever been stored there. It was primarily a place where he kept dreams of power and glory for himself. His Klan robes, his guns, his whips and his knives were kept at home on Pitkin Avenue.

The meeting room contained a podium, twenty folding chairs, a United States flag, a wall telephone, and a stuffed armchair. The flag and the armchair sat on a woven rug behind the podium. Only one decoration graced the wall: a large picture depicting Christ praying in the Garden of Gethsemane.

Sam pushed open the east skylight, then turned and opened the west. He walked about the room, deep in thought, waiting for the hot air to vent. As he neared the wall where metal-folding chairs were stacked, he extended his hand to feel the heat from the chairs. Quickly drawing his hand back, he sucked a gulp of air and reached high over his head to stretch his six-foot-two frame. He bent forward, expelling the pent-up air, and then turned toward the stuffed chair behind the podium. Standing in front of the chair, he raised his head and let his eyes gaze over the vast crowd of imaginary followers, raised his arms and humbly accepted the thunderous applause. When the cheering had subsided, he sat, like a king on a throne, basking in the adulation heaped upon him. With grace and charm, he reached for his cigarettes, lit one, and waited for a breath of cooler air. Minutes passed while he contentedly puffed his cigarette, watched the smoke drift upward and dreamed of the day when he would rule the western part of Colorado—maybe beyond.

While contemplating the curling smoke, he heard footsteps on the stairs outside. He snapped to attention. Stood up. Stepping to the west window, he saw a large heavy-set man wearing blue and white-stripped overalls with a matching railroad engineer's cap. The man's shiny brown oxfords were at odds with the rest of his clothing.

Sam recognized Tom Niles. Tom's watery eyes shifted nervously as he searched for people who might be watching him enter the secret place. From his residence in Delta, Colorado, Tom, a newly appointed Cyclops, commanded all of Delta County. He had driven forty miles for this meeting.

Sam opened the door. Tom entered. "See me coming?"

"Of course," Sam lied. "Nobody gets close without being seen."

"I hope you're right."

Sam reached for a folding chair and handed it to Tom. "Have a seat. Everybody should be here by four o'clock. When did you get my letter?"

"Tuesday."

"Okay. It takes our mail two or three days to go forty miles."

The Delta Cyclops smiled, showing his gold front tooth, but no surprise about the mail service.

"I'm having you and three additional Cyclops attend today's session, Tom. One from Fruita and two from here." Sam sat in his upholstered chair and leaned back. "I didn't want you to send men clear over here just to perform a training mission. But, I did think you'd want to set in on this meeting and see how I organize a raid. In the future, we may have to share personnel, but this isn't one of those times. This way, you'll have some experience in organizing, if you ever want to do something similar. Every meeting or mission we accomplish right now can be considered a training session."

"I appreciate the opportunity."

"After we've finished our local Cyclops business today, I want you to stay. You and I'll have a separate meeting. I'll share a note from the Grand Dragon in Denver. Got some new material, also. Okay?"

"Swell." Tom displayed a sudden flash of memory. "You're going to Denver sometime soon aren't you?"

"Next Tuesday. I need money from the National Republican Party for my campaign. I'm determined to represent this district in the state legislature. Once I'm in, we'll have a more conservative legislative body and beat the hell out of those dammed Progressives. A bunch of Socialists, Jews, and Catholics is what they are." Sam paused to let his words sink in, and then continued. "I'm going to start practicing on Mexicans. The mountains and the bad roads that keep the Western Slope of Colorado secluded and out of touch with our eastern brethren, can help us. That territorial separation will give us a lot of latitude as we organize our part of the Klan. It'll give us the opportunity to shape things the way we want."

"You can count on me doing my share." Tom unfolded his chair and sat down.

"It's too bad we aren't a little farther along with our organizing. More people in the ranks would give me a broader campaign base."

Sam left his chair, crossed to the east window, and then stepped to the west window. "Don't see anyone yet."

Sam returned to the comfortable chair. "Speaking of organizations, Tom, you certainly have my congratulations for the fine job you've been doing in Delta County. You've done a lot of recruiting and organizing since we started a year ago. What's your latest head count?"

"I've got three dens. That's twenty-one men and their families plus four or five fellas that aren't married. All good folks from Delta and the surrounding countryside."

"That's really swell. I got one den in Fruita and three here. A Cyclops leading each den. Have you got a Cyclops for each den?"

"Well ... what's a Cyclops again, Sam?"

Recognizing Tom's need for tutoring, and praising himself for identifying Tom's shortcomings without hurting Tom's feelings, Sam began doing what he liked most: instructing people.

"Well. You're a Cyclops, Tom. You're a leader of a den in Delta, aren't you?"

"Yes. I guess so. You appointed me."

"Okay. You're the boss in Delta, County. Got it?"

"Yeah. I understand that part, but what is a Cyclops?"

Sam gazed long and hard at his recruit. "In Greek mythology, a Cyclops is a one-eyed Titan. Full Titans have both eyes. A Titan commands one or more counties and each county may have several dens, but you need a Cyclops to head up each den. Now, get this: Titans report to the Grand Dragon, and the Grand Dragon governs a State like Colorado. Dr. Locke controls all Klan activity in Colorado. He's our Grand Dragon. Get it? I want to be elected Titan over Mesa County and maybe some of the surrounding counties as well. See?"

Tom shook his head as though he were trying to erase the confusion. The words seemed foreign to him—hard to pronounce. It seemed that before he learned to pronounce a given word, he'd confuse its relationship with the person it designated.

"Well, I guess I'll learn. I just didn't understand 'Cyclops.'"

"These people are all explained in Greek Mythology. Don't worry. We'll have more meetings and iron some of these things out."

Sam and Tom failed to notice two men climb the stairway and approach the door. A loud rapping grabbed their attention. Tom jumped up, stepped behind his chair, and then moved quickly backward. Sam, holding his breath, pressed his right index finger to his lips, raised his left hand signaling Tom to stay put, and tiptoed to the west window. He could see two fellows standing on the platform. The window frame hid their faces and torsos.

Finally, Sam shouted. "Who's there?"

"Ned Benson and Fred Farley."

"They both work for me," said Sam, motioning Tom to open the door.

Sam greeted the men. "Come on in. I see we need to be a little more vigilant. Need lookouts on these windows when we have people in here. We expected you, and you still scared the bejesus out of us."

Reverend Benson extended his hand. "Sorry. Didn't try to scare you." The Minister of the Christian Church removed his hat and combed his pale fingers through his brown, curly hair. Sam knew Ned's gentle brown eyes and soft-looking skin contradicted his true nature, as well as his true intention. He looked like a schoolboy who would, if instructed, dutifully stand in a corner until given permission to move. However, Sam knew while Ned was standing, he'd be scheming about turning the tables on you and when he found the way, he'd cause you more pain than you could possibly dream.

Fred Farley owned the shoe store next door to the Golden Pheasant Restaurant. He would do what he was told. Fred was a typical shoe salesman: pliable and intent on getting more business for his shop. If he thought it would improve his business, he'd join another club. Today, he wore new shoes. One shoe squeaked.

Determined to show himself as a fair man, Sam said, "My mistake, men. I should've been watching the windows. But then, we've learned something, haven't we. Reverend, would you mind taking that north window? Keep an eye out for George Nelson. You know him, don't you? From Fruita?"

"Don't believe so."

"As soon as we get Klarogos elected, we'll have that job covered," said Sam. "But, until we do we'll … just." He gestured toward the north window. "If you don't mind, Ned, would you move from one window to the other and cover them all, as we meet. Just watch for a wiry-looking, little man. He's tough as a pine knot and as mean as hell." On numerous occasions he'd seen George Nelson deliberately place tacks upside down on the chairs of unsuspecting people, then laugh long and loud when his victim sat down on the tacks. Sam couldn't help chuckling when he remembered the pleasure he'd seen on George's face after George had made fools of several people. "The rest of us can sit and talk. You participate in the conversation, if you want Ned, but quietly. We all need to be quiet."

No sooner had the words left Sam's mouth than Ned said: "Here comes your man."

"Let him in, Fred."

When the men were properly introduced and amenities were dispensed with, Sam began his first Ku Klux Klan meeting in the new Klavern.

Standing at the podium, for a long moment, Sam waited for a hush. He looked over the heads of his recruited leaders, and wondered if they were as impressed as he was. "Gentlemen, I won't waste your time. We've talked enough about the Mexican problem in this County. Now we're going to do something about it. I've invited you Cyclops here to meet each other and take an assignment. Your assignment will take place two weeks from this coming Sunday. Between twelve and two o'clock in the morning, you'll burn three crosses in that Mexican settlement at Connected Lakes." Every man in the audience looked with satisfaction at his neighbor. "You'll find most of those greasers at home then. It'll be a strike at scum: the low lifers and the Catholics. We'll let them know that it won't be easy to get us to bow our heads and worship a foreign pope.

"I want you to experience the fact that I may not always be with you as you march for a better tomorrow. So, this time you'll be on your own. I'll be in Denver working for the good of all, and I'll be receiving reports about the good work you are doing here. You'll have your first chance to accomplish something on your own. You'll be doing something without my personal leadership. When I get back, I'll bring word from our great leader, the Grand Dragon of Colorado. I know you'll make me proud in my absence."

Fred Farley chuckled.

"What's so funny, Fred?" Sam scowled, and glared at Fred.

"Nothing, I guess. It just struck me funny that our leader would be out of town when we carry out our first real action."

"Get this straight. I'm not your leader—yet. I'm here helping you get organized. I might be your leader one-day. But, first, you'll have to elect me. Right now, I'm your Kleagle. I work directly under the Grand Dragon in Denver. If you feel this is not serious business, you can get up and leave right now. We don't need you!"

Sam watched Fred lower his eyes and turn red with embarrassment. He thought he noticed Fred's fear of becoming an outcast. It was clear that Fred wanted the camaraderie, the social acceptance and the potential edge he might accrue for his shoe store.

"Sorry, Sam. Didn't mean any disrespect."

Sam glared at his audience. "Anyone else think this isn't serious business?" Each man slowly turned his face away from Sam's stare.

"All right then. You Cyclops pinpoint the spots where you want to burn crosses. Pick places near big clusters of cardboard shacks. Find locations that are easily seen by most of those Chili-peppers. Burn three eight-foot crosses. Wear your robes. Yell your heads off and fire your pistols into chicken coups and whatnot. The chickens will raise hell. Shoot sheds and outhouses while you ride your horses through their yards. Aim high at the outhouses. We don't want to kill anyone this time. That may come later. But, I want those bastards to wake up and see crosses burning everywhere. They'll know the wrath of God is upon them. And when you leave, each Cyclops will take his men in a different direction. You'll just vanish into the night."

"Wow! That'll make 'em think!"

"No need for comments, George," Sam warned. Silence quickly fell over the smirking faces. Sam Isgar let his searing glare sweep the room. "But you're right," Sam finally said. "That'll make 'em think." He paused again to let the men contemplate the perfection of his plan.

Sam continued. "In this operation, we'll be exercising Protocol Number One. This Protocol says, and I quote: 'Right lies in Might. Freedom is an idea only. It must be noted that men with bad instincts are more in number than the good, and therefore the best results in governing them are attained by violence and terrorization, and not by academic discussions.' Any questions?"

A hesitant hand rose—part way. It was Ned Benson. Sam knew that some people, like Ned, hadn't been taught that Right lies in Might or that the best results in governing people is attained by violence and terrorization. He was aware, also, that Ned and some others might be eager to accept the idea, especially where Catholics were concerned, and, that such people might find the philosophy so interesting they could accept it and indulge it. "Where do we get these Protocols from?" asked Ned.

Pleased, Sam smiled at the inquisitive man of God. The answer to this question would give him the opportunity to show his superior knowledge. Also, the answer would further cement his control over this fast growing group.

"Protocols are handed to the Grand Dragon by the Imperial Wizard. The Grand Dragon gives them to the Titans, or in this case, to a Kleagle—that's me—I'll give them to my Cyclops—that's you. We don't have Titans on the Western Slope, yet."

"Tell us about the Imperial Wizard again." Again, Sam found Ned's question laudable.

"The Imperial Wizard commands the entire United States—every Klan in America, Ned. His name is William Joseph (Doc) Simmons. He is, by the way, a former minister of the Gospel."

"Did he write these 'Protocols' himself?"

"Good question. The answer is, no. But the protocols are something we all need to understand if we're to succeed in our objectives. And remember this: there is no question about our succeeding. Very soon." Sam came from behind his podium, leaned an elbow on the lectern. "These Protocols were written by members of a secret Jewish government. They were called Elders of Zion. The Jews laid out a plot for world domination early in the nineteenth century."

Ned stood. "Why are we using Jewish Protocols against Mexicans and Catholics?"

"Sit down, Ned. We're fighting fire with fire. We're going to take Jewish words and make Progressives eat 'em."

"Oh for the love of God, Reverend," George Nelson interrupted. "Don't you see these dammed Mexicans comin' in here pickin' fruit? Then after they're done pickin', they hang around all winter and take the jobs we all need to live on? It's them or us. I intend to see them out'a here."

Sam watched Ned shift in his seat. "I guess you're right. I just hadn't put Protocols, Catholics, Jews and Mexicans all together in one idea. I'm with you all the way. Just wanted to know. I'll bet that basement at St. Joseph's Catholic Church is full of guns."

"Listen. All of you," Sam said, glancing furtively at the windows that viewed the alley. "Keep your voices down. We don't want our first meeting raided by the Sheriff. Of course, I've got some pull there, but loud voices attract attention. Attention we don't want or need, right now."

Fred raised his hand. "Is there a law against it? I mean, meeting like this?"

Sam thought a moment. "Not really. Congress made night riding a crime after the Civil War. And the government used that law once—in 1871. We're on pretty firm ground. The thing is, we don't want to rock the boat while we're getting started. Wait until we control some important state offices. This time, we're organizing differently—not like we did after the Civil War."

"Hell," George said, as though the discussion about law was a waste of time. "You've got to accept some things on faith. You ought to know that."

Ned nodded, "That's true. The gospels require faith."

Sam smiled. "I predict you'll both fare well. You'll go far, Ned, because you ask good questions, and you'll succeed, George, because you accept things on faith. We're going to have a Klan we can be proud of. I promise you that. When we get rid of the Catholics, Mexicans and bootleggers, we'll have a decent community to live in. Let's get back to work."

The men faced the podium, sitting upright in their chairs—all except Ned, of course. He continued his duty at the windows.

Sam searched the upturned faces for faith and acceptance. Deciding he had both, he continued.

"You Cyclops will work out the details of this mission among yourselves. I mean, you decide who burns which-cross-where, and how many men you need. Everything that's necessary for the raid." Sam noticed the Cyclops exchanging glances. He guessed they were wondering how they'd ever get the job done. "Remember, I won't tolerate a breach of orders. You'll carry out my instructions to the letter. Understood?" Sam paused awaiting the nods of understanding.

The men shifted in their chairs. Ned turned his face to the side and coughed. The nods didn't come. Irritated, Sam said, "Nod your heads. Let me know you understand." They all nodded.

"Okay," Sam said. "I want verbal reports from each Cyclops when the job's done. The reports will be used to improve future actions."

The men looked at each other. Sam noticed confusion in their faces, but continued.

"Meet as often as you think necessary to carry out my orders."

George spoke with enthusiasm. "Sam, we want to do it. It's just that … we've never done anything like this before."

"I know. That's why I'm giving you latitude. You want to take responsibility, don't you?" Every man nodded. "You've all had some experience with me. Now you'll put together some of the tactics you've learned and work in a coordinated way with each other. And don't think I won't hear about your mistakes. I get information from sources you fellows don't dream of. I have friends and acquaintances everywhere. When you attack those greasers, they'll probably call the police. If police are called, don't get caught. And in any event, keep your mouth shut. If you do what you're supposed to on the twenty-fifth of September, I'll take care of everything else. Ned, you call the first planning session right away." Sam paused. After a long moment, he asked, "Is there anything else?"

"One thing," Ned said. "What happens if one of us fails … to carry out orders?"

Sam had anticipated such a question. "It depends on how much harm you do to the Klan. I can promise you, my justice will be swift and unstinting. A small punishment could be ridicule before Klan members. A medium sized punishment could be a good lashing with a blacksnake. You could be expelled from the Klan and blackballed throughout the country. It's best not to test me. The stakes are too high. We must win our war against immorality and those who defy God."

Sam drummed his fingers on the podium and waited for someone to comment or ask another question. Ned Benson said, "The first planning session will be in the Christian Church on Fifth Street, Thursday night at eight o'clock. Come in the door on the western side of the church. Every body, please be on time with your individual plans and ideas."

Sam gazed at the group. "This meeting's adjourned. Stick around, Tom."

The men milled about, shaking hands, nodding; but no one uttered a word. Sam handed each man a copy of the protocols and said, "Study this. Keep it out of sight." They all filed out. Ned went last. Sam noticed that the men filed out, one after the other. That method of leaving meetings couldn't be allowed to continue. He'd put significant spaces between their exiting next time.

As soon as the men were down stairs: Sam and Tom were alone. Tom said, confidentially: "I, for one, am glad Ned asked all those questions. I didn't know all that stuff."

"I know, Tom. We all need to study," said Sam. "It takes time and effort to get everything right. But, we'll have a hell-of-an-organization when we do."

"I'm excited. It was a good meeting. Worth the trip. Educational."

"Here. Let me give you a Protocol Pamphlet, Tom." Sam handed Tom a thin, paperbound booklet. "The Grand Dragon wants each Cyclops to have one. He wants us to study the different sections and think about them. After that, we'll modify these ideas to suit our requirements. The basic tenants for domination are good, but the topics need to be tailored to our needs. We're going to model Klan ceremonies after church ritual. Once we've got some preachers in here, we'll appeal to other people like us, people who can rule, people who adhere to fundamental religious principles and disapprove of sinful people who break the law—like the dammed bootleggers with their rot-gut booze."

"Sam, these are heavy ideas. We've sure got lots to think about."

"We'll get to it, Tom. You just read the material set forth in these documents. Digest the ideas and come back to me with some thoughts about how we can implement them. Okay?"

"You bet I will." The railroad engineer from Delta pulled his cap tight over his head. "I've got to get started home. But before I do, I need to tell you about the talk going around Delta County—maybe Montrose, too."

"Talk about what?" Sam felt he could handle any situation.

"About you and yours."

Sam jerked to attention. He didn't like people talking behind his back—not about "him and his." What did Tom mean "About you and yours?" If things were being said in Delta County, in Montrose County: then people in Mesa County might be talking, too. Idle talk was bad. Could hurt a politician. Even ruin him.

"What're they saying?" Sam thought he sounded a little too anxious.

The expression on Tom's face became apologetic. "Keep in mind, these are not my ideas, Sam. You understand. I just thought somebody—a friend—should let you know what people are saying." Tom sounded ominous.

"Tell me, dammit!" Sam smashed his balled fist onto the podium.

"I tell everybody to keep their mouths shut, Sam. Honest! It's just because you're smart and dress nice."

"For god's sake, man, get to it. What are they saying?"

"Okay." Tom shifted his eyes to the pamphlet in his hand. "They say you're queer."

Sam felt as though a tree had fallen on him. He couldn't believe he'd heard the operative word. "You mean … peculiar?"

"No," Tom seemed to wrinkle his nose, "queer."

Sam panicked. He couldn't remember saying or doing anything that would give people the impression he wasn't normal.

His first thoughts blamed Bonnie. Was she in Delta and spreading lies? Surely, she knew he'd kill her. Was she telling people that Harold wasn't his son?

Sam realized that his being an only child had given him special privileges. He knew he'd been pampered, but that hadn't made him effeminate. His parents had built the restaurant business and left it to him, but he'd worked hard, too. Always had lots of girl friends. It wasn't his fault if none of them measured up. He'd always found it easier and less expensive to use a "steady" whore when he wanted a woman.

He'd lost his head over Bonnie. She was so dammed beautiful when compared to other women; she'd swept him off his feet. And, too, he knew he needed a wife if he wanted to be Governor. The only way he could have Bonnie was to marry her. The baby just happened. But hell, that too, had been good for his career, a family man and all that. Now, the little bitch … "Why would anyone think I go for men?" Sam hoped he sounded controlled, even nonchalant. His heart was thumping like a trip-hammer.

Tom Niles hooked his thumbs behind the bib of his overalls. "Well. Women say you're good-looking. Better than most. They say, with your money, a women would have to be nuts to leave you—that's providing you didn't kick her out. Some ask: "Why didn't you get married when you were younger." They're the one's who think you're queer. Others think you just got married to look good in the public eye. Most say you beat your wife once too often. And now that you realize you need her for your political ambitions, you want us to keep our eyes open and tell on her if she comes to town. Another thing. No one thinks she'll come to Delta with anyone—especially, a man. They think Monroe Morgan's a figment of your imagination."

Sam decided to sit. He thought he'd fall, if he didn't. Swallowing hard, he struggled to say something. He needed both Bonnie and Monroe dead. He simply needed time to accomplish it without involving himself. "I can't tell you how stupid these ideas are." Turning away, Sam tried to determine which of his professional faces he'd use in this crisis. He needed a facial expression that would stir sympathy. "Tom. I've got to find her. I want my little boy back. I love my son. My own flesh and blood."

"How about her? Want her back?"

Sam lowered his head, summoned his most pitiful expressions and struggled to bring tears to his eyes. "Yes I do, Tom. I want my family around me!" He opened the Klavern door for Tom. He expected Tom to leave. The conversation was over.

"Did you ever beat Mrs. Isgar—throw her out onto the street?" Tom asked. "Wouldn't let her back in?" Tom, the dumb sonuvabitch, wouldn't take the hint and leave.

Sam closed the door. "Who told you that?"

"It seems to be common knowledge in Delta."

"All right. So we had a little family squabble," Sam admitted.

"Yeah. You kept her outside all night—on different occasions. She couldn't get in to take care of Harold. Her face and arms were black and blue."

"Who told you this?"

"I don't know. I just hear people talking. I thought you ought to know." Tom moved toward the door and Sam opened it again.

As soon as Tom was outside and the door was closed, Sam's mind turned to a new book he'd just purchased: "Poisons of the Southwest." In it, he'd read something about making a deadly poison from Chokecherry leaves and branches. He visualized the large grove of Chokecherry trees growing at the confluence of the Gunnison and the Colorado Rivers just south or town. His mind quickly leaped to Durango and the telephone on the wall.

"I know that dirty sonuvabitch is in Durango. He has to be! And, she's with him," said Sam, out loud. Grinding tension twisted his gut.

Ripping the receiver from its hook, he turned the crank furiously. Waited.

Before the long-distance operator could finish her speech, Sam interrupted. "Get me Durango 335." He stepped back, slapped his forehead with his left hand, whirled aimlessly to his left and returned to his original position in front of the phone, all the while deliberately twisting his face in aggravated grimaces as he moved.

A voice on the other end of the line, said: "Sheriff's Department. Harvey Howe, speaking."

"Hello, Sheriff. This is Sam Isgar in Grand Junction. Is Bob Stout there, please?"

"Oh, yes. How are you, Sam?"

Goddammit! This sonuvabitch wants to visit, Sam thought. "Fine, thanks. But, I'm in a helluva hurry, Sheriff, if he's there?"

"I'll give him the phone. Here, Bob." Sam heard noise at the other end of the line. Then: "Hello."

"Bob, this is Sam, dammit."

"What?"

"Listen, Goddammit! I want you to find my wife and that god dammed sonuvabitchin' Monroe Morgan! They've got to be somewhere in Durango."

CHAPTER THREE

(September and October 1922)

The house <u>was</u> on fire! Monroe couldn't see the haystack. He had no idea about the family—where they were—how they were? Monroe glanced at the sky, tried to estimate time, felt helpless, prayed for rain. Wouldn't you know it, he thought! Two weeks of rain and nothing but clear skies now.

Couldn't someone see the shack burning? Does the fire department know? No phone in the house. Would anyone race across the river to put out a fire in Mexican Flats?

Suddenly, Monroe heard bells clanging. The fire wagon was a long way off, but coming! Must be on Park Avenue … definitely north?

On a dead run, the mules wheeled the wagon over Ninth Street Bridge. Rushing water lapped the girders. He reined the mules south.

When Monroe reached the house, flames were licking the entire building. Fire climbed thirty feet into the sky. He headed the team into the yard while hauling back on the reins and applying the wagon's brakes. Circling the yard, he headed Jack and Jinni back toward Roosa Avenue. Clothes, bedding, cooking utensils and other belongings were strewn everywhere. Mom, bless her, had emptied the house. But where was everybody?

At that moment, Anna appeared in the corral carrying Old Blue's harness. She tried to toss the gear onto Blue's back while Blue stood motionless, but in her anxiety, she heaved the outfit so hard it fell off the other side.

Sliding to a stop, Monroe set the wagon's brake and leaped to the ground shouting: "Ma. Where's Bonnie—the kids?"

Anna let the harness fall. Fear, tension and relief mixed together in her expression. "Oh, Son! Son! Over here." She ran toward the manger. "They're all here. Thank God!"

Monroe dragged the corral gate open and dashed toward the manger only to be intercepted by his mother. The fire hadn't reached the haystack—yet. "Are you okay, Mama?"

"Yes, yes! Everybody's all right. I tried to kill bedbugs. I didn't mean to burn the house down." Monroe watched a tear drop from his mother's chin.

"Don't worry, Mama. Let's make a bed in the wagon and put everybody in it. Grab bedding and clothing from the yard. Put it all into the wagon. I'll bring Bonnie and the boys." Anna nodded and hurried away.

When Monroe arrived at the manger, Bonnie cradled her babies—one on each arm—and smiled. "Are we going to move again?"

Monroe gazed momentarily into the bright blue eyes of this woman he so dearly loved. He kissed her forehead. "And not a moment too soon, huh?"

"Where're we going?"

Monroe lifted Wade, wrapped him in his baby blanket, and clutched him tight against his chest with his left arm. He scooped Harold from his mother's shoulder with his right hand and headed for the wagon. "I don't know, yet," he shouted.

At the wagon, Anna had piled armloads of blankets and clothes that made a bed. She took Wade and Harold from Monroe and ordered: "Go get Bonnie. I'll arrange these guys for traveling and pick up some more stuff."

Back at the manger, Monroe scooped Bonnie and all the bedclothes into his arms and headed for the wagon. "Hang onto your covers," he admonished Bonnie.

Anna began arranging Bonnie and the children for a ride to wherever. "Better get your bed from the haystack, Monroe. Then, we can be off."

47

With Bonnie still smiling, Anna climbed onto the wagon seat and gathered up the reins. Monroe came back with his bedding. "I'll take them to Cascade, Son."

"No, Ma. Not there. Take them to John and Mabel Laurence. You stay there until I come for you."

"They're going to the ranch," Anna said, emphatically.

"Ma. If you're not going to take them where I say, then get off the wagon and I'll take them myself. I don't have time to argue with you."

Monroe watched his mother change her mind. She recognized his determination. "Why hell, son," Anna acquiesced, "you bring my buggy when you finish here." She slapped the reins along the mule's backs. "I'll meet you at Mabel's."

Monroe shouted after his mother. "I think James is in Boulder. At least he was when I last heard." Anna waved and nodded her head.

A curious group of Mexicans scattered as the Firehouse team trotted down Roosa Avenue and pulled water-pumping equipment into the yard. Two men rode the wagon seat. The men paid no attention to Anna, but stared hard at the flames consuming 950 Roosa Avenue.

The roof had caved in. The walls would fall any minute. Glancing about the yard, Monroe saw belongings scattered everywhere. Mostly junk, he thought.

Turning the chuck-box upright, Monroe began retrieving cooking utensils and putting them in the box. He placed the carryall into the buggy between the dashboard and the seat.

"Get that buggy out'a here," a fireman yelled. "Want our pump in there." The fireman looked away, and then looked back. "Is that hay wet?"

"It is," Monroe shouted, running to the corral where he'd noticed Chukaluks and Blue stomping restlessly. He grabbed the harness that Anna had dropped and quickly dressed Blue. He released Chukaluks's halter rope, and then led Chukaluks and Blue to the buggy where he tied Chukaluks to the iron rail on the buggy seat. He backed Blue into the shafts, hitched him in, and knotted the lines at the dashboard. Finally, he led the whole shebang to the far side of the yard, away from the busy firemen, and tied Blue to a young sapling. Still rushing, Monroe, grabbed his saddle from the tack room, threw it on Chukaluks, tightened the girth, and tossed the bridle into the buggy.

With the rig loaded, Monroe gazed at the house—not much left. His mind filled with questions about his liability? If he needed to pay, he'd try to put it off until he earned some money. He wouldn't touch his savings in Grand Junction. Shaking his head, he refused to dwell on it.

He caught a glimpse of two riders approaching. An inexplicable chill ran down his spine. The chill forced a harder look at the men bearing down on him.

Both men moved slowly toward the house. Their actions seemed strange and foreboding. Wouldn't normal men, confronting an obvious emergency, be hurrying to see if they could help? These fellows appeared lackadaisical and unconcerned. Monroe's curiosity heightened when he saw the glint of a Sheriff's star on each man's chest. By god! He knew these guys. Bob Stout and Earl Mills!

Bob, the big man, bubbled over his saddle like a fresh loaf of dough overflowing a bread pan. Bob's feet hung below the belly of his horse, and his head supported a wide brimmed Stetson hat. His whole appearance, when viewed with the horse and all, seemed disgusting, unwelcome.

By contrast, his partner seemed too small. Long blonde hair waved from under the little fellow's brown hat. His legs seemed barely to extend beyond the saddle skirt. Both legs protruded into the air on either side of the broad-backed horse he rode. Though Monroe hadn't seen these fellows for some time, he knew they had to be the ne'er-do-well's he'd avoided much of his life. However, here they were, unavoidable, and headed his way. The mountain and the piss ant: Deputy Bob Stout and his constant companion, Deputy Earl Mills. Both deputies rode into the yard pushing aside the six or seven Mexicans who stood watching the excitement.

When the Deputy's horses stopped walking, their noses bracketed Monroe. He felt like grabbing the reins at each bitted mouth and yank until the riders were either thrown or screaming for mercy. Instead, he simply stared at the deputies while they stared at him. Finally, Bob smiled and said, "Howdy. I've been looking for you." He shifted his gaze to the burned out house. "So, this is my lucky day."

"You've been looking for me?" Monroe asked, voice rising.

Ignoring the question, Bob smiled again and waved his hand at the ashes. "I see you've burned your house down."

"Not my house," Monroe stated as he watched a smile break across Earl's face and reveal a large gap between his two front teeth. "Didn't know you fellows followed fire engines." He couldn't bring himself to pretend friendliness, or even cooperation.

Bob turned his gaze on Monroe. "I thought you were in Grand Junction. How come you're back over here?"

"I'm not," Monroe pointed out. "Can't live in a burned out house."

"That remark and that attitude won't get you anywhere." Bob's voice tightened.

Monroe figured Bob was remembering their school days. Especially the day Bob had pushed too hard and got punched in the nose. That day Monroe had bloodied Bob's nose and made him say "uncle."

"You always was a smart aleck." Bob's anger flared.

Monroe smiled. "Bob. Ever since grade school, we've been growlin' at each other. Why don't we bury the hatchet … let bygones be bygones?"

"I don't think 'bygones' will ever be 'bygones' between us, Morgan. You've done me and my family too much dirt."

"Oh bullshit, Bob. Now, you're talking about your sister?"

"You damn right, I am. And you know it!"

"I've told you a hundred times, that whole thing was in her mind. I never made any advances. It was in her head."

The fire chief sauntered over, interrupting the discussion. "You boys can continue your conversation after I'm gone." His eyes fixed on Monroe. "I think the fire's out. I've sprayed the ashes, the tack room and the hay. So, I don't think it'll be coming back. How'd it happen?"

"Bedbugs. I poured kerosene around to kill the bugs and, I guess, an ash dropped on the floor."

The fireman snapped a twig in his hand. "You might want to watch that hay for a while."

"I'm going to take it with me, eventually. And I'll notify the owner. He lives on Red Mesa now."

"Well. We're leaving." The fireman nodded and walked away.

"Thanks for your help, sir."

Turning back to the deputies, Monroe said, "Now ... if there's some legal business, I'm ready to listen."

"Are you living here alone?"

"Yeah," Monroe lied.

"How come you're not at Cascade? Ain't that your favorite place in all the world?"

Monroe decided to overlook the sonuvabitch. "Well. It's my favorite place all right, but I just signed on to haul coal for Wood & Burnside. Didn't want to make the trip morning and night."

Bob motioned to the buggy. "That's your Ma's buggy. Why's it here?

"Boy! You're just full of questions. All that detecting must make you tired? Why don't you let your little clam talk once in a while?"

51

"Who're ya' callin' 'a clam,' ya' big liar?" Earl Mills face turned beet red.

Monroe struggled to remain calm. "Not a lot of people get to call me 'liar,' Edward. I'll let you get by with it—once."

Bob nudged his horse between them. "All right! All right! Let's not get heated up."

Monroe realized he didn't need a run-in with the law. He'd better try getting along. "Okay," Monroe sighed. "My mother came in to get coal, the house caught on fire, and I sent her ahead with my wagon." Monroe held Bob's stare. He deliberately shifted his eyes and gazed steadily at Earl.

"I don't believe you," Earl whispered.

Believing Bob and Earl were too lazy to ride five miles to check his story, Monroe said, "I guess you'll just have to ride out to Cascade and check it out, won't you?" In any event, Anna had gone to the Laurence's and the Laurence's were on the opposite side of the valley from Cascade.

"We have a friend who says you left Grand Junction with a woman and a baby boy. Is that right?"

"Do you see a woman and a baby here?"

"I think they're both in that wagon your mother drove. I think you're hiding them."

"I can see you think a lot, Bob. I hope it isn't too much of a strain."

Bob kicked his horse in the ribs. The horse jumped forward. Bob swung his quirt at Monroe's head. The lashes ticked the brim of Monroe's hat. The horse galloped away onto Roosa Avenue. "Come on Eddie. We'll have to smoke him out some other way," he yelled.

Monroe strolled around the yard, gazing at piles of ashes and trying to recall articles they'd brought to the house, as well as, the things he'd already picked up.

The bloated river still threatened to overrun the corral, and the water continued to swirl by. Bright sunlight flooded the box elder and narrow-leaf cottonwood trees that stood proudly among the huge boulders bordering both riverbanks. He'd never forget the place. How could he? His son's birth made it memorable.

He checked the knot in Chukaluks's halter rope, released Blue from the young tree and climbed into the buggy. He'd get Bonnie settled at the Laurence's, and then return to the business of hauling coal. As he drove away he checked his watch. "Oh hell! It's 11 o'clock!"

* * *

After crossing Junction Creek on Main Avenue, Monroe turned to West 3rd Avenue and proceeded north again. When he'd climbed a little rise along the way, he was able to see 32nd Street in the distance. His wagon sat in front of the Laurence's and his mother was in the driver's seat. He reached for the buggy whip. "Blue! Giddy up." He cracked the whip over Blue's head. The buggy jumped forward.

Anna turned toward him as he came flying down the street. She continued to stare until the buggy stopped.

"What's the matter, Mama?"

"They're not home."

Stunned, Monroe stared at the house. He hadn't considered this eventuality.

"Well, they're probably down town."

"I thought of that, Roe, but I went next door and asked Betty Howe. She thought they were home—didn't see them go, I guess. James is still in Boulder completing his law degree."

"I wish someone would tell me how I'm supposed to haul coal today." Monroe tried to smile.

"Okay. I'll take every body out to Cascade. It'll be easier."

"Mama. I need the wagon to haul coal with, and you couldn't put everything in the buggy. We can't move to Cascade. I've told you a hundred times: Cascade's the first

53

place Sam Isgar will look. We are certainly beholden to you for the difficulty we're putting you through, but we <u>can't</u> stay at Cascade."

"Why hell, son. You've got to do something."

"I know Mama." Monroe recalled an empty house he'd passed on West Third. "Let's go back. I saw a house on the way out." He stood in the buggy and peeked into the wagon. Bonnie smiled back, quietly.

"Are you okay, Honey?"

"Don't worry about us," said Bonnie, pulling the sheet to shade Wade's eyes. "But we're going to be hungry soon. Harold especially. He needs changing."

"Okay, Honey. We'll look at that house. Won't take long. I didn't notice if there's a place for live stock."

Monroe heard an automobile back down West Third. Simultaneously, he and his mother turned to see a Model "T" Ford sliding and bouncing toward them.

Anna waved. "There they are. Thank God!" She made the sign of the cross over her chest. "Did you ask if you could stay?"

"No, Ma. But I know I can. They've got lots of room. Corrals, barns, everything."

John and Mabel Laurence chugged their Model-T around both stationary rigs while they shouted and waved. Steam hissed from under the radiator cap. Mud balled around the sandbag tires. Mabel's blue, cloche hat framed a happy face with bright eyes and pink cheeks. Mabel loved everyone. Monroe couldn't see the rest of her, but he remembered her as a pretty woman with a bright and peppy personality.

Of course, John hadn't changed a bit. His solid gold tooth still dominated his big smile and his smile dominated his face. His mischievous eyes danced everywhere while his booming voice could be heard from one end of a passenger train to the other. Monroe always figured John got that voice from saying "All aboard" during his many years as conductor on the Denver and Rio Grande Western Railroad. Being retired and raising purebred Morgan horses on his twenty-acre rancho hadn't inhibited his exuberance one bit.

"Well, to what do we owe this pleasure? We haven't seen you for two or more years, my boy." John Laurence shouted his greeting as he and Mabel tumbled from the car and met Monroe and Anna with enthusiastic embraces.

"We've come to impose on you, if we can."

John hugged Monroe with both arms. "You know you're welcome to stay as long as you want. We've told you that a million times."

"Yeah, I know. But I have a wife and two babies now. How do you feel about that? Don't think you have to say 'yes.'"

"Our house is yours. James isn't here, so there's certainly room for our other son."

Monroe turned toward his wagon's tailgate. "Well, come back here, then. Meet Bonnie and the boys."

After introductions, Monroe quickly brought the Laurences up to date on the circumstances that dropped him on their doorstep, and when Bonnie and the boys were ensconced in the house, Anna asked to use the telephone. "Charlie, can you come and get Blue and the buggy?" She paused. "Oh—okay. I'm with the Laurences—on West Third—you know." Another pause. "Well, hell Charlie let that go. Just ride over here and drive the buggy back with your horse tied on behind. I'm going to stay with John and Mabel for a few days and help out." Anna placed the receiver on its hook.

Monroe turned his attention to John and Mabel. "I'm going to continue to work for Wood & Burnside while I find another house for us. I'll do that right away."

"Let's not set any deadlines," John said. "We'll help as long as you need us."

Monroe held the specter of Sam Isgar in his mind, and involving the Laurences longer than a week or two, at most, was unthinkable.

"Well, if you'll all excuse me, I've got a load of coal to haul. Maybe I better go by the office and explain why I'll be working a short day?"

"Better go to town down Main Avenue, Roe. People are stuck all along west Second and Third Avenues."

"And let me make you a sandwich," Mabel said. "You can't go all day without eating."

Monroe glanced at his watch and turned to Bonnie. "Holy Cow! It's one-thirty! I've got to leave right away, Honey."

Mabel offered Monroe a shopping bag. "Here. Take this fruit … stop and get yourself something after you go by the office."

Monroe kissed Bonnie and went out the door. He headed his mules toward Main Avenue and downtown Durango.

Traveling along Main Avenue was worse than Monroe had imagined. He began to wonder whether he'd be better off on West Second or Third Avenue. Main looked like pictures he'd seen depicting a World War I battlefield. The farther he went the more sorrow he felt for stranded people. The cars, mostly Fords, were bogged down in water holes and ditches. Several owners had gone home. Some were trying to push their automobiles; others were pairing up and combining their efforts. All were slipping, sliding and cursing as they kicked each "piece of junk" that provided them so much pride and joy. He had envisioned this scenario when he decided to take Bonnie and run from Sam Isgar. He just thought a team and wagon would be more reliable— more certain.

Right now, there was no getting around, or through, the stuck vehicles. He stopped, sat a few minutes, surveyed the scene and tried to be patient.

One fellow seemed exceptionally agitated. He splashed around his car, tromped from one side to the other, tried to look at the front end. His car had crashed into the cement revetment guarding Junction Creek's north bank. The stylish automobile and the creek bank hung some eight or nine feet above the streambed.

Aggravated, the fellow took off his hat and suit coat. Under the coat he wore suspenders, a white shirt and a tie. His blond hair and pale skin seemed to emphasize his slight frame. Mud completely obscured his shoes— probably oxfords—and collected on his pants. In fact, the heavy mud dragged heavily on his suspenders.

Gazing at the poor fellows plight, Monroe thought perhaps a big hole had been torn in the car's radiator. A headlight appeared broken and a fender peeled back. Might have bent the axle as well.

Climbing down from his wagon, Monroe sunk three to four inches into the mud, depending on where he put his feet. Nevertheless, he made his way to the professional looking man who paced to and fro beside the wrecked car. The man stopped wringing his hands, but he didn't change the exasperated look on his face.

Monroe walked to the edge of the precipice and tried to view the damage. The fellow ceased his pacing and stared dejectedly at the mud.

"I thought maybe I could give you a hand."

The man began wringing his hands again. "I could sure use some help. I don't know what to do. I can't move it."

"I thought I might unhitch my mules, drag you back about twenty feet. That might help. What do you think?"

"My God, man! I'd be grateful." The man's face brightened.

"I don't believe I've seen that kinda car before," Monroe remarked. "Do you live here?"

"No, I don't. I'm from Denver. And that's a Duesenberg."

"A Duesenberg." Monroe shook his head. "Boy, it's a doozy! I've been all over the Western Slope and I've never seen one out here."

"It's too damn big and heavy for these roads—in this weather." The man from Denver splashed to the other side of his car.

"Just a minute." Monroe walked back to Jack and Jinni.

In a matter of minutes, Monroe had dropped the wagon tongue, pulled the kingpin and released the doubletree from the wagon. He let the team drag the doubletree through the mud until the doubletree aligned behind the car. Taking a log chain from the wagon, he wrapped the chain around the Duesenberg's rear axle and hooked it on the chain. Then, using the wagon's kingpin, he attached the other end of the chain to the doubletree. He drove the team forward a few steps until the chain became taut.

"Now, before I start pulling, you better get in and steer as we move away from the revetment. Okay?"

The man stomped his feet on the running board, removing as much mud as possible, then dropped into his seat. "Oh. One more thing," Monroe said, checking his connections. "Where do you want to park it?"

"I don't know. Somewhere out of the way, I guess."

"Okay. We'll put it right over there, near that tree— under it, in fact."

When Monroe had parked the Duesenberg and unhitched the team, three men approached him and ask for help. They simply wanted to move their cars off the street. He couldn't say "no." Then after the last car was moved, the man with the Duesenberg came to him again. "I take it you are going down town."

"Yes, I am," said Monroe. "And I'm awful late."

"I wondered if I could hire you to pull my car to the dealership on Main Avenue. I'll make it worth your while."

Monroe glanced at the sun. It was just edging below the mountains to the west. He fished into his watch pocket. Four thirty-five!

"Why not. I've just about killed the entire day," he said.

"Let me introduce myself, sir. I'm Fletcher Farmer, Assayist, out of Denver."

Monroe extended his hand, but quickly withdrew it when he realized mud covered each hand. "I'm sorry, sir. The name's Monroe Morgan. I'm pleased to meet you, but I better wait to shake."

"Give me that hand." Fletcher Farmer reached with enthusiasm. "I'm proud to shake your hand. You've done a lot of good this afternoon."

Monroe shook the extended hand, smiled, and felt he'd made a friend.

"Do you have relatives here, Mr. Farmer?"

"No. I'm here, on business—with the smelter. We analyze most of their samples."

"Well, gee Mr. Farmer, I'm kinda in a hurry, so if you don't mind, I'll hook your car to the back of my wagon and we'll talk as we go."

"Call me, Fletch."

"Okay. Call me Monroe."

"It's a deal, after I pay for towing my automobile. Okay?"

Monroe nodded his agreement. "I think I'm getting the best of the deal."

With Monroe's new friend sitting beside him, they towed the Duesenberg toward the dealership.

"Do you live here, Monroe?"

"Yes. Always have—pretty much. My folks settled here in 1875. I was born near Pueblo—on one of the many trips my father made between here and Pittsburg, Kansas."

"You're like me, except, I was born in Denver. Never lived anywhere else. Went to school at Boulder, took over my father's business when he died."

"Assayist, you say?"

"Yes. Need something assayed?"

"As a matter of fact, I might have a need, sometime."
Monroe realized he'd never broached this subject

before—not even with his mother. It was about the last conversation he'd had with his father, Henry, and Henry had sworn him to secrecy—after Henry had brought the whole thing up.

"How's that?" Fletch asked.

Monroe held his tongue as his mind wrestled with the thought of telling such a deep secret to a man he'd just met. He did, however, feel more confidence in Farmer than he'd ever felt with any man on such short acquaintance. "On my father's death bed, he told me of a gold mine. I've never been there, but he told me where." Monroe fell silent—a little ashamed. He'd sworn never to tell. Was this a time for him to trust his instincts? He couldn't shake a feeling that he could trust Fletch Farmer. And, somehow, it felt good to have someone to talk to about the mine. He'd had premonitions before.

"I tell you what I'll do, Monroe. When you're ready, send me twenty-five pounds of your ore, and I'll assay it for you—on the house."

"Are assays secret? I don't want this information spread around."

"They can be, if you want it that way. Did your father tell you what he thought the ore was?"

"Gold and vanadium. In that order."

"Okay. I'll give you my business card. Don't lose it."

* * *

Twenty minutes later, Monroe walked into the Wood & Burnside office. The clock on the wall read twenty minutes to six. Herbert Wood was alone. Only the small electric lamp on Herbert's desk lit the room. Monroe walked to the counter and waited. Finally, Herbert looked up and stared at Monroe. "Yes?"

Monroe wasn't sure Herbert would recognize him in the deep darkness that surrounding them. "I'm Monroe Morgan, sir. You hired me this morning."

"Yes." Herbert stood up.

"Well. I want to tell you I couldn't get any coal today." Herbert interrupted. "No coal. No pay."

"Our house burned down. I had to relocate my family. I'll go tomorrow."

Without any hesitation, Herbert Wood said, simply: "Don't bother. You're fired."

"But, I'm willing ….

"Try us again, when you can get something done." Herbert Wood returned to his desk and focused on his papers.

Monroe felt a rush of anger. He whirled from the counter, yanked the front door open and stomped through. When he hit the street, the city lights were on. His mules stood by the curb … tired … dirty. Sure he'd consumed the whole day with things that had nothing to do with Wood & Burnside, but what was a man supposed to do: leave his wife and kids out in the street? Herbert Woods was an inconsiderate sonuvabitch. He could go to hell!

"By god, I'll show them. Hauling coal isn't the only thing I can do." His mind fixed on the whiskey still in Grand Junction—at the vinegar works. Maybe it was time to set up a still here in Durango. Sell booze. He was confident his whiskey would sell. If he hadn't met Bonnie, he'd still be in Grand Junction selling whiskey and making money. Whiskey, wine, brandy … hell, he could make it all!

He thought of several locations where he could build a still. He'd been thinking of homesteading twenty acres on Florida Mesa. That would be a good place for a still. If he found that gold mine in the hills behind Cascade, that might be a good place. Maybe Herbert Wood had done him a favor. By god, he'd get busy. Do it now!

61

CHAPTER FOUR

November 1922

Bob Stout leaned his overweight body against a telephone pole in the dark alley behind Durango's Mason & Ambold Grocery. He'd tried the store's back door, but couldn't get in. His ears were freezing. Indian summer had left in mid-October and winter was here. They'd had four inches of snow in two days and most of it was still on the ground. No wind to speak of, just a steady breeze pressing a deep chill into every part of his body. He hunched against the pole.

Snow had been piled against the building and that pole was the only place Bob could find to hide. The dammed porcelain-shaded bulb that hung over the grocery store door flooded the alley with light. If he'd been able to find a light switch, the dammed thing would be off. He didn't want anyone to watch him skulk the alley.

He'd told Carméllo Basíllo and Earl Mills to be at the store before nine o'clock. They were both late. Bob shifted his weight toward the building. He couldn't understand why Carméllo wasn't there: Carméllo was the store's janitor.

In Bob's opinion, the Ambold Grocery storage room was a good place to meet because it was centrally located. Now, since Sam Isgar was so all-fired determined to get his wife and kid back, it seemed like a perfect time to have a Ku Klux Klan meeting, as well.

Earl's being late didn't surprise Bob. Earl was making a habit of being late. Probably a phase he was going through. He liked to play games. Keep people off balance.

As Bob gazed south, he heard someone in the alley. Earl passed through a pool of light a half-block back. Bob watched the little shit kicking along through the snow like a kid without a care in the world. He wondered why he remained a friend to the little devil.

Earl Mills kicked his way to within earshot. Bob kept quiet. He'd surprise the squirt. But, it was obvious Earl wasn't stopping. He kept scuffing along. Bob couldn't believe his eyes. Earl, in the middle of the alley, looking neither left nor right, just tramping on by.

"Hey! Where you going, Shit?"

The small figure halted. He didn't turn around. Just stood still.

"What the hell's the matter with you, Asshole."

Earl whirled laughing. "Ha! Ha! Thought you'd catch me, didn't you? But I fooled you, didn't I?"

"I did catch you, Asshole! If I hadn't, you'd have gone on up the alley kickin' snow until you ran into the river north of town."

"Oh hell, Bob. I saw you trying to hide behind that toothpick. If you really want to hide, you'll have to get a bigger pole. In fact, you big prick, you'd need a bunch of poles." Earl doubled over laughing. He staggered around holding his stomach. While kicking his overshoes through the snow, he laughed as though he were having a fit.

"God dammit. Shut up! You'll wake the dead." Bob left his place behind the power pole and grabbed Earl by the collar. "Be quiet, you little bastard, or I'll throttle you right here."

"What're ya' doin', boys?" Bob stepped back, whirled and bumped into Carméllo Basíllo standing tight against his chest. Carméllo's nose almost rubbed the third button down on Bob's sheepskin coat.

"God dammit, Car, you scared the shit out'a me," Bob exclaimed. "I don't know why I associate with you two. You're going to get mc in a world of trouble, sure as hell."

Bob glanced up and down the alley. No one. He didn't expect to see anyone because he knew only drunks and prostitutes inhabited the alley after dark. The low-lifers couldn't be expected this early.

"Come on, Car. Let's get this thing started."

Carméllo unlocked the door, reached in, found a switch and turned an inside light on. Pushing the door, he went in, then turned quickly and beckoned Bob and Earl. As Bob crowded into the narrow isle, he felt Earl jabbing hard at his butt. He elbowed the little piss-ant.

"Get in. Get inside ... so I can close the door," said Carméllo, anxiously.

When everyone was in, the slender janitor, closed the door, locked it and sidestepped around Bob. He scooted between wooden boxes stacked on both sides of the isle until he vanished into a small doorway on his right. Bob followed by sucking in his stomach as he entered a tiny room lined with more boxes that made the room seem smaller than it actually was.

As Earl crowded in, Carméllo flipped another switch. A dim light lit. Bob saw a small wooden table, four straight-backed chairs, a coffeepot, a can of condensed milk, and a galvanized, water bucket with a blue porcelain dipper hanging from the rim.

Surprised at the close quarters, Bob said, "Good thing we don't have claustrophobia."

"Damn you, Bob! How do you know I don't have it? What is it?" Earl's face twisted into a grimace while Carméllo looked unconcerned and pretended to know what the big word meant.

"Oh, for Christ's sake! You haven't got it, so don't worry."

"How do I know I haven't if I don't know what it is?"

"Trust me. You haven't got it." Bob removed his Stetson with one hand and raked his wavy brown hair with the other.

"Want some java?" Carméllo pointed to the coffeepot.

"Yeah. Don't mind if I do." Both Bob and Earl spoke at the same time. Bob complained. "You don't have to say the same thing I say at the same time I say it."

"It wasn't me saying what you said, it was you saying what I said." Earl's eyelashes batted up and down.

"Oh shit, Earl! Forget it. Sit down. I want to get this meeting started."

"Well. Do you want me to sit down or make the coffee? I can't do both."

"You go ahead, Carméllo. Make coffee, but listen while I talk. We've got a lot to cover."

Bob backed into a corner and seated himself. He hoped for enough room to lean back in his chair. That way he could stretch a little. He hated tight places where he had to watch for things he might bump into or knock over. Trying to catch things before they fell, and/or paying for them if they broke, was a real pain in the ass.

"Now you men are my first Ku Klux Klan recruits. As such, I hold you both in very special regard. An Indian and a white man. I've got all bases covered … I hope. Mexicans and Catholics don't count for nothing." For a moment, Bob held that thought, then recalled that some people thought Carméllo was Mexican. "Anyway," he said, "the orders we get from higher up in the Klan are going to be carried out. You understand that, don't you?"

Bob took a "yes" answer for granted, and wiggled in his chair, seeking a more comfortable position.

"By the way, Car, I know you're part Ute, but what's the rest? What kind of white man's mixed in there?"

"Italian, I guess. I don't think about it. But I know my Dad worked on the railroad out'a Chama. I've always lived in Ignacio, even after my father died. He was a good Christian."

"Your mother was Ute, wasn't she?"

"Oh, yeah. Still is."

Earl kept nodding his head as if agreeing with everything said. All the while, Carméllo seemed to be completely occupied with lighting the kerosene burner under the coffeepot.

"Well, we've got a job to do right away." Carméllo turned toward the table and Earl leaned forward.

Bob continued. "I've heard from Sam Isgar, our Kleagle in Grand Junction. He wants us to look for his wife and kid here in Durango." He looked directly at Carméllo. "Earl and I <u>saw</u> the bastard who brought them here from Grand Junction, just the other day. I reported the sighting to Sam and he called back today with his instructions. So, listen up."

Both Earl and Carméllo nodded. Earl belched a question. "Why'd he wait until today?"

"Shit! How the hell should I know? Probably wanted to check with other Klaverns before he made a decision."

Bob leaned back in his chair, causing the darn thing to squeak so loudly he became afraid it would crack, so he rocked forward and folded his hands on the table. "Earl, you already know the man. But you, Car, you're going to have the pleasure of becoming acquainted." Carméllo shifted, nervously.

"I'm going to tell you about him—describe him to you. When I get through, you'll know him. You'll know what he looks like. You'll be able to recognize him when you hear people talk about him. Okay?" Both Earl and Car nodded.

"His name is Monroe Morgan. Ever hear of him ... or meet him, Car?"

"Nope. I don't know the name." Carméllo slid into his chair.

"Anyway, commit the name to memory, Car. You too, Earl. We're going to be looking high and low for him. He'll have a woman with him ... she'll probably have a baby with her."

Bob leaned back, took a sack of Bull Durham from his shirt pocket, and gestured to Carméllo. "Go ahead. Pour some coffee."

While Carméllo served, Bob continued. "Morgan is big, not heavyset like me, but big, kinda muscular. He's dark complexioned, like a Mex—darker in the summer. He's got straight black hair. Parts it in the middle. His eyes are black. Women think he looks like Rudolf Valentino. Jesus, if I keep talking like this: I'll vomit! Well, anyway, he always dresses good. I mean his shoes are shined, his clothes clean, and his hat brushed and shaped. And he's been out working since grade school. I mean … railroading, mining, ranching and such.

"I understand, he's been in the booze business in Grand Junction. I think he had his still in the Vinegar Works where he was the Supervisor, so you know he's slippery.

"Well, he met Sam's wife, Mrs. Isgar, one night when he was delivering booze. Her name is Bonnie. Sam and Bonnie were having a family argument and this guy, Morgan, interfered. She's supposed to be a real looker! Red hair, blue eyes, good figure. Not very big. Sam says she's got a mind of her own … and uses it. Can't tell her anything. She'll have a kid with her. The kid's Sam Isgar's boy. Sam wants 'em both back.

"Oh, yeah! I almost forgot. Morgan's nickname is "Blackie." You may hear people call him that around town. And don't forget another thing. He's got the worst temper in the world. He gets so god dammed mad he goes crazy. Blacks out. Don't forget that."

Earl raised his hand. "Why'd she take the kid with her when she left Isgar?"

"How do I know?" Bob growled. "I'm just telling you to look for a good lookin' young woman with a baby. The kid's about two years old, Sam says."

Bob gazed around the room, flicked his ash on the floor and tried to gather his thoughts. "Okay. Let me tell you about Morgan. He and I went to school together. His father lost an arm in a dynamite accident, and after that, Monroe quit school—that was during seventh grade—and he went to work to help his mother. The Morgan place is called Cascade Ranch. It's about five miles out East Animas Road.

"Monroe, or Blackie, as we called him in school, was a goddamned smart aleck. Always trying to help people like God 'a mighty. When his Dad got hurt, he wanted to be the big breadwinner. Now he probably thinks he's saving Mrs. Isgar from Sam, or something.

"Always made good grades, but he thought he was God's gift to women. He also thought he was the best-goddamned baseball player on the team." Bob swallowed hard trying to continue.

"Was he?" Earl asked.

"Used to piss me off so bad!"

"Was that when your sister fell in love with him and he wouldn't give her a tumble?"

"Oh. Bullshit, Earl! She didn't fall for him. She just thought she did! And the bastard didn't treat her right. Now, quit interrupting!"

Bob took a sip of coffee. "Now, let's see. You know what he looks like; you know what she looks like. Red hair, blue eyes, peaches and cream skin. Sam says she won several beauty contests before coming to Grand Junction. She sang and danced in a Chautauqua. That's how she got to Grand Junction.

"When Earl and I saw Morgan last week on Roosa Avenue, he was stumblin' around trying to get organized after he burned his house down. I've been kinda keepin' an eye on Cascade, and I haven't seen him. Sam Isgar thinks they're all here in Durango. So do I. That's our job. Find Monroe, find Bonnie and find the kid. As soon as we smoke 'em out, I'll call Sam and tell him. After that, Sam'll tell us what he wants us to do with 'em."

"What kinda guy is this Morgan? I mean: does he act different in any way?" Carméllo asked.

"Well, no," said Bob shaking his head. "But I can tell you he's not going to be easy to get a grip on. The reason I say that is because he's full of stubborn pride and sneaky as hell. He tries to pass himself off as a-goodie-two-shoes, but he's not. We didn't like each other in school and we don't like each other now."

"He whipped you when you were kids, that's why," Earl said.

Bob glared at him. "No one whipped me, 'cause I'm still fightin'."

"Maybe it's because you got too big to sit a saddle in those bronc bustin' contests and had to give up?" Earl persisted.

"Shut-up, Asshole! We're not here to discuss my private life." Bob looked away in disgust.

"Get this. Monroe Morgan is one stubborn sonuvabitch. Once he sets his mind, he won't quit until he's forced. Another thing to keep in mind: he's honest, when he wants to be. He likes to tell the truth. That's why you have to believe everything he tells you. You can't afford to test him or think he's lying.

"Now, I'm going to give you your assignments." Bob pursed his lips.

"Earl, I want you to spend as much time as you can keeping an eye on Cascade. Anna Morgan may be hiding them. If you see anybody except that one-armed Indian or Anna Morgan, I want to know it pronto. Got it?"

"I'll have to find a place in the hills east of the house. Right?"

"Right. I think the best time of day for you to be there would be early in the morning or late in the afternoon, during chores. If something comes up in the office, I'll cover for you. Use your own good judgment, then go ahead."

"And you, Carméllo. We're going to cover the town. Some of the people we talk to, or some of the people we overhear, may be talking about 'Blackie,' keep that in mind." Bob paused. "As I said before: we don't know exactly where he is and we can't follow him until we do. Right now, it's like he's left town. Anyway, we've got to find him. So, ask people about him—not straight out, but lead them into talking about him. Let what they say be information you didn't ask for. We're not really lookin'. Get it?

"Put every bit of time you can on this and be as cunning and clever as possible. If you find anything, let me know immediately. If you call the Sheriff's office, ask for me. If I'm not there, leave messages. Tell me where you'll be and I'll find you. We'll meet here next week, at the same time, unless we learn something sooner. Is everything understood?"

Carméllo and Earl yawned. Both men stood up to leave.

* * *

An entire week passed. Neither Carméllo nor Earl came to Bob with news about Bonnie or Monroe. It was as if the earth had opened and swallowed the two fugitives. Bob received three phone calls, all from Sam Isgar, complaining about no word. Now, Bob had called another meeting. This time there'd be no kidding around.

Bob slipped into the store's back door, laid his hat on a crate of apples, removed his sheepskin coat, took off his overshoes and lumbered down the narrow isle to the tiny meeting room. "Howdy, Earl. Made it on time, I see."

"Thought I'd surprise ya'."

Bob sucked in his stomach and slid into a chair. "Well men, I haven't seen Morgan, and I take it, you haven't either, or you'd have said so. The question is, what to do next. Sam's anxious as hell. He can't understand why we haven't found 'em.

I've checked the hospital, courthouse, newspapers, and rentals, everything. Nobody has seen them. Either that or everybody's keeping awful quiet. How about you two? Got any ideas?"

"Not me, Bob," Carméllo said. "I rode up 'n down streets, looked in backyards, talked to people, and nothin' even made me suspicious. And you know me, I get suspicious easy." Carméllo poured coffee.

"I've been settin' on that knoll just south of Cascade every day—early and late—and sometimes in between. I see the mother and that one-armed Indian, that's all," Earl said.

Bob pulled his coffee closer. "I guess we're going to have to smoke 'em out. Sam'll blow up if we don't. Patience isn't one of his long suits. He's got people searching the entire Western Slope—Grand Junction, Montrose, Delta, Ouray, Silverton, Telluride, and now Durango—nobody's seen 'em. I know they're here, dammit! We <u>saw</u> him, didn't we?" Bob looked to Earl for verification.

"Hell, yes," Earl answered. "We should have arrested him then."

"For what? Nothing? Can you see me walk in with Morgan and charge him with setting his house on fire when he wasn't even there?"

Earl pointed a finger. "You said, we gotta satisfy Sam."

"Well, he's got enough power and money to make it tough for us if we don't. He's one ambitious son-of-a-gun, and he's smart enough to make us wish we hadn't crossed him."

"What's he doing in Grand Junction?" Carméllo asked.

"He owns the best restaurant in town and he's running for State Representative in his district—he'll probably win. His folks died and left him wealthy. He's organizing the Ku Klux Klan on the Western Slope."

"Okay then. What do we do, now?"

"We're gonna to do two things, Car. Number one: you're gonna set up a whiskey still on that property you homesteaded last summer."

"On Florida Mesa?"

"Yeah. It's about eight miles from town—a cabin with water, huh?"

"Yep—well, I have to carry the water."

Bob sipped his coffee. "That's going to be our ace in the hole when we need money to offset Klan expenses. I can see we'll go broke selling memberships. And, Number two: Earl and I are going to make a midnight call on Cascade to see if we can light a fire under our friend, Monroe Morgan. We're going to try our new robes. Maybe get somebody up in the middle of the night to protect that little woman he stole. Whata ya' think of those apples?"

"Wow!" Earl gasped, slapping his hands together. "You've been doin' some heavy thinking."

"We'll let the weather dry up over the weekend and do it Monday. I want to get it done before it snows again. Are you with me?"

He saw excitement glow in Earl and Carméllo's eyes. They nodded their heads. They extended their hands to shake.

Earl put his hand on Bob's arm. "I've been anxious to get started. Didn't think it would happen like this … but it's fine with me."

Car nodded. "Me too. But it's going to cost a lot to get the still started."

"We'll get the money, don't worry," Bob said. "You find the equipment we need. Okay?"

"Okay, I will."

"Earl, we'll meet in the sheriff's office tomorrow. Make decisions about changing the landscape at Cascade." Bob stood up, waiting for questions. "Okay, let's get out of here. There's a Masonic meeting tonight."

* * *

When God fashioned the Colorado Rockies, He looked at his handiwork and found a region where life and beauty could co-exist in freedom and grandeur. Through the San Juan Mountains, He caused a river to flow and dig the earth, widened the valley and turned it into a perfect garden spot, filled it with dark rich soil, caused the stream to flow through solid rock and caused it to be called Animas Valley. He surrounded the entire space with red-rock wall—walls that touched the sky and left this piece of heaven for man to enjoy.

So ... on a ledge, high above the lush valley floor, a pair of sharp-eyed eagles built their aerie. To this precipice, the giant birds brought fish, reptiles and mammals, for food. They fed sumptuous meals to their young, and while adults, lived monogamous lives in peace and security.

Each day, the eagles sharpen their curved talons before unfurling seven-foot wingspans to search the magnificent land below. Year after year they entered this verdant habitat because food was abundant, air was clean and fresh water was plentiful.

There, on that cliff, five miles north of Durango, America's Emblems nested and watched over the land fed by the river of lost souls.

A thousand feet beneath the eagle's nest sat a white, two-story ranch house. The people who dwelt therein call the place "Cascade" in deference to the delicious water that spilled over the red rocks and plummeted into a shady glade above the house. During the summer, the white fences and outbuildings sparkled like diamonds in a world green with timothy grass. From the gracious buildings, backed by scrub oak, quaking aspen and ponderosa pine, the land slopes gently across a large front yard that fills with yellow daffodils each spring and terminates at a north-south road called East Animas. West of the road, the property continues to glide down past a large hay-barn and corral that provides residence for fat horses and contented cows. The Animas River gurgles and laughs a mile away, while it combines the rich timothy pastures spread between the road and the river.

The Denver and Rio Grande Western Railroad puffs and exhales its way through the valley as it provides a connection between Durango and the mountain town, called Silverton.

It would have been a waste of time and energy for the eagles to dream of a richer, more beautiful place, because none exists. But, on a late October night, in 1922, when the barn was dry and crisp: pestilence attacked Cascade Ranch. The plague arrived like a hellish inferno. The fire ravaged the place and created never heeling wounds.

At 2:30 A.M. Two devils dressed in white bed-sheets rode black horses around the barn, shouting and torching everything incendiary. Anna Morgan awoke to the screams of stalled horses and a fire that shriveled her peaceful world … a world that would never again, truly live.

Anna watched in horror as her barn exploded. Bright red and yellow fire mixed with black smoke. Dry hay fed the raging blaze that shot high into the night sky. Frightened cattle rammed their heads into corral fences, bellowed, and tried to run again, only to be stopped by a fence once more. Barn boards crackled. Hungry flames sucked juice from the wood.

In the holocaust, Anna saw hooded riders whip their horses from place to place as they searched for tinder. One of the men, a big, bulky pillager, made the size of his horse seem minute by comparison. The other fellow was a little man, with stubby legs that flailed his horse's sides like an insect trying to keep aloft.

Then, suddenly, there it was! A burning cross! Placed at the south corner of Anna's expansive lawn. She'd heard of the Ku Klux Klan, its shenanigans, its burning crosses and all, but she hadn't dreamed that it could happen in her front yard. Anger pushed aside Anna's original fear and rushed like a tidal wave through her gentle mind and body.

In the light from the fire, Anna saw One-armed Charlie run, half-dressed, from the bunkhouse toward the barn a hundred yards away. He threw his good right arm across his face to shield against the intense heat as he neared the barn.

Anna shoved her feet into a pair of slippers, wrapped her robe around her body and tied it off. She grabbed her rifle from the chifforobe, pounded downstairs, out the front door, knelt on her front steps and fired at the marauding men. Hearing the shot, the dwarf flung his torch high into the air, turned abruptly and galloped south toward Durango. Anna fired again and watched sparks shower from a burning board not two feet from the remaining rider's head. The giant dropped his torch, beat his horse toward the road, and thundered after his friend.

Anna saw Charlie running a circuitous route to the corral behind the barn. He'd release the cattle to safe pasture away from the burning hay.

Racing to the barn, she heard her precious horses, panicked by the flames, squealing and kicking the sides of their stalls. She must get them out! A sharp rock punctured the sole of her thin slipper, but on she ran to the wide barn doors and swung them open. Through the doors and into the burning barn, she ran. Near the door, she grabbed a saddle blanket and threw it over her head. The heat and smoke forced her back, but her horse's cries urged her on.

She fought her way to the first stall. It was empty! Jumping to the next—the one reserved for Blue—she found her wonderful buggy-horse crowded into the far corner, scared to death. Her heart broke. "I'm coming!" she cried, then watched the wild eyes of her darling horse turn in her direction. "Oh baby!" she called, while taking the saddle blanket from her own head and tossing it over Blue. She tightened the blanket about Blue's head, and pulled him away. Outside the door she released him. He lunged through the exit to freedom and the night.

In a matter of minutes, Anna had freed three horses. The fourth, Blister, a favorite of her dear departed Henry, had been placed in a stall under the loft. Burning hay from above had dumped into Blister's stall. Her heart ached for dear Henry's remarkable cow pony, as Blister's body lay twitching and kicking in the burning hay.

Sobbing, Anna turned and ran through the burning door. She didn't stop until she reached the road fifty yards away. Her slippers were gone and her feet burned with cuts and tares.

Quickly, she forgot her painful feet when she remembered Charlie. Turning toward the barn, her gaze tried to penetrate the smoke, the fire, and the night. There he was! Running through smoke. Charging in her direction. His right arm held high to shield his face from the fire. He seemed to be looking for her.

"Over here, Charlie!" Anna yelled while waving her arms and jumping up and down.

Charlie raced toward the burning barn doors yelling: "Are you all right? Are you all right?"

"Wait! Wait! I got them out! They're all out!"

Charlie stopped on her command and turned with eyes searching into the night. He pointed to his red roan standing in the corner of a barbed fence that terminated the barnyard. His finger moved to Blue and Chelsea. He ran toward Anna. "Where's Blister?"

"He didn't make it, Charlie. Don't go in there."

"Dead?"

"Yes."

Anna stood dazed. She stared at the dwindling flames. Much of the barn had caved in. The hay still burned brightly. Dark smoke climbed hundreds of feet into the air.

"Henry built that barn with his own hands, Charlie. It was one of his proudest possessions. And Blister was his favorite horse." She covered her face with her hands and sobbed. Tears dripped through her fingers. "Oh how he loved to show his Blister off in calf-cutting contests."

Charlie turned his face toward the hills and listened. "I remember."

"Why hell, Charlie," Anna said, raising her head and swallowing a sob. "Let's see if the horses are all right. We don't have a snowballs chance of stopping that fire. The barn's lost."

Anna walked toward Blue and stumbled. "Why hell, Charlie. I better get some clothes on ... especially shoes ... and it is kinda' cold ... now that I think of it."

"Yes, Ma'am." Charlie followed her to the fence where Blue stood.

Blue tossed his head as Anna approached. She circled his neck with both arms. "How are you ... ?" A shot tore a hole in the night! She heard a thud. Felt Blue's body shudder. Blue's entire weight dropped like a huge sack of grain. She had no way to escape. No one could help her. The big horse tumbled kicking and jerking on top of her. She heard bones in her right leg snap. She saw Charlie grab Blue's head and pull the horse to one side. And old Blue, bless him, tried to regain his feet, but flopped again in another direction. Dead only three feet away. But not on her ... thank God!

Bang! Another shot split the dark and went whining through the air. Charlie yelled. "We're between them and the fire. Stay down!"

Bang! The third shot tore into Charlie, knocking him some six feet across the yard. "Ma'am! I'm sorry." Charlie clutched the big muscle atop his left shoulder—near his neck. "Goddamn," he groaned. Anna knew pain had gripped him. "Don't move, Anna," Charlie warned.

They lay panting and moaning quietly. Silence fell.

Charlie spoke, quietly. "How bad're <u>you</u> hurt?"

"It's my right leg. I think it's broke in a couple places. Maybe more. It's getting numb." Anna hesitated … fearing the worst. "How about you?"

"Bullet went through—my neck. Felt it come out the other side. Bleeding like hell. I'm trying to stop the blood— with my hand."

Anna couldn't imagine Charlie stopping blood from two bullet holes—one on either side of his body. "Are your legs straight out, Anna—and close together?"

"They're together, but the right one is bent back at the knee, I think."

Suddenly Anna heard the sound of hooves pound the road going to Durango. "Do you hear that?"

"Yes. Only one horse, though. Maybe the other guy's still here? Where'd you leave your rifle?"

"I dropped it by the barn door."

"I'll get it, if we hear someone coming."

Anna felt excruciating pain in her hips. "We've got to get to the phone and call Monroe. I don't think I can walk. Can you?"

"Roe don't have a phone, does he?"

"No. But if we call John Laurence, they'll get Monroe."

"Okay. You stay put. I'll walk … or crawl … whichever. I'll get blankets and make the call. The heat from the barn might help you, 'cause I may take a while. So don't move." Charlie grunted with every move as he struggled toward the house.

"Find a string, a rope, or something … and a knife. I'll try to stop your bleeding." Anna clinched her teeth as a pain shot up her side. "Don't move too fast. You're loosing to much blood."

Charlie crawled toward the house. Anna watched while he labored. She saw him try to walk … then stumble. He moved faster. The darkness swallowed him.

The next thing Anna knew, someone covered her with a quilt. "Oh Charlie! I was out … like a light. I must have fainted. Did you get Monroe?"

"Yes and don't move. It's getting colder."

"How about string?"

"Got binding twine, your scissors and some dishtowels."

"Good," Anna said. "I've got to set up. Raise me and put some blankets behind my back, then give me your belt."

Anna put pressure on Charlie's wounds and fell back exhausted. She gazed lovingly at Blue. "Oh! Look at Blue. God, how I loved that horse."

"He knows it, Ma'am."

Anna saw blood running down both sides of Charlie's body. She feared for his life. "Charlie. Lie down until they get here."

"After you're covered and laying down."

Anna's emotions were running rampant, her brain seethed with plans for revenge. It had to be Bob and Earl. Suspicion wasn't enough. She needed proof. She'd let Monroe handle it.

CHAPTER FIVE

November 1922

Monroe awakened to a heavy pounding on the front door. It was four o'clock in the morning! Monroe heard Bonnie say, "Who's there?" He opened his eyes to see Bonnie sitting straight up in bed, silhouetted in the dim night-light left for the babies. He sleepily climbed from the bed and crossed the room, heading toward the disturbance. Harold began to whimper.

Monroe opened the front door a crack. He didn't immediately recognize the person outside. Realizing he hadn't put on pants, he pushed the door shut. Somewhere between the door and the bed, he'd questioned the time-of-night and the house he was in. Finally, he remembered they'd left the Laurences—moved to a rental house on West Third.

"Wake up. We got problems!" An excited voice came from beyond the door. It sounded like John Laurence? Didn't look like him.

Monroe shouted over his shoulder. "Just a minute!" He stubbed his toe on the way to his pants, cussed, and struggled to wake up.

"John! Is that you?" Monroe asked, shoving his right leg into his pants.

"Yes, it's me!" John sounded irritated. "Charlie called."

Monroe, still on bare feet, rushed to the front door trying to figure why Charlie would call in the middle of the night. He opened the door slowly and stared hard at the man pushing his way into the house.

"Hello, John. You don't look right in that hat."

"It's your mother and Charlie, Roe. They're both hurt. It was Charlie that called." John edged his face close to Monroe in the deep shadows. "Somebody burned your barn." John began pacing aimlessly.

It was as though a 2-by-4 had flown out of the night and struck Monroe right between the eyes. He hadn't spoken to his mother for three days, but he didn't think he had a reason to be worried about her.

"What happened?"

"Get dressed. I'll tell you on the way." John gripped the doorknob.

Monroe dashed to the bedroom. "What happened, Roe?" Bonnie asked from the middle of the bed where he'd left her.

"I don't know, Honey. Mama and Charlie are hurt. John says someone burned our barn."

"Oh, my God! I'll get dressed."

"No. You stay with the boys. I'll go. Be back as soon as I can. Mama's hurt worse than Charlie or she'd have made the call." Monroe grabbed more clothes with the idea he'd dress in the car.

"But you said Charlie was hurt?"

"I know. Mama must be worse?"

John's agitated voice came from the other room. "Come on, son. We need to get going. The Ford's running."

Monroe bent and kissed Bonnie.

* * *

On the way north along East Animas Road, John proceeded to reveal all he knew. Monroe could think of only one man: Sam Isgar. The whole idea boggled his mind.

"I can't thank you enough for what you're doing, John. You and Mabel have been a godsend. And this car … well, it'd take me more that an hour to get the wagon out here."

"Well, we're wide open, my boy. Probably doing about 25 miles-an-hour. I hope we don't hit a deer or have a flat tire."

"If we do have an accident, I'll run on ahead," said Monroe. "You come when you can." Both men fell silent.

John rounded a corner in the graying light and Monroe saw thin streamers of smoke rising from the ashes where the barn should be. He sucked a cold breath of air as his chest spasmed and he turned his eyes away to the dark mountain shadows that seemed close enough to touch. No matter how fast they were going, they weren't going fast enough.

When he focused on the barn again, he smelled smoke. Old wood and burnt hay. Flames were flickering and dying … devouring debris. Still standing among the ashes were several huge vertical logs that had supported the structure. John yanked hard on the steering wheel. The car careened into the driveway on their right. Headlights lit the house.

John gawked to his left and yelled: "There they are!" He crammed the brakes, reversed the car while spinning the steering wheel, and strained to look back at the barnyard. "They're down there."

Sure enough, while concentrating on the house, Monroe had missed Charlie standing several feet below and left of the roadway. A blanket barely covered his left shoulder while he waved his right arm. After another sharp turn, the Model "T" came to a sliding stop about ten feet from Charlie. A large bundle of blankets lay at Charlie's feet.

"Where's my mother, Charlie?" shouted Monroe while leaping from the car.

One-armed Charlie stood twisted. He reeled as though dizzy. In the headlights, Monroe saw Charlie's white teeth and his brave attempt to smile. Then suddenly, Monroe lost his temper. Uncontrollable rage consumed his mind. He wanted to hurt someone.

"Right here, Roe." Charlie wobbled.

Monroe grabbed Charlie by the shoulders. Shook him hard. "What the hell happened, man?" He felt his right hand slip in Charlie's blood. He jumped back.

Charlie's eyes widened, shock registered in every expression. "God, Roe. I didn't do it!"

Confusion gripped Monroe. He felt deep and abiding shame for manhandling Charlie. Helpless, he fell to his knees beside the pile of bedding. As he looked up to ask for Charlie's forgiveness, Charlie swayed and fell to the ground. John leaped forward, trying to catch him.

John kneeled beside Charlie. "There's a tourniquet across his left shoulder, Roe. Bet your mother put it there." John retrieved Charlie's blanket. "You take care of her. I've got Charlie."

"God, John! I didn't mean any of that. I shouldn't have grabbed him ... shook him."

"He knows you're out of your mind with worry. He's already forgiven you."

"Mother?" Monroe carefully peeled blankets from the pile.

Finally, Monroe heard Anna's quiet voice. "Son? They ... burned a cross in our yard. They burned the barn. And they killed old Blue. Blister, too." She sobbed. Then, ever so faintly, she began to repeat herself. "They burned a cross. They burned the barn. They killed Blue ... "

Tears flooded Monroe's cheeks. "Where does it hurt, Mama?"

"My leg. My right leg. Broke. Below the hip ... and below the knee. I think."

"We'll take you to the hospital, Mama." Monroe hugged her shoulders.

"I'm not going to no hospital. Just get me to the house."

"Mama! You've got to go to the hospital. You've got broken bones."

"Well. I'm not going. Get a doctor out here. Somebody has to take care of Cascade."

"We're not worrying about <u>Cascade</u>, Mama."

"You better worry, Son. It's number one. Don't forget it!"

"I'm not forgetting Cascade, Mama. Honest, I'm not. I just want you in the hospital."

"You take Charlie. I'm gonna take care of our home."

"I know, Mama." Monroe thought of all the sacrifice his mother and father had made for this spot of earth and, then, he thought of all the planning he'd done to keep Bonnie away from Cascade—to keep her safe. He knew now he'd have to re-plan everything—the homestead on Florida Mesa, the sampling of the gold mine. But, regardless of the cost, he'd satisfy his mother. "I'll stay here, Mama. I'll take care of Cascade."

"You'll move here—with Bonnie?"

"Yes, Mama. Until you're on your feet again." Monroe began to think that maybe he should have taken Bonnie to Cascade to begin with. Maybe he should quit running and meet Sam Isgar head on—and maybe, just maybe—there was something else. Maybe Sam didn't want to find Bonnie and Harold as urgently as he tried to make his Klan members think.

"How'd this happen, Mama?" Monroe asked.

"I was hugging Blue when I heard a bullet hit his head. He just shuddered and fell on me. He tried real hard to get up. But all the strength went out of him, and he fell again." Anna began to sob uncontrollably. When she tried to talk again, her voice was so weak Monroe could hardly hear her.

"Don't talk, Mama. Just rest." Monroe stood up.

John put his hand on Monroe's shoulder. "Charlie is bad hurt. He must have caught a bullet after they shot Blue. He's unconscious."

Monroe stalked the car, trying to visualize both his mother and Charlie in the Ford's back seat. John followed.

"Charlie's lost a lot of blood, Roe."

"I think if we lay him on the back seat and tie him with something, we can put Mother on the floor. What do you think?"

"How're we gonna do that? Your mother's right leg is shattered—maybe her hip. The seat isn't wide enough."

"Let's find a wide board. Long enough to support her hips and legs. Let's tie rolls of blankets over both legs and the board—so nothing moves. Okay?"

John nodded.

"Let's try it. She'll tell us if we can't—won't you Mama?"

"You do what you have to," Anna said, weakly. "Charlie and I can make up the difference. Can't we Charlie?" Charlie didn't answer.

"Why, hell, Son. Charlie's been the best help a woman could have." Monroe heard his mother's sniffle. "Don't let me hold you boys up. Charlie should be in the hospital."

"Who did it, Mama? Do you know?"

"It looked like that big deputy, Bob Stout, and that little pipsqueak, Earl Mills. They both wore bed sheets and pointy hoods, so I can't say for sure."

Monroe moved toward Charlie and turned to John. "I'll help you with Charlie, then I'll get a board for Mother while you lay Charlie flat on the back seat. Tie him there if you have to."

After Monroe had found the right board—wide and about three feet long—he picked up the binders twine and returned to the car. John, with a piece of twine in hand, had Charlie on the back seat. Each man worked silently, intent on his own project.

Finally, Monroe looked up. "John, when you finish tying Charlie to the seat, you can help me with Mama, okay?

Moments later, Monroe took his position at Anna's head and John moved to her feet. "Okay. Just stay where you are. I'll open the back doors on either side of the car and leave them open."

When Monroe returned, he crouched and slipped his hands under his mother's shoulders. "When I count three, we'll carry her to the car feet first. Okay. One, two, three." Monroe and John lifted Anna off the ground. John shifted his body to one side and pointed Anna's feet toward the nearest rear door.

"You put her feet in and go around to the other side. We'll scoot her in as far as possible and close the far door.

"I'm ready when Anna is," said John, glancing toward Anna.

"Why hell, Fellow's, let's go," said Anna.

When the fancy moves were completed, Anna lay in the car. Monroe, holding Anna's shoulders, gradually raised her head, bending her, ever so slowly, at the waist. When her head seemed to clear the inside of the car door, Anna exclaimed: "Isn't that enough?"

"I think so, Mama. Let me put a blanket under your shoulders."

John grabbed two blankets from the ground, folded both and Monroe stuffed them under Anna's shoulders. Monroe closed the car door and said: "How's that, Mama?"

"Well, I'm glad it's over. Can we go now?"

"I'll get more blankets from the house, John. You start the car and meet me at the road." He headed for the house.

* * *

When Monroe returned, the Model "T" was still where he'd left it. It wasn't running.

John cranked and cussed. "Damned thing! It usually starts. May be it's flooded."

Monroe went directly to the car, covered Anna and Charlie with the blankets. "Are you two getting any heat from these bedclothes?"

"I think so," said Anna. Charlie didn't reply.

Monroe placed his hand on Charlie's chest. "Buddy, I hope you're still with us?"

"I'm right here, Roe," Charlie whispered.

Monroe touched Charlie's hand. "Hang tight, my friend."

At the steering wheel, John adjusted the spark one more time. "Now. Let's try that."

As luck would have it, when John cranked, the motor chugged twice, backfired, and failed to start. John, panting hard, slipped the crank into its slot and spun. This time the engine fired. John ran to the steering wheel, adjusted the spark while climbing into the seat. Monroe leaped in beside him. The automobile, with its desperate passengers, made a half-circle in the barnyard and headed for Durango.

* * *

Neither John nor Monroe spoke as they made good time over a partially dry road—smooth in places and rutted in others. Monroe noted the morning had brightened. He began planning his move to Cascade.

The danger to Bonnie and the boys would definitely be increased. He didn't like that, but he'd still be able to look for a homestead on Florida Mesa and it would be easier to search for his gold mine. His whiskey still could go somewhere in the hills behind the house. And it would be easy for Sam Isgar to find Bonnie.

Monroe guessed it had to be. He'd promised his mother he'd look after Cascade and, by God; he'd do it and keep Bonnie safe, as well. He'd just have to plan on confrontations with Isgar. The length of their stay at the ranch would depend on Anna and Charlie. The degree of risk would increase with the length of time.

Suddenly, the Ford's right rear dropped. Monroe thought a wheel had come off. The loud banging against the fender startled Monroe. "What happened, John?"

"Oh shit! We've got a flat tire!"

"What do you mean—a flat tire? I thought these tires had sand pillows and they couldn't go flat."

"They've got sandbags. But sometimes if you hit a rut or turn a corner real fast, the tire opens at the rim. The sandbags come out like a string of sausages."

John was obviously mindful of the patients as he tried to stop the car quickly. Nevertheless, the loud noises made by the sandbags crashing against the car fender and the lurching automobile brought moans and groans from both Anna and Charlie.

Finally, the car came to a stop in the middle of the road. John leapt from the Ford. "Anybody traveling by will have to go around."

Monroe turned to the back seat. "Are you two, okay?"

"Why hell, Son, I thought we were going to roll over, that's all."

"I'm okay," Charlie said, weakly.

John leaned over the rear door. "Damn, I'm sorry, Anna. We'll get going again real soon. At least we've got daylight."

Monroe glanced at the sun as it touched the mountaintops on the west side of Animas Valley. The sky was blue. The air was crisp. Monroe sniffed the fragrant timothy hay.

"Roe. Notice how I managed to stop over a level spot. Get that flat rock over there while I get the jack out, will you?"

Monroe headed for the rock. "Can't we just lift the wheel up and set the jack under the axle?"

"Well. Maybe you could—you're probably strong enough—but what if it slipped. We don't want to jar Anna or Charlie any more than we have to, do we?"

Monroe didn't think he'd drop the car, but maybe shortcuts should wait for another time. He couldn't imagine Anna and Charlie's pain, and surely they didn't need any more. "You're right, John. Let's not gamble."

Soon the wheel was off it's axle and the tire removed. They re-stuffed the 30 x 3½ tire with its sand pillows, tightened the rim and set the tire on the road again. John hurried to the steering wheel, adjusted the spark and moved on to the front of the car to begin cranking. "Now if we can get it started again, we'll be on our way." The crank clicked into its slot, John spun the handle twice and the engine started.

* * *

John drove directly to Mercy Hospital's front door, stopped the car and kept the engine running. Monroe jumped out, but before he got to the door, he noticed a sign: "Emergency, This Way." An arrow pointed to the left. He whirled mid-stride, waved for John. "We need to go around here."

"Yeah. I think you're right." John gunned the Ford.

Monroe rushed through the only door on the left side of the building. A sign on the wall read: "Emergency Room." He stepped into the room and spied a wheelchair, a gurney, a cot, a small table, and a cabinet. The emergency room was church-mouse quiet.

Monroe stepped into the hall and shouted: "Hello, the hospital." His voice reverberated through the building. He took three steps forward. Stopped. Looked around. Filling his lungs, he prepared to shout again, but a starched, crisp nurse hurried down the stairs at the far end of the hall.

"Please, be quiet. You're disturbing patients." The tall, slender nun would maintain control. She wore a black robe with a stiff, white wimple and veil.

"I'm sorry, Sister, but my mother and her foreman may be dying."

The Nun folded her hands below the crucifix that dangled on her chest and pursed her lips in concentration. "Bring them into the Emergency Room and I'll look at them."

"They're hurt bad, Sister. It's going to take a doctor … maybe two. My mother's leg is broken and Charlie's been shot in the shoulder. I don't know if my mother is bleeding inside, but Charlie has lost a lot of blood."

"I'm alone."

"Can you call someone?"

"Maybe I'll have to. But bring them in so I can see."

Having spent a significant part of his early life under the tutelage of nuns, Monroe knew when to follow instructions. He turned, immediately, and headed for the car. John had untied the twine that bound Charlie to the seat.

"They're both unconscious," John announced.

"Let's take Charlie first," said Monroe.

As they arrived with Charlie, the nun held the outer door open, then, she went quickly ahead into the emergency room.

The Sister indicated the gurney. "Put him here and get your mother. Put her on the bed in the room across the hall. I'll meet you at the door."

"Thank you, Sister."

The Sister reached a piece of paper in her pocket. "I'm Sister Agnes. Be good enough to put both their names and addresses on this piece of paper, then you stay in the waiting room across the hall?"

Monroe took the paper. "Yes, Sister." Monroe crammed the paper into his pocket. "Can I do something to help get a doctor, please?"

"What's your name, Sir?" Sister Agnes had a strong suggestion of reproach in her voice.

"Monroe Morgan."

"Then, Monroe, you can help by being patient. If I need a doctor, I'll get one. Now, go get your mother."

Sister Agnes turned her attention to Charlie. Monroe, along with John, didn't break stride until they reached the car. There, they opened the car's rear doors and began removing Anna.

Anna's condition seemed to have worsened. Her face was chalky-white. Her lips were blue. She lay listless … perhaps, unconscious? Monroe felt panic enter his heart and looked hard at Sister Agnes standing at the door.

"Let's hurry, John."

"I've called Doctor Miller," said Sister Agnes. "He'll be right over. Charlie will need a surgeon. Just follow me with your mother." Sister Agnes led them into the room across the hall. "Now you two men go to the sitting room at the end of the hall and wait for me. If bones are broken without tearing blood vessels or nerves and she's not bleeding internally, that's good. There's a small chapel next to the waiting room. Feel free to go there if you wish."

Monroe and John sat in the small room without speaking. Finally, they heard a rustle as though someone might be entering the hall through the side door. Monroe ducked into the hall and witnessed a man handing his hat and overcoat to Sister Agnes.

Monroe turned to John. "Is that the doctor?"

"That's Doctor Miller."

"Do you know him?"

"No. But I've heard he's good."

The gurney rolled out of the emergency room. Charlie was on it. Doctor Miller and Sister Agnes wheeled him to the elevator. The elevator door closed and an electric motor whirred.

"What do you make of that, John?"

"I think the operating room is upstairs."

"The bullet must have cut a vein or an artery. That tourniquet Mama put on may have saved his life. I wonder how she's doing."

"How old is she, Roe?"

"Sixty-seven."

Sister Agnes walked into the room. "Mr. Morgan, do you have those papers I asked for?"

"Oh. I'm sorry, Sister. I'll do it right now. How's my mother?"

"We're still working, but I think she'll be all right— eventually. There doesn't seem to be any internal bleeding.

Her leg is fractured above and below the knee and her hip is out of joint. It'll be some time before she's able to move around and quiet a bit longer before she can walk. She's suffered shock. Will need rest."

"And Charlie?"

"He may not survive. Gone into secondary shock. We think the bullet tore the subclavian vein that returns blood from the left side of his body. It's a very deep wound. Only time can tell."

"Is he in the operating room, now?"

"Yes. Doctor Miller will close the vein and the wound. How did he lose his left arm?"

"We were riding broncos in a rodeo. A horse fell on him and broke it. They had to cut it off."

"Well, there's nothing you two can do here. Both of you might as well go home. Please, fill out the information and bring it to me in the emergency room, will you, Mr. Morgan?"

"Yes, Sister. Right away, but can I see my mother— or Charlie?"

"I'm sorry. They're both unconscious. It would be better if you came back later. We'll know a lot more then."

"Okay," said Monroe. "I'll fill out the paper and bring it to you."

Sister Agnes smiled. "Pray for Charlie ... and your mother. Charlie needs it most." She turned toward the emergency room.

* * *

When Monroe and John exited Mercy Hospital's side door, a white Stetson seemed to float above the far side of John's car. The hat contrasted sharply with the Ford's black hood. Monroe recognized the hat instantly. Bob Stout had to be squatting on the other side of John's automobile. Monroe glanced at John. "What in the hell's he doing here."

John glanced about. "Who?"

Monroe quickened his pace. "Let me do the talking, okay?"

"Sure," said John, confused and falling back a step.

As Monroe rounded the car, he found Deputy Bob Stout on his haunches examining the left front tire. Bob looked up, smiled, moved his hat to the back of his head. "Glad to see ya'." His gaze turned to John as he spoke. "I didn't know this was your car, John, but I knew your traveling friend was here."

"What the hell're you doin' here, Bob?" Monroe asked, deliberately staring.

"Now don't get excited, Monroe. I've always wondered about these tires. Now, I know they're 30 by 3½."

"Well, we're pretty busy. So we're gonna keep moving."

Bob put out a hand, palm up. "Now don't run off, Mr. Morgan. I've had a couple of phone calls about some trouble out at Cascade. How's your mother?"

"She's in the hospital—with a broken leg—and Charlie's in there with a bullet hole in his left shoulder. Does that make you feel better?"

Bob seemed taken aback. "Why should it make me feel better?"

"Because the two sonzabitches that did the damage looked a lot like you and that little piss-ant you run around with, that's why." Monroe recognized his anger was getting the best of him because he could hardly see. He knew he might lose control, and when everything went black, he couldn't remember anything afterwards. It frightened him, but he'd never been able to do anything about it. He felt himself slipping.

"Now wait a minute. Are you accusing me and Earl Mills of burning down your barn?"

"Did you? You sonuvabitch!"

"No. Dammit! Now get a hold of yourself." Bob backed away, extending both hands defensively.

Monroe knew he wasn't handling this confrontation well. He began pacing in front of the Ford ... trying to control himself.

"Get in the car, Monroe," John said. "Let's go!"

Somehow Monroe heard John's voice through the rage. He tromped stiff-legged to the car's radiator. "Get in, John. I'll crank."

Monroe cranked the car so hard it couldn't help but start. He walked to the passenger seat and climbed in. "Let's go."

Bob took a step toward the car and smiled. "So, where you living, now?"

As the car made a U-turn, Monroe stuck his head out the window. "Go to hell!"

CHAPTER SIX

December 1922

Bonnie took her coffee into the front room, made her way to the bay window and looked west across Cascade's front lawn, then over the road to the barn's gray-black ashes, and into the far distances of Animas Valley. Beyond the burned-out barn, the corral's white board fence and two watering troughs stood stark against three haystacks that had not been consumed by fire. Attached to the white fence posts that formed the stockyard, she saw barbed wire fencing that terminated the barnyard at the road and returned to the corral's white fence. Inside the enclosure, near the watering troughs, Chukaluks stood with Monroe's black mules, Jack and Jinni. She searched for Monroe in the meadow. When she could not find him, she supposed he'd come back to the house and finished his walk-around. Probably gone to the tack room down by the bunkhouse. She knew the cows had been milked because she'd separated the cream.

Bonnie's mind turned to yesterday and how quickly she'd packed. She smiled. Even though she'd worked feverishly to save the daylight for her first look at Cascade, her anxious efforts had gone for naught, because by the time they'd driven to Cascade, darkness had fallen. Monroe had barely enough time to milk the cows and assure that appropriate stock could be contained in what was left of the corral and the barnyard fencing.

Now, she just wanted to sit in the large window seat, sip her coffee, puff her pipe, and gaze across the valley as the sun came up. How she loved Colorado!

To Bonnie, Colorado seemed the cleanest, the freshest; the most beautiful place she had ever lived. She loved it more each day. She reasoned that if these terrible problems had to be hers, she might as well be surrounded by breathtaking beauty. And after having lived a patched-together life for twenty-six years, she felt she deserved to live in this majestic spot.

Of course, she didn't remember much about home, i.e., Kentucky. She didn't remember much about the state, or Rochester, the town. She did remember the heat. She remembered being there—and she'd been told she was born there.

Her parents had moved to Kansas City, Kansas, when she was twelve. And, being the only child in the Matthew Gunn family, life seemed perfectly pleasant until that frightful day when everything turned upside down … literally.

She had been on the train with her mother and father, in a Pullman-roomette, traveling home from Chicago. They'd just finished admiring the sunset and they'd begun to prepare for dinner. Suddenly, everything seemed to slip and slide. The train buckled, derailed, and the cars began running into each other at a river crossing. The car, in which she and her family rode, turned upside down, crashed into the coach in front of them and got smashed by the cars crashing in behind. Bonnie survived, but her mother and father died. Her mother, Esperanza Cortez Gunn, and father, Matthew Gunn, were buried in Kansas City.

With no family members, the Kansas City authorities arranged a home for her at St. Joseph's Orphanage. Since she was Catholic, the choice seemed correct.

And, at the orphanage, she had achieved an eight-grade education while the Sisters taught her cooking and sewing. She sang in the choir. Her obvious singing and dancing talents made her a standout in school theatrical events. At sixteen she entered and won her first beauty contest.

Two years later, her enthusiasm for the theatre caused her to enter another beauty contest sponsored by a traveling Chautauqua, which needed a dancer-singer. Bonnie won. To her great delight, she began traveling the Chautauqua circuit from Chicago to San Francisco via Kansas City, Denver, Salt Lake, Reno, Sacramento, and selected smaller towns' in-between. The show, when its schedule allowed, made short stops in places like Grand Junction, Colorado. For several years, she had enjoyed the traveling and the excitement of show business.

But finally, at age twenty-two, in Denver, she began thinking of leaving the show. She'd visited Denver several times, but this was the first time she'd visited a town with the idea of staying. And, this was the first time she spoke her thoughts to her Director and Stage Manager, Mr. John Sturdivant.

After that conversation, Bonnie didn't have long to wait for her chance to leave the show. The Chautauqua stopped in Grand Junction that year and, there, she met a man whose name was Sam Isgar.

Sam was the committee chairman who brought the Chautauqua to Grand Junction. He gave the cast an opening night dinner at his Golden Pheasant Restaurant. He requested an introduction to Bonnie and John Sturdivant obliged. The introduction began an intense courtship.

At the time, Bonnie found Sam attractive, charming, and wealthy. Sam was a good catch for any girl, she thought. When he proposed marriage, she accepted. She wanted to get married. She'd thought about it a lot. But mostly, the circuit had lost its allure, and Sam seemed to be a truly good man.

Bonnie later learned that Sam needed a wife to further his political ambitions. She also learned that his political friends had raised questions about his being thirty-two-years-old and unmarried. The Ku Klux Klan and his desire to organize a political base on the Western Slope came later.

Sam promised to marry her in the Catholic Church, but when the time came, he made excuses. Bonnie realized, too late, that that was the time she should have backed out of the engagement. Instead, she settled for a wedding before a justice of the peace. Now, however, Bonnie was happy she'd married before a justice of the peace, because getting a divorce through the Catholic Church would be impossible.

Now, Bonnie had only two ambitions in life. First, she'd be the best wife Monroe could ever have, and second, she'd be a very good mother for both her boys.

And then, yesterday, when Monroe asked her to gather up the babies and move to Cascade, Bonnie's heart leapt with happiness. She saw an opportunity to help Anna and to further her own ambitions.

Last night, she had moved their meager possessions into the house while Monroe milked three cows, fed livestock, and rode Chukaluks a mile up the road to the Jackson Ranch. When Monroe got back from the Jackson's, he said the Jackson's had volunteered to care for Harold and Wade whenever she and Monroe needed to go some place together. In fact, he said, Mrs. Jackson was coming over this morning to watch the boys while she and Monroe went to the hospital.

Hearing a strange noise outside the house, Bonnie tiptoed across the front room and peeked through the window toward the back of the house. There in an attached shed, she watched Monroe twisting the crank of a Model "T" Ford, and if the engine indicated that it might start, Monroe would scurry back and forth adjusting the spark and the gas levers attached to the steering wheel. After each adjustment, he cranked again. The car chugged but never started. Seemingly frustrated, Monroe strode to the rear of the car, yanked a tarpaulin forward over the car, and tied the tarpaulin off at the car's wheels and headed for the house.

In the house, Monroe hung his hat on a wall-peg and plopped into a kitchen chair. "Tried to start Dad's car," he said.

"Try again after breakfast," Bonnie encouraged, kissing his cheek.

"Ah, I'll just hitch Chukaluks to the buggy. We'll take that. Need to get him used to the buggy anyway." Monroe went to the basin and washed his face and hands. "You'll have to learn to hitch that rig, when I'm gone."

Bonnie spooned two bowls of natural whole wheat and sat a pitcher of cream on the table. "No problem. I love horses. I bet you only have to show me once. Chukaluks likes me."

"I may be gone a day or two at a time, you know. Think you can handle things?"

"Milking may be a problem for a couple of days. But if other women can do it, I can."

"No doubt."

Bonnie poured cream on Monroe's whole wheat. "And don't worry about me getting the harness on Chukaluks. I may be a little short, but I can stand him by the granary dock and drop the harness over him."

"Okay. How about the shafts—to the harness?"

"Don't worry. I'm plenty strong. I'll show you when you're ready to hook up this morning."

"Okay. I'll be watching. But, can we leave for the hospital as some as Mrs. Jackson gets here?"

"I don't see why not. I'll feed the boys and get them ready for her."

Bonnie could hardly wait to meet Mrs. Jackson. She wanted to know all of Monroe's friends, but she particularly wanted to know the ladies living in the valley.

* * *

In the hospital, Sister Agnes met Bonnie and Monroe. After introductions, Sister Agnes ushered them into her tiny office.

"Folks, I don't have good news." She looked at Monroe. "Mr. Eagle and your mother are going to be here for some time. His shoulder wound and his loss of blood, as well as your mother's broken leg, and her age, might have been too much. The weather only added to the problem. No one knows how long recovery will take. It's just too soon to tell."

Monroe leaned forward. "They aren't going to die, are they?"

"No, I don't think so. We'll know more later."

Monroe reached for Bonnie's hand. "How long, Sister?"

"Probably six weeks—maybe more."

Bonnie stared at Monroe. "That means they'll be in the hospital through Christmas and into January."

Sister Agnes agreed. "I think so. You shouldn't hurry them. Charlie might come around sooner, but your mother will probably need every bit of the time. And there's something else I need to make you aware of, if you're not already."

"What's that, Sister?"

Sister Agnes left her desk and walked to the window. "We're getting a lot of flu cases. It acts like the Spanish Influenza we had a few years back. It strikes when you least expect it. We have four cases, now. So, take care of yourselves." She adjusted the window blind for more light.

"Could Anna or Charlie get it," Bonnie asked.

"Anybody can get it, but I was thinking of you two … and your children."

Both Bonnie and Monroe remained silent as they focused on their potential health problems. "Thank you for your concern, Sister," Bonnie said, rising from her chair. "May we see Anna and Charlie?"

"Of course. But please don't stay long. They're very weak. Charlie's in Ward D and Anna's in Ward C. Both upstairs. Be very quiet."

"Thank you Sister." Monroe smiled, nodded and followed Bonnie.

Bonnie and Monroe walked along the hall, peeking into large rooms on either side. Since Bonnie had helped out in a Kansas City hospital, she felt quite at home and walked along counting beds. Of the twenty beds she counted, only five were empty.

Anna appeared to be a sleep when they arrived. Her face was ashen. Bonnie could see the neck pulse pounding rapidly. As they approached the bed, Anna turned her face to them.

"Oh," Anna said, opening and closing her eyes.

"Hi, Mama." Monroe touched her hand and kissed her forehead. "How are you?"

"Better than yesterday." Anna tried to smile. "I go in and out. Can't seem to get rested."

"Well, Mom, you've got nothing else to do, so just relax." Monroe took a firm grip on her hand.

"Have you moved to Cascade, Son?"

"Yes, Mama."

"I love it," Bonnie said, eagerly.

Anna looked sideways at Monroe. "You have to milk the cows, you know."

"Don't worry, Mama."

Anna's forehead furrowed. "How's Charlie?"

"We'll see him next, Mama."

Bonnie bent closer. "What can I do, Anna?"

"Oh, Dear, if you take care of the house and your family, that'll be enough. How are you?"

"I'm fine, Mama," said Bonnie. "Getting better every day. I just want to help you, if I can."

"Why hell, child. I feel the very same way about you." Anna tried to touch Bonnie's hand and failed. "You better go see Charlie, now." Anna slowly closed her eyes.

"We will, Mama. And we'll see you tomorrow."

Anna kept her eyes closed, but when Monroe kissed her nose and turned toward the door, she said: "Did you drive the automobile in?"

"No, Mama. It wouldn't start."

"Get John to help you … and use it."

"I will, Mama."

On the way to Charlie's room, Bonnie grabbed Monroe's arm. "Can I drive it?"

"What do you mean?"

"I want to drive the car." Bonnie was emphatic.

"Can you crank it?"

"I can try."

Monroe smiled and hugged her shoulders. "Of course, you can drive it. You can try anything you think you're big enough to handle—just don't break your arm cranking."

Bonnie's first glimpse of Charlie caused her to turn away. She had seen his robustness and steadfast independence when he retrieved the buggy from the Laurence's. She remembered his dark good looks and his strength when he drove the buggy away allowing Anna to stay with her and the babies. She hadn't seen many Indians, but she liked Charlie right off. Now, his cheeks were sunken and the ruddy glow of color and health had gone from his face. The high cheekbones were greatly emphasized and the deep-black eyes gleamed in a pale gray skin. He appeared smaller and thinner than she remembered. As Monroe walked closer, a look of recognition, then happiness crossed Charlie's face.

"Roe!" Charlie weakly raised his right hand off the bed.

Monroe stepped quickly to his friend, leaned over, and grasped the extended hand. "Charlie! I'm missing you already! I had to milk those dammed cows all by myself last night."

Charlie barely smiled. "You doin' the chores?"

"Who else? You go down. I step up—and vice versa."

"Mostly vice versa." Charlie glanced at Bonnie.

"He misses you, Charlie."

"I know it." Charlie gazed at Monroe.

"How do you feel?" Monroe asked.

"Like a cloud. Floating."

Monroe smiled. "White or black?"

"White. It glows pink in the sunset."

"Ah, my friend. You'll be running free in no time. White clouds are good."

"I'm too darn tired, Roe. No strength." Charlie seemed reluctant to admit physical weakness.

"You lost a lot of blood, my friend." Monroe gently touched the bandage near Charlie's wound.

"Don't do anything until I'm up. Okay? I want a hand in the next round.

"Trust me." Monroe nodded his approval. "I go nowhere without you."

"Good." Charlie moved his eyes to the doorway. "I'll hold you to it."

The sound of footsteps caused Bonnie and Monroe to glance toward the door. Charlie's eyes never left the face of the man who entered the room. He was tall—maybe six-four—and dark complexioned. He wore a black Stetson hat and a sheepskin coat. He was clean-shaven except for a heavy black moustache. He moved deliberately to Charlie's bedside. A silver star gleamed below his sheepskin's collar.

"Good morning. I'm Sheriff Harvey Howe. I apologize for interrupting your visit." He looked at Monroe. "But I'm pressed for time, and I want to ask Charlie, some questions. You folks mind waiting in the hall for a few minutes?"

Bonnie resented the intrusion. She immediately disliked the Sheriff.

"All right, just give us a minute. We were saying good-bye." Monroe stepped forward gently touching Charlie's chest. "We'll see you later, Charlie. Get some rest."

Monroe turned to the Sheriff. "Don't stay too long, Sheriff. He's had enough pushing around."

Bonnie felt Monroe's hand on her arm guiding her from the room. She noticed the glint in Monroe's eyes as he blanched white around the mouth.

"What's the matter, Roe?"

"Remember," Monroe whispered. "Mama said the men who burned the cross on our front lawn looked like Deputies Stout and Mills? Well ... they work for him ... Sheriff Howe! And he's the same size as Bob Stout."

"What are you thinking?" Bonnie asked, peeking sideways into Charlie's room.

"That man could be running the Klan in Durango. Maybe he rode with Earl Mills instead of Bob Stout?"

Bonnie hadn't liked the sheriff's attitude when he entered the room. Now, if Sheriff Howe was a friend of Sam Isgar and if the Klan in Durango was helping Sam ... well ... it was too much. She tried to think what to do. She was ready to fight, she just didn't know whom to hit first. She was glad, however, that the Sheriff knew she was in town. "When he's gone, let's go back."

"Well ... I'm anxious to know what the Sheriff wanted, but not if it creates more stress for Charlie. We'll ask our questions later."

* * *

The following morning, Bonnie eagerly proceeded with her divorce activities while assuming responsibility for the boys and the ranch, as well as, hospital visits, and Monroe continued to implement his plans for homesteading Florida Mesa, locating his gold mine, and establishing a whiskey trade. They had agreed that the whiskey business would be temporary.

Monroe had already called John Laurence, started the Morgan Model "T" and headed into town to begin the Florida Mesa land-filing process. Bonnie had washed the breakfast dishes, put a boiler full of dirty clothes on the stove and bathed both boys, but her mind was mainly on Mrs. Jackson.

Bonnie picked up the telephone. She cranked three longs and a short. Mrs. Jackson just might enjoy a little visit over the phone.

"Hello. This is Barbara Jackson on East Animas Road."

"Hello Mrs. Jackson, this is Bonnie Morgan. We didn't get to visit yesterday."

"I know! I'm glad you called. We want to help where we can."

"Well, I need to tell you again how grateful I am that you were willing to take the boys yesterday when we went to town."

"Oh, it's nothing. What are neighbors for? We're glad to have you and Monroe back home. How's Anna this morning, do you know?"

"No. Not yet. Monroe's in town today, so he'll stop by the hospital and see both of them—Anna and Charlie. You know Charlie, of course?"

"Oh, sure. He's special."

Suddenly, for the first time that morning, sunshine flooded the valley and bathed Cascade in crisp, bright sunlight. Bonnie reacted joyously. "We're having our first direct sunlight. I just love the way the mountains control shadows in this valley."

"And the weather, too. Have you noticed how all the storms come from the north?"

Bonnie thought, briefly. "Well maybe I have. But, do you know, I don't think I've been here long enough to recognize very much, Mrs. Jackson."

"Oh please. Call me Barbara. We're going to be friends. I just know it."

"I certainly hope so ... Barbara. I'm anxious to make time for a visit. And you must call me Bonnie, will you?"

"Of course. Tell you what. I'll just run over and have a cup of coffee, right now ... if it's okay?"

"I'd love it."

"I'll be over within the hour. I <u>love</u> that house."

Bonnie replaced the receiver, glanced around the house while she wondered what needed to be done before Barbara got there. Her excitement soared. She hurried from room to room, touching furniture, inspecting for dust, straightening a doily here, a tablecloth there. Finally, she ran upstairs to the boy's room; they were fast asleep. Turning to a closet, she selected a fresh dress: a print she liked. She quickly brushed her hair, checked her lipstick and hurried downstairs. According to the grandfather clock at the foot of the stairs, nine minutes had passed. "Well, I'm ready. Whoops!" She headed for the coffee pot.

As Bonnie fussed, she recalled Barbara Jackson's remark about the house. She said she "<u>loved</u> that house." What was so special about <u>this</u> house, Bonnie wondered?

Finally, after many glances up the road, Bonnie saw a brown horse loping along. Mrs. Jackson! Harold began to whimper. Darn! She knew if Harold were awake, Wade would soon follow. "Perfect timing," she said aloud, as she prepared to greet her new friend.

Barbara Jackson, healthy, hearty and big in the hips, tied her horse to the hitching post outside the kitchen door, shouted a greeting and hurried forward while she expressed an urgent desire to use the bathroom. With greetings and salutations gushing, Bonnie ushered Barbara to the downstairs bath, then waited until her guest returned. She let Harold fuss.

Barbara exited the bathroom. "Oh, I do love this house so very much! It's such a pleasure to go to the toilet inside the house! You don't know how lucky you are!"

"Doesn't everyone have inside plumbing?"

"Heavens, no! This is the only house in the valley with piped-in water and bathroom facilities."

"I guess Monroe hasn't had time to tell me everything, has he? If I want cooking or drinking water, I just go to the faucet in the kitchen and turn it on. The little creek across the south side of the yard goes under the road to the barn and the stockyard. We've been as busy as ants, Barbara, especially with Anna and Charlie in the hospital." Bonnie gazed intently at Mrs. Jackson's moon face and soft-brown eyes. Monroe had said that Barbara was at least twice Bonnie's age and that she'd been one of the original valley settlers.

Barbara continued to gush. "Did you know that there's a pond on the other side of those haystacks?" Then, without waiting for an answer. "The pond has a valve on the far side that either holds water in the pond or allows it to go on down for irrigation."

So the day went, with Barbara Jackson informing Bonnie about the Jacksons and the valley and Bonnie acquainting Barbara with herself and the children. Bonnie learned of the shock and surprise felt by valley ranchers when they heard about the Klan's attack on Cascade. In fact, both women became so comfortable with each other that they left very little out of their conversation.

But when the postman brought the mail at 3 o'clock, both ladies noted, with astonishment, that a huge amount of the day had lapsed. Especially when it became clear that they had not finished talking. However, the mail gave Barbara Jackson an opportunity to say she needed to go home, and the letters piqued Bonnie's curiosity, so, the ladies terminated the happy meeting by resolving to get together often. Either home was made available for their next meeting. But, according to Barbara, Bonnie's house was preferable.

When Bonnie approached the mailbox, it was stuffed. She thought the volume of mail represented several days' accumulation. After carrying it all into the house, she dumped it unceremoniously on the kitchen table and carefully sorted through each piece, noticing the return address and stacking it according to date. Nothing in the pile was from Douglas Downey, her divorce attorney. One letter from the First National Bank of Durango held her attention and she didn't know why. The children were taking their afternoon nap.

While watching the western mountain shadows move toward the river, Bonnie heard "the fliver" churning up the road from town. She watched Monroe round the last bend before turning into the gate. She felt excitement just watching the easy way Monroe's big shoulders moved, rhythmically, as he went about doing things—such as now, when he effortlessly turned the steering wheel and maneuvered the car into the yard. She could see his black eyes searching the windows to get a glimpse of her. It was thrilling to watch him come home and know he wanted her. She ran to the kitchen door as Monroe backed the car into the shed.

"I'm going to leave it uncovered until I finished the chores. Don't let me forget to drain the radiator. It'll probably freeze tonight." He swept her into his arms and kissed her eager mouth. "Now, what have you been doing all day?"

"After you tell me about your mother and Charlie."

"No change. They're still touch and go. Now, you."

"Oh, Roe! I've got so much to tell. All good. Don't worry. But you better get your chores done first. I don't want to be interrupted."

"Okay." Monroe smiled and gazed at the last of the day's sunshine. He went onto the porch to get the milk buckets. "Did you happen to get mail today?"

"Yes. I did. And there's a lot. Nothing from my lawyer, though."

After dark, when the chores were done, and supper was over, Monroe sat down with the mail. He moved the electric table lamp closer to his elbow. Bonnie watched as he opened piece after piece. Some letters they discussed and saved, others they opened and discarded. Finally, Monroe picked up the letter from the First National Bank of Durango. Monroe ripped the letter open. He read the letter and then looked away.

"What's the matter?" Bonnie reached for his hands.

"Oh, Honey. I didn't realize." Monroe fumbled for words. "I had no idea."

"What is it, Roe?"

"Cascade!"

"What about Cascade?" Bonnie rose and moved to his side. She reached for the paper. He let it fall from his hand. She stared incredulously and moved the letter closer to the light.

"They're going to foreclose on Cascade! They're going to take Cascade away from us—in thirty days. I can't dump this on Mama. I'll have to take care of it myself, if I can."

* * *

Early, the next morning, Monroe entered Main Avenue at Tenth Street, a block north of the First National Bank. A city water wagon passed. It was spraying the street's powdery dirt with formaldehyde. Monroe remembered they'd done that in 1918—for the flu.

Vacant stores screamed "hard times." Boarded-up saloons yelled "Prohibition." Continuing to glance left and right, Monroe kept Chukaluks clear of the few people who walked the street. No automobiles anywhere. "Doesn't look like anyone wants to be here, big fella."

Monroe tied Chukaluks to the hitching rail in front of the bank, stepped across the boardwalk, cleaned his boots on the scraper and opened the front door.

As the bank door creaked inward, a string of sleigh-bells jingled. Monroe saw no one. He smelled the musty air, the oil-soaked floor, the coal soot, the writing ink and the aging paper. He heard a sharp, cold wind strike the building as the dark-gray clouds deepened the shadows.

"Morning. Can I help you?" The voice came from inside a corner room, in back. A small metal placard on the office door read "John McGovern, Vice President."

Monroe opened a swinging gate, passed two empty desks and stopped at McGovern's door. Peeking in, he said, "Sir, I'm Monroe Morgan—son of Henry and Anna Morgan?"

"I know who you are. I remember your father."

The banker, in his late fifties, leaned his tall, slender frame against the back of a shiny red leather chair and let the light from a green-glass desk lamp flood his face. Resting his head against the chair, he gazed at the ceiling. His forehead was as pale as the large white handkerchief that covered his nose and mouth. A salt-and-pepper goatee extended below the white cloth. Deep brown eyes peered from beneath heavy eyebrows.

"Name's John McGovern. Have a seat." McGovern's waving hand indicated a straight-backed chair and his gaze never left the ceiling. "Hang your derby on the rack."

"Thank you." Monroe realized he held his hat in his hands.

As Monroe removed the foreclosure notice from his pocket, his red bandanna fluttered to the floor. He scooped the errant rag. "Do you want me to cover my face?"

"Suit yourself. You're the one at risk."

Monroe cleared his throat. "Sir, with my Dad's recent death and my mother in the hospital, there've been bills. It's hard to make ends meet. Last week somebody burned our barn." McGovern's eyes didn't leave the ceiling. Monroe forced himself to continue. "Well—about the mortgage. I'd like to pay interest on the principle each month and pay taxes when they're due."

John McGovern's eyes shifted to Monroe's face. He leaned forward in his seat, palms pressed flat on the desk blotter. "Not so fast. The bank is in a position to foreclose today. We want payment in full."

"I thought we could talk it over."

McGovern looked away then stared directly at Monroe. "You mean negotiate?"

Monroe hesitated. "Well, I don't have much money. Only a month's interest."

"But that's your problem, isn't it? Your father said he'd make payments on time. Right?"

"Yes."

"Well? You Morgan's have missed payments all along."

Monroe's mind raced. He felt he needed to say the exact right thing. He didn't know what his mother may have said on previous occasions or whether she had ever conversed with McGovern about financial difficulties.

"If you don't want to discuss it, I'll see a lawyer and try to decide what to do," said Monroe. He hoped to keep the discussion going.

"Why don't you sell it, Young Man? Farming and ranching haven't been profitable. Even during the war, we mostly traded among ourselves. This is a mining community—when we don't have all these damn strikes." McGovern flipped a pencil across the desk to emphasize his point.

"You mean ... sell Cascade?" Monroe gazed beyond McGovern to a painting, which glorified Animas Valley.

"I couldn't make that decision, sir. Cascade belongs to my mother and she's in the hospital."

"Cascade? That what you call it?"

"Yes, sir."

111

"Sell it. You're young and strong. You could take care of your mother and save yourself a lot of trouble. You're reasonably intelligent, if I'm any judge. How old are you?"

"Twenty-nine."

"So. You were too old for service in the war. But you're not too old to start over with a nest egg."

Monroe couldn't imagine why McGovern brought his age and World War I into the conversation. Cascade wasn't his "nest egg," it was his mother's home.

"I don't know what Mother would do, if she could decide, but I'll tell you right now, if it were up to me, I wouldn't sell. That's right up front, Sir. I, personally, don't want to leave the valley and start over, either. My plan is to earn money right here and pay the bills I owe … and the bills my mother owes."

Monroe felt his chest tighten. He sat silent not knowing how to proceed. Finally, he remembered a talk he'd had with his father just before his father died.

"Mr. McGovern, Cascade is very special. My Dad, on his deathbed, made me promise to keep it. We've got family graves there. Grandparents on both sides. A brother. A sister." He lowered his voice. "I plan to live there and raise my own family."

"Family graves … and you're not the type to roam. What else keeps you from selling?"

Monroe thought a moment. "Well, I don't want my mother worrying about it right now. That's why I'm here."

"But you might burden yourself for life if you try to pay your folks debts."

"The river runs right through Cascade. Waters our stock year 'round."

"That river runs through a lot of farms."

"There's a gold mine in our canyon. It'll make money someday. We've got the mineral rights to all one hundred acres."

"Means a better price when you sell. You'd have cash left over."

Monroe exploded. "We're not going to sell! And that's that!"

"If you don't pay the bank, I'll foreclose and sell it for you. You understand that?"

Monroe gulped for air. "Yes, Sir! I understand that." Monroe cleared his throat. "I want to pay the interest each month until I can catch up all at once."

Time seemed to stand still. Monroe looked at McGovern. McGovern stared back.

"The bank needs money, son. I can't keep that front door open and carry every rancher in Animas Valley."

"You won't lose money on me. I'll pay interest in advance, taxes on time—and the entire principal in four years."

McGovern leaned back in his chair again. "Can you make two interest payments now? Today?"

"Would I have to?"

"That's the only way I'd make another agreement with you. I think I'm being pretty fair, don't you?"

Monroe knew he had the money, but he didn't want to spend it. He had purposely come to town without money. His plan was to establish a bank account if there was some reason for it, but until he saw some benefit; he'd keep his money under his own control. Now he wondered if he shouldn't establish an account with a small amount of money. Might give McGovern more incentive to write a new contract.

"Maybe I could get the money, today, but I might have trouble getting back into town. Did you know they're checking people again? Like they did with the Spanish Influenza a few years ago. There aren't many people moving around out side there."

McGovern nodded. "Who's doing the checking? The Sheriff?"

"I don't know. No one stopped me, but I saw them at a distance."

McGovern stared at his desktop. "Tell you what." He swiveled his big chair and took a thick binder from a shelf. "We'll make a new contract. I'll write an attachment to your father's contract. You'll pay principal and interest this month plus interest for next month. Then you'll pay interest every month, in advance, for two years. After two years, you'll pay the principal in full."

Monroe couldn't believe his ears. The entire debt in two years! How would he do that?

"Mr. McGovern. I've got this month's interest, but I don't have the principal."

"I'll give you 'til Friday to get the rest. That's two days. It'll take that long to modify the contract."

"But the letter said we had thirty days until foreclosure," Monroe reminded McGovern.

"Oh, let's get it over with," McGovern said.

"I don't have it." Monroe heard the tension in his voice.

"Sell something." All expression had left the vice-president's face. His mouth held steady.

Monroe made the Sign-of-a-Cross. "Could we figure exactly how much money I'd need Friday?"

"Sure. Just a minute." McGovern seemed relieved. "Let's see. Two interest payments of $13.71 plus a principal payment makes a total of $64.71. After keeping up your interest payments each month, you'll owe $3, 248 at the end of two years. If that's agreeable with you, I'll draw up the papers so the interest will be due on the first of every month. Come in Friday with the money and sign a new contract. All right?" McGovern extended his hand.

"It'll have to be. Could I pay the principle in three years instead of two?"

"No. Two years seems fair to me—under the circumstances." Monroe stared directly into McGovern's eyes. "But, so there's no hard feelings, I'll make it two years and six months."

114

Resigned, Monroe relaxed his shoulders. "Well. I don't know how I'm going to accumulate $3,248 in two-and-a-half years, but I'll tell you right now: I'm going to do it."

"Look at it this way, young man. You can sell Cascade right now and wind up with some cash or you can sign a new contract. If you pay off the mortgage, we'll both be happy." McGovern left his chair and came around the desk. "We'll meet here Friday. Agreed? Or the deals off."

"Yes, sir."

"And let me warn you—just so there's no confusion—the bank <u>will</u> foreclose if you are late for this Friday appointment and we'll <u>foreclose</u> if you're a week late with the interest payments."

"Now, why would I be late?"

"I don't know, but I understand you have a tendency to put things off. You could have come in before we sent you the notice. You knew the money was due."

Monroe now suspected that his mother had been warned before and hadn't mentioned it. She had evidently been having difficult times.

"Who told you I put things off?" asked Monroe, recognizing one of his failings.

"No one in particular and everyone in general. The bank wondered whether you'd make this appointment today. You've had it a month."

My god! Had Anna forgotten an appointment with the bank she'd had for a month? Did he simply stumble onto the foreclosure notice after his mother had missed appointments?

"Today is different. Cascade's at stake," Monroe said.

"Friday?" McGovern smiled and nodded. Extended his hand, again.

"I'll be here." Monroe took McGovern's hand. "Eleven o'clock. With money." Inside his head, demons seemed to be smashing themselves against the hot rocks of Hell. He walked to the door. "God, help me," he breathed.

* * *

115

When Monroe's feet hit the bedroom floor Friday morning, his head ached. He hadn't felt well since he'd talked to John McGovern last Tuesday. Bonnie said the negotiation caused his illness. But no matter what, his eleven o'clock appointment would be kept.

He pushed himself to do chores, saddle Chukaluks, and leave early. Bonnie's parting words were: "Come home when you're through at the bank and go to bed. All right?"

The day was cold and windy. Looked like snow. Everything seemed strangely quiet.

At 10:25 A.M. he entered the bank.

Monroe found himself signing his name to whatever papers were placed before him. He rose. His legs shook. Sweat ran down his face.

"Are you all right, Morgan?" McGovern looked concerned. He hurried around the desk and placed a hand on Monroe's shoulder.

"Yes. I think so. Haven't felt well—this morning. Walk with me to my horse, please." McGovern adjusted his handkerchief over his face.

Monroe, with McGovern's help, climbed aboard Chukaluks and headed out of town. He gripped his legs tight to the saddle skirt in an effort to keep from falling.

Chukaluks's hooves sounded like a bass drum as he crossed the Main Street Bridge. Monroe realized he shouldn't be on the bridge at all. He'd gone too far. He should have turned east at 15th Street.

Monroe looked toward the sky ... its swirling clouds ... the blurring hills. Smeared colors streaked by. Gray. Green. Black. White. He couldn't breathe.

Grabbing his pigging string from his saddlebag, he wrapped the string around both his wrists and cinched the string tight to the saddle horn. "Take me home, big-boy. Guess I should've covered my face with something."

* * *

From Grand Junction, four days later, Sam Isgar phoned Bob Stout in Durango. He hadn't had a report from Durango in over a week. Something had to give.

Bob answered the phone. "Goddammit, Bob. How come I never hear from you?"

"Oh. Well. Here I am," came the deputy's answer.

"Yeah. I know you're there, but I never hear from you." There was silence on the line.

"How about the letters I write?" asked Bob.

"That's good," said Sam. "They give us a chance to detail things and send copies of stuff—newspaper clippings, handbills and the like. They help clarify things, but right now I need something more current. It takes a week or more to get a letter over here. There are things happening in Durango that I need to know about."

"Like what?"

"For Christ's sake, Bob," growled Sam. "Bonnie and that Asshole, Morgan!"

Sam could hear someone talking to Bob on the other end of the line. In exasperation, he waited for Bob to come back.

"Okay. That was Sheriff Howe. He wants me to check on some flu cases at the hospital. Prisoners we had here in jail."

"That's another thing. I shouldn't have to talk with you while you're at the jail. Too damn many ears."

"I hear that. Never have liked it."

"Okay," Sam said to his henchman. "Here's my idea. Might work out good. You call me every Friday between 4:30 and 5:00 P.M. and reverse the charges. That way you can call me from anywhere you happen to be and you can arrange some privacy. I'll take the call here in the Klavern. We'll both be able to talk freely. What do you say? Can you do that?"

"I don't see why not. Sounds good."

"Okay. We'll start this coming Friday. Agreed?"

"I'll do it, Sam."

"Now, one more thing, Bob. Keep this under your hat. I'll be over there in a couple weeks, or so."

CHAPTER SEVEN

December 1922

When Monroe opened his eyes, he felt weak and disoriented. It was dark. He thought it best to lie still and listen. No need jumping up until he knew where he was. Wherever he was, it smelled like formaldehyde. The place had been disinfected. Must be a sickroom!

As his vision improved, the room took shape. A kerosene lamp, turned low, on a table across the room. He could see a dim chimney ring reflecting on the ceiling. No sound anywhere.

Suddenly, he remembered. He'd been riding Chukaluks. Let's see. He'd finished with the bank and headed home. Maybe he was home? He couldn't remember coming in.

"Hello. Anybody here?" He touched a cotton mask covering his nose and mouth. While wrestling with the questions created by the mask, he listened. Silence everywhere.

A door opened. Someone stepped quietly into the room. The light brightened. Bonnie!

"Honey! Oh, God! I'm glad you're here. Where are we?" He stared across the dimly lit room while talking through the cloth.

Bonnie hurried across the room. "Cascade. We're home, Honey."

"Really? I'm home?"

"The Logan boys came along and found the two of you in the ditch beside the road." Bonnie bent and kissed him. "They couldn't wake you, so they brought you home. They helped me get you into the house."

"Which room is this?"

"The one at the top of the stairs—in the front part of the house—overlooking the valley. Remember?"

"Yeah. It's my old room—when I was a kid. Did they carry me?"

"No. I kept you downstairs for a day, and then Mr. and Mrs. Jackson helped me."

"Have I been unconscious all night?"

"You've been 'in' and 'out' for three days and four nights," Bonnie said. "This is the fourth night. Don't you remember?"

"Remember what?"

"What you said," she smiled. He couldn't imagine why Bonnie was smiling. "You talked about all kinds of things," she continued. "The bank—several times. I fed you broth for three days. You've been drinking a lot of whiskey. And, incidentally, whiskey's done more good than anything else. The doctor said to take it."

As far as Monroe could remember, he'd just left the bank … around noon. "Oh, my God! I've put you through hell, haven't I?" He threw the covers back. Determined to get up. "What's the matter with me?"

"Now, now!" Bonnie's voice rose for the first time since entering the room. She pushed his shoulders down. "You're not to start worrying. Hear? I'm fine—the boys are fine—everything's fine."

As he leaned back and relaxed against the pillow, Bonnie replaced his covers and moved into the chair beside his bed. Bonnie's facial expressions gave him concern. She swallowed hard. Trying to remain calm, he thought. "Let me try to answer your questions, Roe. We'll get through this." She reached for a drinking glass with a golden liquid in it. Whiskey? "Now, listen," Bonnie, continued. "You haven't been a burden to me. Believe it or not, I've loved caring for you."

Monroe lay still. His mind turned to the hospital. "How are Mama and Charlie? Have you seen them?" Bonnie put the glass back on the table.

"No, but John and Mabel Laurence have. They say Charlie's doing well."

"And Mama?"

"Not so good."

"Oh, God! What's wrong?" asked Monroe, anxiously.

"Some kind of fever—they say."

"Prairie Fever! Did they call it Prairie Fever?" Monroe raised his head to see Bonnie's face.

"Roe, Honey. You've got to relax. You're not well." Bonnie reached for the glass. "Barbara and the doctor both said you have flu symptoms. But you haven't hemorrhaged or lost your breath, so maybe it's something else. I've been doing what the doctor says."

"What's that? Feed me a lot of booze?"

"Feed you plenty of warm broth, make you wear a mask—here let me take that off—and give you whiskey to drink." Bonnie smiled. "You'll be proud to know you've drunk the better part of a gallon."

"Have you been doing the chores?"

"Who else?"

"Oh, Honey! Can you forgive me?"

"There's nothing to forgive. It wasn't exactly singing and dancing, but it was definitely a part of the show. I'm glad I could do something."

Monroe chuckled. "That reminds me of a fella in the north valley who had a wife and six girls. The girls all got scarlet fever at the same time, and the wife came down with it, too. Then one day, when he was on the roof trying to fix a leak, he fell to the ground and broke his arm. When he felt his arm go, he said it crossed his mind—just for a moment—that he might should try to get a doctor."

"Oh, oh. You're feeling better!" Bonnie smiled as she tucked his blankets under his chin. "I feel like singing. I would, too, if the kids weren't asleep and the snow would let up for a while."

"Is it snowing?"

"It started before you got home last Friday and it's been snowing off-and-on ever since."

"Damn! How deep is it? I wanted to get back into the hills and find my gold mine."

"You can wait a few days. See how you feel."

At about 10:00 o'clock, Monroe decided to get up. He wanted to bathe and shave. His determination carried him through the bathing, but when he was through shaving and combing his hair, he was happy to take a chair.

"Honey," he said, "I'm going to look out the window for a while. I want to see our valley—white with snow. Is that okay?" Bonnie helped him turn his father's big, red-leather chair toward the bay window.

"I'm going to plan my trip to the mine," Monroe said. "I think I can see Mama and Charlie tomorrow, then leave soon after. Okay?"

"Whatever you do, don't rush it. You may have over-done to begin with."

"I'll take it easy for a couple of days, while the trails are clearing."

* * *

Three days later, Monroe leaned his elbows on the breakfast table and began to wonder whether they'd have snow for Christmas. His life was back to normal. Twice, he and Bonnie had visited the hospital. Each time they re-learned what they already knew: Charlie was coming along fine—in fact he was talking about visiting his family in Window Rock—but Anna still fought her fever. She remained Monroe's chief worry. Her respiratory problem prevented her from talking and he certainly didn't want to mention the financial changes he'd made at the bank. He did feel her condition would allow him a brief trip in search

121

of the mine. "Honey, I'm going to take Chukaluks, and ride east along our creek, past the waterfall, and over the hill into the valley beyond. Pa said the country opens into a beautiful valley with a big lake. The valley over there is supposed to have chimney rocks, natural caves and a climate all its own. If it wasn't so far from town, Pa said, he'd rather live there than here in Animas Valley."

"Do you think you should go today?"

"Yes, I do. I feel fine." Monroe rose from the table and walked to the bay window in the living room. "The weather looks good. I'll travel light—a bedroll, my side arm and a rifle, some jerky, a canvas water bag, some matches, my prospecting pick, my saddlebags—that's about all—tobacco, I guess. I ought to be able to go right to the mine. If not, I'll come on back. Pa's instructions seem clear enough. I don't suppose anything has changed."

* * *

Monroe rode Chukaluks to the waterfall behind the house. He'd cleaned and maintained the water system over the years, but he'd never gone beyond the falls. He was anxious to see what was up there.

At the base of the falls, he gazed at the small reservoir holding the water that would eventually go into their house. He remembered the wild strawberry patch that grew on the surrounding slopes. Every summer, as a kid, during strawberry season, he'd spend lazy days lying on his back in the strawberry patch, watching fleecy white clouds float in the azure sky, while he extended his hands and picked luscious strawberries for his salivating mouth. On those occasions, John L., his great sheep dog and constant companion, lay beside him, waiting patiently, while Monroe filled himself with fresh strawberries.

Monroe looked for John L's grave near the strawberry patch. He'd buried John L there right after Henry died. He visualized the animal as he moved near the dog's grave. "Hi, John L. How ya' doin'?"

Moving on to the pond's edge, Monroe pulled back on the rains, paused, leaned back in his saddle and scanned the top of the falls. He wondered why he'd never taken this trip before. Just had other things to do, he guessed. His father had said it wasn't easy getting beyond the falls, but once up there, a person would find animal trails following a gradual slope along the creek and leading directly to the hidden valley beyond.

But, in order to reach the spillway above, Monroe had to dismount, lead Chukaluks behind the plummeting water, and climb on foot. Just skirting the falls left Monroe and Chukaluks dripping wet. Then, as if the cold splashing were not enough, they had to climb some thirty feet up a narrow dear trail, and angle slightly north through red shale, sandstone and mudstone. Resolutely, they proceeded up the cliff in stair-step fashion. Monroe and Chukaluks zigzagged back and forth along the cliff until they reached a broad cutout from which the creek spewed over the cliff. The path they had to follow gave Monroe pause, and Chukaluks wasted no time in registering his objections. But, slowly, with a minimum number of glances down, they made their way to the summit.

On the top ledge, the grand valley's vast expanse could be viewed. The scene was breathtaking. Monroe estimated himself to be six hundred feet above his house—at an altitude of at least 7,500 feet. He could see Durango on his left. The majestic San Juan Mountains reached skyward on his right.

He wanted to stay forever, but when he'd caught his breath, he patted Chukaluks's bulgy neck. "Are you ready for the next six hundred feet, big boy? If so, I'll walk a short distance, then ride, again."

Chukaluks seemed grateful for the rest, because he turned immediately and headed east along a deer trail that undulated along Morgan Creek. The terrain was surprisingly flat for about a hundred yards, then, it rose gradually. Only patches of snow remained on slopes facing south while almost a foot of snow covered slopes facing north.

Small clumps of scrub oak interspersed groves of Aspen, while long, dead blades of tangled grass overlaid the floor of a wide-and-rising gorge. Monroe hurried to walk in front of Chukaluks.

Rabbit and deer sign appeared everywhere. Bright darts of light, shot from the snow, like evil little sparks attacking his eyes. The exposed and subdued grass tended to sooth the pain. Clear sweet air and delicious solitude reminded him that he was in God's theatre now, and the curtain was going up.

Finding a place to set his feet became a distraction, so he decided to ride. He'd let Chukaluks do the walking while he did the looking.

The ridge ahead—probably half-a-mile away—appeared to be a rise that would fall away on the other side. Since his objective couldn't be more then three miles away and he had plenty of daylight, Monroe felt no urgency. But when he reached the crest, the earth slowly rose again to the brow of another hill further on. In the depression between the ridges, a grove of Aspen sheltered a bull elk and his seven cows. The elk leapt to their feet and bounded away as Chukaluks approached. Monroe turned in his saddle to watch the magnificent animals clear high bushes and make ninety-degree turns as they landed. He remained in his turned-around position in order to view the country through which he'd just traveled. It occurred to him that he should leave marks as he went along to jog his memory when he returned.

"Whoa, boy. Take a breather." Monroe reached out and broke a branch near at hand. He squinted at the sun. Late morning, he thought, and rode on.

From the top of the next rise, he looked into a vast, fertile valley. Pine, Spruce, Aspen—all thrived. Far in the distance, red cliffs, tall spires and jutting rock walls punctuated the basin. Morgan's Creek rushed at him from his right. It appeared to tumble from the plateau some two hundred feet above.

"There's a lake on top of that bluff, my boy. We can't see it, but Papa said so." Monroe eyed the hillside trying to see the creek's path, but the heavy growth of trees and bushes hid the secret. He turned his attention to the business of orienting himself in relationship to the mine. "Somewhere," he muttered, "Papa said I'd find a huge monument at the north end of this gigantic bowl—a solid piece of granite poking a hole in the sky. Near the tower, he said I'd see a big natural cave that would appear like a yawning piece of midnight in the green hillside. And if the sun were just right, I should see a rockslide beside the cave."

Straining his eyes, he searched for details. "And if there's gold ore down there, it better be real high-grade, or it'll cost more than it's worth to bring it out."

Moments later, Monroe stood in his stirrups and stared hard into the distance. "There's the big spire, Chuky! See it?" Monroe heeled Chukaluks' flanks. "Come on, boy. Let's go down—see if we can find a gold mine."

Almost immediately, the grassy slope became a forest. Fewer scrub oak, heavier groves of Spruce and Pine, vast fields of Aspen, all living together in God's miraculous design.

Monroe looked for an opening in the foliage. He wanted to see the great rock. Taking the first opportunity to head in that direction, he watched for a rockslide. What he needed was some idea of the terrain, the quality of the ore and the transportation difficulties he might encounter.

Chukaluks seemed to enjoy going down grade. He executed the various direction changes with ease.

When they arrived at the base of the obelisk, Monroe failed to recognize the outcropping. Its foundation was so massive; he mistook it for the sheer side of a mountain. But as he rode, he caught a glimpse of the rockslide. The sight of the slide awakened him to the fact that he had almost passed the granite monolith. His father had said the cave was near the top of the rocks. Therefore, he headed Chukaluks up hill. The going got tough. On several occasions he wished he'd worn chaps to protect his legs and a bearskin coat would have fared better than the sheepskin he wore.

Eventually, Chukaluks stepped from tall brush onto solid rock. Monroe found himself on the lip of a huge cavern—a large, open clamshell with a flat floor. "Well, whata' ya' know?" His voice reverberated in the hollow room. "Hi ya'! Anybody home?" Again the sound resonated. "We're going to build a fire. Live here for a day or two. Whata' ya' think?" No response, except the harmonics of the cave. "Anybody here?" he persisted. "Bears … Coyotes … Snakes … anyone at all?"

Monroe stepped down, lifted his canvas water bag from the saddle horn, pulled the cork and drank. Holding the bag, he led Chukaluks along the edge and looked for the spring his father had mentioned. Sure enough, water bubbled into an icy pool on the north side of the cavern. A healthy stream gurgled and dashed into the underbrush. "You're battin' a thousand, Papa."

Confident of his near proximity to the mine, Monroe removed Chukaluks' saddle and bridle. He lassoed the big stallion's neck, fashioned a halter, and tied him in the grassy glade near the spring.

Returning to the cave, he decided to search for critters that might be loitering on the premises. Better safe than sorry.

As he kicked a notch piled tight with debris, he discovered the remains of a campfire. He wondered if his Pa had fired those sticks.

Monroe remembered the day he came home from school and a neighbor lady explained how Henry went into Durango to buy dynamite for road construction. Henry had purchased one-third stick of dynamite and put it in his coat pocket to free his hands while riding back to the work site. Along the way, he thoughtlessly placed his lit tobacco pipe into the pocket with the dynamite. They theorized that hot ashes had ignited the dynamite. Anyway, the blast destroyed his father's right arm and damaged his torso. His father lived several months, and then died. Monroe quit school during his seventh grade and became the "family bread winner." As such, he'd taken a job mucking ore in The Gold King Mine. Next, he stoked coal on the Denver & Rio Grand Western Railroad. Eventually, he arrived in Grand Junction and took a job in the Grand Junction Vinegar Works. Because of his interest in chemistry, he quickly progressed to supervisor. While in the vinegar business, he'd learned to make various alcoholic beverages—wine, brandy, and whiskey—and if he'd never met Bonnie he'd still be making and selling vinegar and booze.

He returned to the business at hand by deciding to take a short walk north of the cavern, and move up the west side of the rockslide. "Papa said I'd find a flat shelf about a hundred yards up from the cave and see the vein exposed in the slide."

He took his prospector's pick and left the cave. Chukaluks whinnied as he passed.

"You stay here. I'm gonna look for a gold mine."

The snow was deep in a gully north of the cave. Trees shaded the entire area. He fought through the deep snow and reached higher ground. Once he started west up the mountain, his passageway became easier. He constantly glanced northward, toward the rockslide, hoping to see "the flat shelf" his father mentioned.

Finally, he saw the ledge, but the distance he'd covered, surprised him. He wished he'd marked his path. However, the shelf was there—leading to the vein, maybe … "just staring at you" his father had said.

He made his way across a stretch of hillside covered with tight growing Mountain Mahogany. Several Gooseberry bushes clumped tight on either side of a trail that featured large rocks under his feet. The mine should be very near, he thought!

Moving forward about fifty feet, he saw a face of earth peeking out, split open, and pulled apart. He leaned forward … squinted. Deep shadows obscured the embankment. He touched the exposed face. "Thanks, Papa. I'm here. But it's too dark to see. I'll have to come back tomorrow."

Gazing to the east from his darkened dell, Monroe saw the last rays of sunlight glow on a far away peak. Mindful of the coming darkness and unwilling to trust to the uncertainties that could befall a man on a strange mountain, he turned quickly and headed back.

When he finally heard Chukaluks snort and tug his halter rope, Monroe began to gather firewood. By the time he'd started his campfire, he was on a first name basis with a hoot owl that continually demanded his attention. No wind, no moon—just stars—hands full of bright, sparkly little devils—all strewn about the sky. He couldn't expect a moon until early morning.

Monroe huffed and puffed as he dragged a thick log near the fire. Next, he retrieved his water bag and his jerky, and then sat down.

Even though full of expectations for tomorrow, he was experiencing a great desire to tell Bonnie that he'd arrived and that he'd found the mine. So he cupped his hands to his mouth and shouted, "Honey! I love you!

I'm here!" Not even an echo returned. Chukaluks' fire-filled eyes stared back at him. "Oh well, I'm here," he mumbled, chewing his jerky and unrolling his bed.

* * *

Meanwhile, at Cascade, Bonnie returned to the kitchen after changing Wade. It felt good to have the chores done. She was expecting a quiet evening at home. After washing her hands, she reached for a towel. A loud knock at the kitchen door gave her a start and she forgot the towel. Her first thought: Mrs. Jackson from down the road! She flipped the switch for the porch light and yanked the door open. Sam Isgar stood there smiling! Hat pushed back and blonde hair shining. His blue eyes crinkled with glee. She reeled back … clinging to the knob.

"I want to see my son." Sam strode toward her, pushing the door to one side with his right hand. All joy engendered by thoughts of Barbara Jackson, turned to panic.

"No! No! Get out!" Bonnie screamed, but she couldn't oppose Sam's strength. She staggered back to the living room and eyed the rifle above the kitchen hat rack. "You're not coming in here!"

"I'm already in," Sam laughed. "Who the hell do you think you are? He's my kid." An ugly smile twisted Sam's mouth. "Couldn't wait to see my faithful wife and child."

"Roe will be here any minute," Bonnie threatened.

"Not tonight, my dear. You never could lie. You better forget that guy—come home where you belong."

"And let you browbeat me every day?"

Bonnie looked for something to throw. She edged toward the cook stove.

"Come on, Sam. Now, you've seen her. Let's go." The voice came from the yard.

"Who's that?" Bonnie asked, sensing help.

The voice in the yard spoke again. "I said I'd show you where she lives and now you're breakin' and entering." The screen door opened. Deputy Bob Stout ducked into the kitchen. Monroe had described him well.

"Oh, all right, Bob." Sam stood glaring at Bonnie. "But, I'll be back whenever I feel like it, Mrs. Isgar ... and when you least expect it. Got that, <u>Mrs. Isgar</u>. You haven't seen the last of me. I'd kinda like to have this ranch—especially, since you're here."

* * *

Chukaluks nickered. Monroe opened his eyes, lifted his head, and looked around. Strong sunlight everywhere. He left his bed, fully dressed. Must've been tired last night, he thought.

"Okay, my boy. You got me up. I'll drain my radiator and be right with you." When he walked toward the spring, he noticed Chukaluks' big hoof prints among the shattered pieces of ice.

"So you broke the ice yourself, huh? Then, what are you neighing about—see something?" Monroe looked around—carefully—slowly. "Just lonesome, big boy?"

Assured that Chukaluks was all right, Monroe returned to the campfire. He felt the ashes hoping they were cold. He drank from the water bag and shoved a piece of jerky into his mouth. When he'd gathered his equipment, he headed for the mine.

"Now you stay here and watch the camp, Chuky. I'll be back as soon as I can. Don't over eat."

Arriving at the mine, Monroe struck the embankment's face in several choice places. The vertical vein branched in all directions. No one could miss it. The wide trunks of quartz crystals probably held iron and gold. But, among all the minerals, was a yellowish ore he'd never seen before. It seemed to be in flat crystals. Sometimes powdery.

Desire swept over him. He wanted every bit of that vein. And getting a sample of the thick part would be fairly easy … but from the fingers … well, that would be something else. He'd get the sample, and then he'd scout the area. But what <u>was</u> that yellow stuff?

He wedged his sack of jerky into a crotch on a pine branch and took a three-foot square of canvas from his saddlebag. With his prospectors pick he'd corral some of that yellow stuff or know the reason why.

Hours went by while he chipped away. When he relaxed, he moseyed about calculating the size and direction of the vein. He ate jerky, worked and slaked his thirst from the water bag. Noontime passed.

Almost without notice, clouds enclosed the valley. Sunlight faded. Only when it began to snow did he stop work. He looked at his watch. Three o'clock!

Quickly, he tied his second sample, tucked it into a saddlebag, grabbed his belongings, and headed for the cave. The bushes were wet. The snow began to fall faster and the flakes were bigger.

By six o'clock, the valley was white. Chukaluks' hooves clattered over the stone floor as Monroe moved him to a tree at the cave's edge. "You don't need to stand in the snow. No. Not my Chuky."

After gathering more wood, Monroe re-built the fire. He'd stay one more night in the cave, scout the neighborhood in the morning and get home tomorrow night. Reflecting, he realized that blazing a trail had been a good idea.

Morning dawned still and gray. Four inches of new snow spread a deep hush over the woods. Thinking he'd scouted the neighborhood enough and that getting home was a priority, Monroe broke camp and headed home.

Beyond the grade, which led down into Animas Valley, he found no additional snow. A white Christmas in Animas Valley seemed remote.

Monroe and Chukaluks descended the treacherous slope from the falls spillway to the reservoir, and Monroe rode directly to the kitchen door before he yelled: "Hello, the house. Any one home?"

Bonnie came crashing across the separator porch, knocking down cream cans and fumbling with the latch. She stumbled off the steps into the yard and stood straddle-legged with imploring arms. Monroe felt his jaw drop. He stared as tears ran down Bonnie's cheeks. "Oh, Roe! Thank God, you're back!"

In one quick motion, he leaped from the saddle and gathered her in his arms. "What's the matter, Honey? Mama?"

"No, no, no." She stared down and away as though she wanted to hide. She took a moment, then: "I'll just say it." She buried her face in his chest. "Oh, Roe! Help me!"

"Sweetheart, I will! It can't be this bad." Monroe struggled to think what might cause such agony ... such hysteria. "Whatever it is, we'll handle it. Trust me." He tried to intercept her darting eyes. "What's wrong?"

"Sam Isgar. He was here!" Bonnie pushed herself away. She grasped his arms and shook. "Right here ... at Cascade! Can you believe that?"

Monroe gulped. He scanned the area half expecting to see Sam Isgar! Pulling Bonnie back into his arms, he tried to console her. "Honey, it's all over. I love you and I promise we'll take care of it once and for all." He stroked her head as he continued to glance around.

"But, just think, now we know he's in Durango, don't we?" he said, with a certain degree of satisfaction. "We'll do something ... definitely. Court papers or something. Don't worry." Then, trying to change the subject. "How about Mama and Charlie?"

"Oh, Roe! Charlie's out of the hospital. He left today for Window Rock, Arizona. He thinks he'll recover quicker on the reservation. Said he'd be back." Bonnie sniffled, but seemed to be regaining her composure. "And your mother is worse. She's barely breathing."

Monroe mulled over Bonnie's news. His being gone had made the situation worse. But, in his mind, he argued that Sam might have come to Cascade whether he'd been home or not. After all, Bonnie <u>was</u> married to Sam, and Harold <u>was</u> Sam's son. Staying home wouldn't have benefited his mother. In addition to her broken bones, Anna was suffering from Prairie Fever contracted years ago when she and Henry traveled between Durango and Pittsburg, Kansas. And Charlie's decisions—well, they were Charlie's decisions.

"Honey, I'm home now. We'll think of something. Sam's not going to continue to upset you. I'm sorry I left you alone." Monroe kissed her, smiled, and gently released her. "How are the boys?"

"They're just fine. We're blessed with two healthy boys. At first, Sam said that he'd come to see his son, but after he busted into the house, he never mentioned Harold again."

"Your leaving him has embarrassed the hell out of him."

Bonnie stood on her tiptoes and kissed Monroe. "I'm glad you're home. Don't ever leave again."

"If I have to go someplace, you'll go with me. Okay?"

"Put your horse up and come inside." Bonnie gave him a winsome smile and nodded toward the door.

* * *

Next morning, gray clouds hung low over Animas Valley. In silence, Monroe went about his chores. When he'd finished, Bonnie had prepared breakfast and gotten the boys ready for Mrs. Jackson. They left immediately for the hospital. Both Monroe and Bonnie arrived in the hospital just after eight o'clock. Anna was having a difficult time.

133

In Anna's room, Sister Agnes said, "She may not live the day. It would be grand if one of you could stay."

"Didn't realize how bad she is, Sister," Monroe said, taking note of his mother's sunken cheeks, her sallow skin and her labored breathing.

"She took a sharp turn for the worse last night." Anna opened her eyes and weakly beckoned Monroe.

"Yes, Mama," Monroe said, bending to his mother.

"My bottom dresser drawer—my will. Cascade is yours. I love you all." Anna closed her eyes. Monroe and Bonnie pulled chairs near the bed, while Monroe asked: "May we have a priest, Sister?"

"Father Conley attended her yesterday," Sister Agnes said, leaving the room.

Monroe and Bonnie watched and prayed for three hours while Anna breathed her last. She never opened her eyes.

"Sister, I'll have Hood Mortuary come for her," Monroe informed the Sister. "She'll be buried in Greenmount Cemetery before Christmas." Monroe turned to Bonnie. "Can you think of anything else, Honey?"

* * *

They scheduled Anna's funeral for 2 P.M. on December 24, 1922. The day dawned with snow falling in a valley already covered with snow.

"Roe, I want the boys to attend their grandmother's funeral. Do you have any objections?"

"No, Honey," Monroe answered. "In fact, I've been thinking how we can do just that."

"And?"

"I'm going to hitch the mules to the sled and put jingle-bells everywhere. We're going to trot to town and we're going to trot home. Anyone, within earshot, will know we're coming. Mama's going to have a merry

Christmas … and so are the boys. You make fudge and popcorn when we get home, okay? I'll get a tree and we'll decorate tonight."

"Oh, Roe! I love you, so! We'll remember your mother forever."

* * *

In Greenmount Cemetery, Monroe noticed Father Conley's face brighten when attendees continued to arrive. The small group of mourners, seen at the church, had grown to at least one hundred and fifty people at the gravesite. Folks Monroe hadn't seen in years.

Monroe saw James Laurence in the crowd. Home from Denver, he guessed. James looked taller. His blonde hair and blue eyes peeked from under the black brim of his hat. It didn't appear that the law degree had changed the open look on his face. Monroe was anxious to enlist his help with Bonnie's divorce.

And surprise of surprises! Charlie was back from Window Rock! It seemed that everyone was here to honor and say goodbye to Anna.

After the service, Monroe walked through the crowd accepting condolences and saying "hello." He thanked each person for coming. Meanwhile, Bonnie took the children to the sleigh, tucked them in and prepared for the ride home.

Finally, Monroe approached James. He noticed the professionalism and the reserve his friend had acquired at school. He also found the warm glow of friendship he'd always known.

"Thanks for being here, James." Monroe reached for an already extended hand. "I want you to come to the ranch the day after Christmas, if you can. We need a meeting. Okay?"

"Sure," answered James, with questions showing in every facial expression.

Monroe gestured with his thumb. "Follow me, Buddy. Let's go see Charlie."

James grabbed a handful of Monroe's shoulder. "Lead on."

Charlie stood quietly near the statue of the great, bull elk, which parts the road as one enters the cemetery. As they approached, Charlie smiled, and stuck out his hand.

"I loved your mother, Roe. She was a fine lady."

"I know. She loved you, too, Charlie. I didn't know if you'd heard?"

"It was on the wind—with the drums." Charlie shook James's hand and continued to smile.

Monroe placed a hand on Charlie's shoulder. "You're going home with us aren't you?"

"Yeah, but I'm going to ride my horse. See him?" Charlie pointed to a black stallion tied further up the slope.

"Wow! He's a beauty!" Monroe was impressed.

"Not bad for an Indian, huh?"

"Where'd you get him?"

"Running wild in the Chuska Mountains. Same as Chukaluks."

"Did you catch him, yourself?" asked James.

"No. I'm too weak. My brother had him and couldn't break him. I just stood by the corral and he came to me. After that my brother said he was my horse. He's never bucked me."

"What's his name?"

"Nakaii. It means, Blackie—like you, Roe." Charlie's face lit with a sly grin.

"Well, I'll be dammed." Monroe wrapped an arm around Charlie's shoulders and gave a quick squeeze. "Did that hurt?"

"Only when I laugh."

"Then let's go. I brought the sleigh."

James held back. "I'm here with Dad and Mom, so I'll see you, Friday. Good to see you, Charlie."

Charlie waved.

* * *

Friday, Monroe stood at the bay window in his living room at Cascade. He was thinking dark thoughts about Durango's police force and Sam Isgar. Scanning the countryside, he noticed a black speck moving across Trimble Lane toward East Animas Road. The person and the horse were too far away to recognize, but Monroe guessed it was James Laurence.

Monroe headed for the bunkhouse to notify Charlie. He knuckled the wooden door and heard Charlie say: "I'm coming, Roe."   ·

James reined into the driveway and Monroe motioned him to the hitching rail beside the porch. Charlie closed the bunkhouse door and crossed the yard as James cinched his reins to the rail.

"Let's get some coffee, men," said Monroe."

James ducked under his horse's neck. "Sounds good, Roe. Hi, Charlie."

"Cómo está, amigo!"

"Fine. Fine." James raised a hand to Bonnie on the porch. "Hi, Bonnie."

"Come in and get warm. Just hang your hat and coat on these wall-pegs, James."

"Gosh! It's good to be back. Haven't been out here in a while," said James, removing his coat and hanging it beside his hat.

"Glad you're back where you belong. Sure proud of you," Monroe said. "We thought for a while you were going to open your law office in Denver."

"Almost did, but Dad prevailed on me to give Durango a try. From what I hear, you need a good lawyer." James winked at Charlie. Both men smiled.

"Well, there are a couple of things that need your attention. Bonnie and I want to talk to you about Bonnie's divorce, and the three of us want to talk to you about the two hooded-riders that burned our barn. Bonnie's hired Douglas Downey in Grand Junction to represent her there—because Sam Isgar lives in Grand Junction—but we've learned that Isgar is organizing the Ku Klux Klan and, of course, the Klan has long tentacles. Sam can reach nearly every town on the Western Slope."

Monroe interrupted himself. "Sit down fellas." Charlie and James took seats facing the bay window.

"Bonnie and I need help, James, and we want you to know right up front that we're determined to pay. It won't be a free service you'll be rendering."

Monroe watched James nod and smile while Bonnie glanced shyly away. Charlie gazed unconcerned through the large bay window.

"We're serious James," Bonnie said, emphatically. "You can't start your practice by giving your service away." She waited with hands on hips. When no further words followed, she turned toward the kitchen. "I'll bring coffee. Take cream or sugar, James?"

"Black's fine."

Monroe followed Charlie's stare out the window and proceeded to take a seat in his father's red-leather lounger. "I've always liked this view of the valley, but it was better before they burned the barn, shot Charlie and crippled my mother."

"I can't believe it," James said, peering in the direction of the barn. "Right here in our peaceful valley."

"You can see what remains of the cross they burned." Monroe pointed to the black sticks on the lawn. "I'm not going to clean that up until I've done something about the people who put it there. And that's the main subject for today."

"Glad you waited for me," said Charlie. He could barely be heard.

"Well, I'm asking for your help, both of you. I feel fortunate to have friends I can ask. But I don't want to take you for granted, either. If you'll give me your opinions and then give me a hand, I'll be grateful. I want you both to feel free to say 'no' about anything. I understand that this is my fight, and that you may have something to lose by involving yourself."

Charlie leaned forward in his seat. "I know what I want to do. No one takes a shot at me—or mine—and walks off scot-free. If you weren't doing something about it, I would be. As it is, we'll go together."

That was a long speech for Charlie, Monroe reasoned, as he and Charlie both turned expectantly toward James. "What're you both looking at me for?" James asked. "I'm in."

James leaped to the window scanning the valley. "Thought I saw some elk." He moved back to his chair. "You need legal counsel and I need clients. I'll help—any way I can. You'll be my first clients."

"Include me in this army," said Bonnie, as she emphatically put cups on the coffee table, and then returned to the kitchen.

"Didn't mean to leave you out, Honey. After all, this is mostly about you."

"I know it," Bonnie said, coming back into the room. "I'd change it if I could, but I've gone too far. As a matter-of-fact, I can't turn back." Bonnie sat a coffeepot on the table. "Help yourselves, gentlemen."

Monroe reached for Bonnie's hand. "We're not crying over spilt milk, fellas. We're admitting our mistakes and doing our best to rectify them. Okay?" Monroe pulled Bonnie gently to a seat on his right.

"Now … you know the barn-burning story," Monroe continued. "The question is what are we going to do about it. I've thought a lot, as I'm sure Charlie has, and I'm willing to side with my mother who said she believed it was Bob Stout and Earl Mills. What's your take, Charlie?"

"I'll go along with your mother," Charlie said. "She may have seen them better than me—longer than me. One was big—the other was little. It looked like Bob and Earl, in bed sheets."

"All right, then … a problem. They both work for Sheriff Harvey Howe. He's big, like Bob. What if they're all Ku Klux Klan members—and it does look like a Klan job because of the sheets and the burning cross—the question is: is the Sheriff a Klan member? Was he riding that night, or was Bob." Then without pausing, Monroe let it all gush out. "And since we know Sam Isgar is a Klan organizer, is it too far fetched to think that Sam Isgar is behind everything?"

"Wait a minute. Wait a minute." James gestured for silence. "How do you know Isgar is a Klan organizer?"

Bonnie interjected. "I know he is. I learned that when we lived in Grand Junction. He's in the business of organizing the whole Western Slope. He plans to use the Klan as a political base when he runs for Governor—this—or the next election."

"My God! This is serious." James fell back into his seat. "I had no idea!"

"There's more here, James, than just beatin' the hell out of a couple guys who burned a barn and tried to kill two people. This has ramifications that involve the whole state."

"Well, you don't know that Sheriff Howe is a Klan member, do you?" James stared at Monroe. "You don't know that he's working for Sam Isgar, do you?"

"No. We don't know anything about the Sheriff."

"Okay, then." James seemed to be thinking. "We need to talk to the Sheriff. If he's working for Sam Isgar, that's one thing. If he's not, he may be fair—and he may be a help rather than a hindrance. Let's talk to him—feel him out. You should have gone to the Sheriff by now anyway."

"I agree, James. We were just waiting for things to come together. You know: Charlie needed to get well and you needed to come home."

"Ho, Ho, Ho," said James, pretending laughter. "You waiting for me before you decide to do something. That'll be the day."

"Wait," Monroe said, turning to Charlie. "There's something else I wanted to ask Charlie. Remember when Sheriff Howe saw you in the hospital? What did he want, if it's any of our business?"

"Well, yes." Charlie glanced thoughtfully out the window. "He wanted to know if I knew who shot me. I said not for sure."

"Well, how'd he know you'd been shot? How'd he know you were in the hospital?"

"I asked him that very question."

"And?"

"He said he'd asked the Sisters to notify him whenever they got gun shot victims."

"Okay. That makes sense. Doesn't tell anything about where he stands, though. Anyway, next subject: Sam was here at Cascade last week." Both Charlie and James leaned forward. Their mouths dropped open. "He took advantage of my being gone. Tried to get Bonnie to take Harold and come back to him. When she said 'no' he threatened her."

"Well, there's nothing wrong with a man trying to get his wife back," said James, "but threatening her could be something different. What'd he threaten?"

"He said he'd break Monroe in a million pieces; take the boys from me and take Cascade from Roe."

James grimaced, hunched over and said to Bonnie: "Taking your boys might be pretty hard. He'd have to prove you 'unfit.' Not many Judges would rule in his favor even though you're a run away. He was abusive." James turned to Monroe. "Can he get his hands on Cascade—bank loan or anything?"

"Yes, I suppose he could. My folks have had a tough time since Dad lost the use of his arm. They've borrowed money. First National Bank of Durango."

"Would the bank sell the note to Sam?"

"I don't know. I just signed a new contract making me responsible for the debt. Ma was in the hospital. The bank wanted us to sell Cascade."

"You've got to keep that contract current. You know that, don't you?" said James.

"Yes, I do. But above all, I've got to keep Bonnie and the kids safe. I'm not sure I can do that while we're living at Cascade."

"Well, let's go see the Sheriff first thing in the morning, then we'll talk to the bank. Agreed?" James looked at Monroe and Charlie. They nodded.

CHAPTER EIGHT

January 1923

Monroe glanced back and forth as he rode west on Fifteenth Street, and then he reined Chukaluks south on Main Avenue. James had promised to be near the intersection. If he were, he wasn't visible. Monroe spotted Charlie, sitting like a peacock, astride his prancing Nakaii.

Even though the snow and ice had begun to thaw, the ruts were still frozen. Main Avenue had not been graded.

Stressed, but at peace, Monroe moved toward a rendezvous with his friends. He and Bonnie had spent a restful holiday. He'd paid a visit to the Trimble Springs Resort and he'd offered them peach brandy in whatever amount they wished. The owner-operators had jumped at the chance. He now had his first liquor customer in Durango, but he needed to deliver some brandy as soon as possible. Price was not an issue.

Monroe looked for James again. He wanted to pigeonhole the Sheriff as soon as possible and get on with the business of acquiring his booze making essentials. If he could figure out how to haul the brandy from the vinegar works in Grand Junction, he'd have the biggest part of his problem solved. But, first things first: this morning, he'd strike a blow against the men who attacked Cascade.

"Where's James?" Charlie asked.

"Right there," said Monroe, as he glimpsed his friend rounding the corner. James galloped toward them.

"I hear him. Ridin' fast." Charlie didn't bother to look around. Nakaii was sidestepping—hoping to run.

James hauled back on his reins. His horse slid to a walk. "Where're you fella's goin'?" he asked, cheerily.

"We're on our way to see the Sheriff." Monroe's words sounded rhythmic, like a nursery rhyme. "Want to come along?"

"Don't mind if I do." James squinted at Charlie and Nakaii. "Who's this fellow with the high priced horse? I don't know anyone who can afford a horse like that."

"Let's keep our minds on the Sheriff, boys," said Charlie, displaying a lack of joy.

"Oh, oh! Pretty serious, huh Charlie?"

"I don't like Sheriffs, James. And I don't like jails." Charlie straightened Nakaii to move down Main Street.

"We're going to start a conversation that may put someone else in jail," said Monroe. "Have either of you had any new thoughts since we talked last week?"

Both Charlie and James shook their heads. James reiterated, "We've got two things in mind. First, we want to know if Sheriff Howe is a member of the Ku Klux Klan. Second, we want to know what he intends to do about the raid on Cascade."

No one spoke. It was ten minutes to ten when they turned east on Ninth Street, heading for the jail. Monroe returned his watch to its pocket.

Charlie finally broke the silence as they wrapped their reins around the hitching rail in front of the stone building on Second Avenue. "I don't like Sheriffs, and I don't like jails."

"You've said that before," James reminded him. "Ever been in jail? I mean 'tossed in' for something you did wrong?"

Charlie didn't answer right away. Monroe interceded. "Hope the Sheriff's in. It'd be a pain in the ass if we have to wait. He could be out of town."

When Monroe entered the Sheriff's office, he found himself in a large rectangular room. It sounded hollow. About three-quarters of the way back, a long counter divided the place into a reception area and an office space. A bolted gate was the only access to two desks and a small office that appeared behind the counter. The reception area gave people a place to sit while they waited their turn at the counter. File cabinets lined the rock wall behind the two desks in the office space. Two doors interrupted the string of cabinets on the back wall. The door on the left was solid steel, painted green and cemented into the wall. Probably an entrance to jail cells. Earl Mills sat at his desk in front of the green door. He appeared to be alone and writing something. He never looked up. The other chair was empty, while sheets of paper and periodicals littered the desk. This had to be Bob Stout's desk. A standard door remained open behind Bob's desk, and through the adjacent plate glass window, Sheriff Howe sat, in what appeared to be his office. Monroe glanced around the reception area, noting several groups of straight-backed chairs lining the wall.

Earl Mills wiped his nose on his sleeve without looking up. Monroe placed his hands on the counter, stared at the miniature deputy and cleared his throat. James and Charlie leaned on the counter. Earl ignored them.

Monroe began to seethe. Sheriff Howe raised his voice. "Earl, see what the gentlemen want."

Earl Mills rose from his desk, keeping his attention focused on his paper. He walked to the Sheriff's door. "What can I do for you, Sheriff?" he said, solicitously.

"Not me. You've got people waiting."

"Oh, yeah. I know. I'll get to them right away." Mills didn't look in the direction of the counter, but he returned distractedly to his desk and sat down. Eventually, he turned slightly in his chair, stared into the distance above Monroe's head, and heaved a sigh of resignation. He lowered his eyes to stare directly into Monroe's face, then, ran his stubby little fingers through his kinky red hair.

"And what can we do for you, gentlemen?" Earl sneered.

Monroe's view of Earl began to blur. A kind of darkness clouded his vision. Anger flooded his being. He fought against it, but pent-up hatred was gaining the upper hand. He turned to James and hissed through clinched teeth, "Would you talk to him?"

James immediately turned to Earl. "We'd like to see the Sheriff, if we could?"

"Who're you?" Earl asked, while staring at Monroe.

"I'm James Laurence, Mr. Morgan's attorney. You probably don't remember me, being in the same school with me for four years, and all."

Earl didn't bat an eye. "Well, can I help you? That's what I'm here for."

"Oh, I'm sure you could," said James, "but we had our hearts set on talking to the Sheriff. You see, the Sheriff visited Charlie in the hospital, and we want to continue the conversation."

Earl approached. His chin barely cleared the counter top. He grasped the edge of the counter with both hands and flexed his arms as though he were doing a push-up. "Well, I don't know," he drawled. "Let me see." Finally, he slouched away. His boots scrapped the floor as he made his way to the Sheriff's door.

"Bring 'em on in, Earl," Sheriff Howe cut in.

Monroe reached over the countertop, unlatched the swinging gate and stood aside while James and Charlie walked through. In the office area, James and Charlie deferred to Monroe, who refused a glance at Earl Mills, but led the way into the Sheriff's office. Though Monroe continued to struggle with his anger, he was able to smile amiably when they took their seats before the Sheriff.

"Thanks for seeing us," Monroe said. "Hope we're not interrupting."

"No, that's fine. I want to tell you how sorry I am about your mother," Sheriff Howe said. "I intended to ride out for a talk. Could have saved you a trip."

"Have you done anything to catch the people?" Monroe asked.

"Well, Charlie didn't give me much to go on. He was pretty weak, and after I tried to talk to him, I thought it'd be better to wait for him to get stronger—then he went to Arizona. That right, Charlie?" Charlie nodded. The Sheriff continued. "I didn't know your mother was in the hospital or that she was involved until just before she died. By that time, she wasn't talking to anybody. I found out from Sister Agnes that she was hurt during the barn burning incident."

"Did you know they burned a cross in our yard?" Monroe asked.

"Well. Little by little, stories have come to me. People I've met have passed things word of mouth. I don't know what's true and what's not. That's why I planned to ride out and see you—see if I can get something going," said the Sheriff. "What're you doing here?" The Sheriff aimed his abrupt question directly at James. "How do you fit in?"

Monroe uncrossed his knees. "Sorry, Sheriff, I should have introduced James Laurence."

"No. That's all right," said the Sheriff. "I know who he is. I just can't figure how he fits into this business."

"Well, let's start over." Monroe turned to James. "James is one of my oldest and best friends. He's about to open a law office, and I want him here for his legal advice, and help, as we go along."

"Well, I don't see a problem with that," said the Sheriff. "I knew some of Charlie's story, James, and I was wondering if you were out there, that night, as well." The Sheriff extended a hand to James.

James shook the Sheriff's hand and said, "Like Roe said, Sheriff, I'm trying to help. If the people who committed this crime are found, they should be punished. We don't disagree on that do we?"

"I intend to catch 'em. The law will punish them." Sheriff Howe cleared his throat. "Now, where were we?"

"Sheriff," Monroe said. "We want to tell you the story from our side. I can give you my mothers story, Charlie can give you his. My mother and Charlie were the only people there, except the sonzabitches who did the job."

"May I interject a question, here?" James asked.

"Go ahead," said Monroe, glancing at the Sheriff.

"I just wanted to ask the Sheriff if he's aware of Ku Klux Klan activities here in Durango?"

"Yes. They've burned a few crosses around. Mostly up on Smelter Hill. That's about all. No damage that I know of. Why do you ask?"

James said: "They're getting politically powerful, especially around Denver. Establishing a real base. Some Democrats and Republicans are worried. I'm not privy to a lot of it, but I've been wondering what's going on in Durango."

"Well, far as I know, they haven't broken any laws, and I can't do anything until they do. But, I'll tell you this: if they ever break a law, they'll have me to contend with. I'm not a member and I don't intend to become a member."

"I think we've got enough problems without a bunch of bigots raisin' hell, Sir," said Morgan.

"How's that, Morgan?" the Sheriff asked.

"Well, I was thinking about the people who are striking for higher wages and companies that are trying to keep wages as low as possible. I was thinking of the saloon doors closing—more jobs lost—things like that. I just don't think we need a gang of bigots running around picking on Mexicans and Catholics. The two men who burned our barn and shot Charlie wore sheets with pointy hoods." Sheriff Howe had been leaning back in his swivel chair, now he leaned forward with intense interest.

"Is that right, Charlie?" The Sheriff stared hard at Charlie.

"Yes, sir."

"How many men?" asked the Sheriff.

"Two."

Monroe leaned back in his chair and stretched his neck for a good view of Earl Mills. The little shit wasn't writing. He appeared to be listening, intently.

"Did you recognize 'em," Sheriff Howe asked, "anything about 'em?"

"One was a real big man—the other was a real little guy."

Sheriff Howe looked flabbergasted. Of the five thousand people living in Durango, the description fit only one famous twosome.

"What did Anna see?" The Sheriff seemed to be preoccupied.

"She said she thought it was Bob Stout and Earl Mills." Monroe kept tight control of his voice.

Sheriff Howe's complexion turned ashen. "Are you sure?"

"I'm sure my mother thought so."

The Sheriff turned to Charlie. "How about you, Charlie?"

"Sure looked like 'em."

"Are you accusing them? Do you have proof?"

"No," Monroe said, quietly. "We're only telling you the facts as we know them."

The Sheriff rose from his chair, glanced quickly in the direction of Earl Mills, and returned to his seat. "It's a fact that your mother thought the men were Bob and Earl. That what you're saying?" asked the Sheriff. Monroe nodded and the Sheriff tapped a pencil on his desk. "Let me look into it. In the meantime, be careful who you accuse."

"There were hoof prints, I'm sure, but they've probably weathered by now," James said.

"The bullet went right through Charlie's shoulder. We never found it. Don't even know the caliber," Monroe said.

"Did a horse fall on your mother?" It seemed the Sheriff wanted to change the subject.

"Yes. Whoever the bastards were, they shot old Blue while my mother had her arms around his neck."

"That right, Charlie?" the Sheriff asked.

"He fell on her. Broke her hip and leg." Anyone looking at Charlie would have thought him calm and relaxed, but considering the way he disliked sheriffs and jails, Monroe knew this was a terrible ordeal for Charlie.

"Charlie saved my mother's life that night. He made the phone call that brought John Laurence and me."

"Who did take your mother to the hospital?" ask Sheriff Howe.

"John Laurence took Charlie's phone call and picked me up in town." Suddenly, Monroe saw an opportunity to suggest a relationship between Bob Stout, Earl Mills and the Ku Klux Klan. "Do you know a fellow by the name of Sam Isgar—from Grand Junction?"

"Met him the other day," the Sheriff replied.

"He's a very influential man in Colorado's Ku Klux Klan. He might have been introduced to you by another Klan member." Here the inference seemed natural enough. Especially if Bob Stout were the one who introduced Sam Isgar.

"Who said Sam Isgar was a Klan big shot?" asked the Sheriff.

"My fiancée. Sam Isgar's former wife." Monroe felt guilt and shame for the life he was leading; as well as for the suffering he might be causing Bonnie. "She's in the process of getting a divorce."

Sheriff Howe leaned back in his chair and stared at Monroe. His brown eyes gazed at James and then moved to Charlie. His heavy black mustache wobbled back and forth.

"The reason I'm telling you this, Sir," Monroe added, leaning tensely toward the Sheriff, "is because Sam Isgar came to our home, unannounced and uninvited—while I was away. He isn't welcome at Cascade, and I want you to know that I intend to tell him so. He's not welcome any time, for any reason."

The Sheriff contemplated Monroe and the strong feelings he saw there. Eventually, he said: "What you people do with your lives is your own affair—when you break the law, it's mine." The Sheriff appeared to have his mind elsewhere. Finally, he said, "Now, I'm going to look into this Klan business. I want to know if the Klan is involved in your property damage and I want to know about my deputies. I'll do my best to be fair. I haven't anything to go on except your suspicions, so I'll probably be out to look around. I want to find out where the shots came from. Maybe there's something I can hang my hat on. If there is, I'll take action. Especially, if they are my people. I wouldn't be much of a Sheriff, if I didn't."

Monroe rose from his chair. James and Charlie followed suit. "We'll help where we can and we'll keep in touch. If we learn anything we'll tell you about it."

"Give me your names, addresses and phone numbers, will you?"

James reached inside his coat and produced a pencil. Each man honored the Sheriff's request. The Sheriff extended his hand as they filed from his office. Earl Mills sat smirking.

* * *

At the hitching rail, Monroe spoke, "Let's ride and talk."

Quickly they moved down the street. When out of earshot, Charlie turned in his saddle. "Anybody know where Isgar's staying?"

"I don't. Do you, James?"

"Nope. Shouldn't be to hard to find, though."

Monroe questioned, "What do you think about the Sheriff's involvement?"

"I think he's pretty straight," James responded. "Don't think he's a Klan member, do you?"

"He's not in the Klan," Charlie concluded. "He's gonna shake Bob and Earl hard. You could see him zero in on those two assholes when we said 'big' and 'little.'"

Monroe interjected. "I'd like to kick-the-hell out of both of 'em. Did you see the smirk on that little bastard's face when we left? In my heart of hearts, I know my Mother's right."

"I'm <u>gonna'</u> kick shit, if I get the chance," said Charlie. Charlie looked at James. "You wanna' help?"

"Set it up," said James, nudging his horses' flanks. "I have a long memory when it comes to Bob. He was a bully in school and I suspect he's a bully now."

"You better stay out of this, James. You're my lawyer. It wouldn't do to have you in jail for fighting with a deputy." Monroe eyed James, half-serious, half-joking.

"I tell you what, Roe," interrupted Charlie, as he stopped Nakaii dead in his tracks. "If you'll describe Isgar to me, I'll stay—I'll sneak back—and find him. Give me today and tonight. I'll tell you where he is and what he's doing. Then, we'll decide what we wanna' do about him, okay?"

Monroe hesitated. "I was thinking of something like that. But I'll do better than describe him. I brought his picture." He reached inside his coat. "He's about my size, a couple inches taller, light colored hair. Blond, I guess you'd say. About my age. Got pale blue eyes. Could be wearing anything. But normally he wears a regular felt hat and business suit. Probably an overcoat. He's got money, and he looks it."

"Let me see that dammed picture." Charlie extended his hand, took the picture and studied it. "I can change my appearance: untie my hair, throw a blanket over my head, look like an Indian. After I've walked a block with my head down looking half drunk, no one will notice me."

"Want to do it, Charlie?"

"Dam' right. You want to give him the word before we do anything else, don't you? If I play my cards right, I might pick up something about Bob and Earl."

"What do I get to do?" James's eyes shifted from Charlie to Monroe.

"You get to go home and wait," Monroe said. "No. I really do want you on the outside, James. Sam may get heavy, or he might be with one or two of his henchmen when we nail him. We'll keep you posted one-way or another."

"Sounds like a plan, I guess." James reined his horse north. "Somebody has to stay clean. I might as well start acting like a lawyer."

"I could stay with you, Charlie," Monroe suggested.

"Nah. That wouldn't work. A white man and a drunk Indian … " Charlie laughed out loud. "Anyway, you're too well known. No disguise. Better go home. I'll either come back to the ranch or call you."

"Yeah. You're right, Charlie. How do you feel?"

"I feel good. Best in weeks."

"Okay," Monroe said. "Let's all go down this alley, between Tenth and Eleventh. James and I'll come out the other end. You drop off, Charlie. I don't think anybody followed us, but just in case: watch yourself. And don't get into trouble until we're together again."

"Trust me." Charlie rode a few yards into the alley, held Nakaii back, and then turned back toward town.

* * *

Monroe and James walked their horses across Eleventh Street and turned up Main Avenue without saying a word.

When they reached Fifteenth Street, James stopped his horse. Monroe turned Chukaluks to a position near James' right hand.

"Well, my friend, be careful," said James, pensively. "Charlie will find Isgar and set him up—tonight or tomorrow. That means you'll be talking to Sam shortly. Don't lose your head. Mr. Isgar won't roll over and play dead. Whatever you do, keep control. No black-outs, okay?"

"I don't normally 'black-out' when I'm calling the shots. I lose it when someone shows contempt, like that smirking little sonuvabitch this morning."

James smiled and extended his hand. Monroe took the hand, and said: "I'll call you. Thanks for going with us."

"Tell Bonnie I wrote Downey a letter telling him that I'm on the case. Should get a response in a week or so."

"Good enough." Monroe headed Chukaluks toward East Animas Road while James went west, and then north.

* * *

The early afternoon seemed unusually cold. No automobiles anywhere. The soot from the smelter and the smoke from the trains had turned the once pure white snow into a dirty gray and black blanket. Monroe evaluated the sky constantly.

As he turned into Cascade's driveway, great white clouds were forming in the north and the west. "Better get the chores done early today," he breathed, fully planning a trip back to town if Charlie called.

Then at one o'clock the next morning, he found himself awake, sitting in the bay window, staring at the road into town. His mood didn't allow him to think it strange that he should do this, but when his eye caught a rider, in the moonlight, moving along the road, he sat up and took notice. Charlie coming home!

Monroe jumped from the window seat, threw his sheepskin coat over his long johns, crammed his hat on his head and hurried into the cold night air. His toes gripped his house-slippers as he moved over the packed snow between the kitchen porch and the tack room.

Charlie waved. "He's staying at the Strater." Charlie's voice crashed across the moonlit yard. "Went right up to his room. Third floor. Got undressed and went to bed."

"Where were you," Monroe asked, with a lilt of happiness in his voice for a job well done, "waiting in his room?"

"Nah," said Charlie. "Standing in the vacant lot across Seventh Street, north of the Strater. I crossed Main and looked right into his room. Saw him turn his light on; saw him turn his light off."

"Through the window?"

"Yeah."

Monroe studied the ground. "I guess we can't go in there and pull him out of bed, so it'll have to wait for tomorrow."

"That's what I thought. I'll pick him up first thing in the morning."

"Good work, Charlie. Good-night." Monroe turned toward the house. "I'm going in before I freeze to death."

Charlie had already stored his saddle in the tack room and was leading Nakaii toward the corral.

* * *

By nine o'clock next morning, Monroe and Charlie were at the Stater's reception desk asking to see Mr. Sam Isgar. They were told: "yes", Mr. Isgar was registered, but he'd left the hotel. "No", no one had picked him up. "No", he hadn't rented a horse. He'd simply walked out the front door and down the street. "No", no one knew when he'd return.

Standing on the front steps of the Strater, glancing up and down Main Avenue, Monroe and Charlie resolved to have breakfast and watch the hotel. They walked to the Mandarin Café, which occupied the corner diagonally across the Strater intersection. From their window booth, Monroe could see all entrances, front and side.

They lollygagged through breakfast and had two cups of coffee after the meal. Sam Isgar didn't show. Monroe began to feel self-conscious about holding the table.

"Okay. What do we know?" he asked. "Sam can't meet people in a saloon. All the saloons are closed. There's whorehouses, barbershops, grocery stores, libraries, clothing stores … what else?"

"Maybe he went for a walk?"

Monroe eyed Charlie. "Maybe he went to a bank—or Western Union?"

"How about I change my appearance a little and make the rounds?"

"Sounds good," Monroe said. "I'll walk over and sit in the lobby. He'll have to pass me if he comes in."

"Does he know you?"

"Oh yeah. We haven't had long conversations, but he knows me. I'll invite him outside to talk. Don't want to start anything in the lobby."

Charlie nodded. "And I won't be far away, but if I find him, I'll come back, walk up to the front door, look in until you notice me, then hike over to the vacant lot across the street. You follow me and we'll talk."

* * *

Shortly after six o'clock that afternoon, Monroe was tired, irritated. He'd called Bonnie three times. Something had to give, and soon. Suddenly, Charlie appeared in the door and winked. He'd found Sam!

Monroe followed Charlie across the street. In the vacant lot, hushed and anxious, he asked, "Yeah?"

"I know where he is." Charlie whispered, needlessly. "It's funny though."

"What do you mean?"

"Come on, I'll show you." Charlie walked briskly toward the alley running north and south between the railroad tracks and the back doors of Main Avenue stores. Packed snow crunched beneath their feet. Two blocks ahead, a string of idle boxcars sat west of the alleyway.

"Let's get in the boxcar with the open door." Charlie walked hurriedly toward the open car and jumped in. "Hurry up!" Monroe clambered in. "Keep out of sight," Charlie instructed. "You stand on that side of the door and look north; I'll stand over here and look south. That way we can see people coming and going. Okay?"

"Okay. But what are we looking for?"

"Anybody using that door." Charlie pointed to a door with a sign above it that advertised <u>Mason & Ambold Grocery</u>.

"Is Sam in there?"

"Yep."

"When?"

"About twenty minutes ago."

"What the hell's he doing in back of a grocery store?" Monroe asked.

"I don't know, but Earl Mills is in there with him."

"How do you know that?"

"I watched the door after Sam went in—just in case he came back out and went somewhere else. I saw him open the door and let Mills in."

Monroe continued to look north. "Then we really don't know who or how many people are in there. We just know Sam Isgar and Earl Mills are. Right?"

"Yep."

"Well. They've been in there quite a while." Monroe slipped his watch back in his pocket. "Maybe they're having a Klan meeting. Could be women in there."

157

"Looks like a secret type meeting."

"Why do you say that, Charlie?"

"When Isgar came to the back door to let Earl in, he kinda sneaked peeks up and down the alley, like he didn't want to be noticed."

"Shall we just bust in and raise hell?"

"You want to start a riot, Charlie?"

"I don't care."

Monroe smiled and looked sideways at his friend. "Well, just between the two of us: I'm not too particular either."

The city lights snapped on. Now the light above the grocery door sharpened the dark shadows living in the alley. Monroe chose not to look at his watch again. They'd stay the night if they had to.

Suddenly, the door cracked opened. A huge head in a large Stetson hat cautiously gazed around the partially opened door. Slowly, the man wearing that hat emerged. Bob Stout! He glanced south. Then north. Evidently satisfied that the way was clear, he stepped into the alley and moved north. A minute later, the door popped open again. A much shorter man exited. Earl Mills! Charlie and Monroe nodded to each other with satisfaction as their minds connected Bob Stout, Earl Mills and Sam Isgar. The black of night swallowed Bob and Earl.

Time passed before their revelation became complete. But, when the door opened again, Sam Isgar cautiously stepped forth. He wore a dark felt hat, an overcoat, and galoshes. He stepped into the center of the alley, glanced about, and turned south toward the Strater.

Monroe jumped from the boxcar. "Just a minute, Isgar. I want to talk." He hurried across the railroad tracks and headed straight for Sam.

Sam's jaw dropped as he whirled quickly toward Monroe and began crabbing sideways down the alley. He shoved his hands deep inside his overcoat pockets.

"Wait a minute you sonuvabitch." Monroe leaped the three-foot ditch between the railway ties and the alleyway. While trying to maintain his equilibrium, he said: "I'm Monroe Morgan. You visited my ranch a few days ago."

Monroe noticed Charlie walking straight to the grocery door. Sam hesitated. Monroe approached Sam while watching the overhead light clearly illuminate Isgar's face. Surprise and even fear seemed to stand out in Sam's twisted countenance. "We're going to have an understanding."

Sam thrust his hands deeper into his coat pockets, hissed something between his teeth, flared his nostrils as he sucked in cold night air and said distinctly, "Fuck you."

"Keep a civil tongue in your head and listen. I'm only going to say it once," rasped Monroe. "You're going to stay away from Cascade. Don't ever step foot on my property again. Hear?" Monroe stopped within two feet of Sam and thrust his face forward.

"As long as you've got my wife and boy, I'll do pretty much as I damn well please. So go fuck yourself," growled Sam.

Monroe glanced over his left shoulder when he heard metal squeak at the grocery door. He saw the door opening. A pale light, radiating from the bulb above, let Monroe see Charlie's head snap in the direction of the door. Confident, Monroe returned his gaze to Sam. At that moment, Sam's right hand streaked from its hiding place and swung a stinging blow to Monroe's head. The blow struck with unusual force. Monroe went down. His hat slid some six feet away. While struggling to regain his feet, Monroe realized that he'd been hit with a blackjack. His hatband had deflected the blow. His feet slipped from under him and he fell backward just in time to feel the searing pain of a left hook delivered by a balled fist with brass knuckles in place.

Monroe's vision blurred. "You sneaky sonuvabitch!" he cursed as he scrambled for firmer footing and prepared for Sam to strike again. Sam leaped in his direction, swinging his blackjack as though it were a whip.

Charlie charged like a bull. "Keep it fair, you sonuvabitch." His head struck Sam full in the rib cage. Sam momentarily slid sideways then fell to his knees and eventually rolled onto his back in the cinder-ditch beside the railroad track.

On his feet, Monroe moved toward Sam. "Thanks, Charlie! Watch that asshole comin' out." Bending, Monroe scooped a handful of ash-filled snow and leaped on Sam. Grabbing Sam's hair with his left hand, he smashed the cindered snow into Sam's face, and then ground back and forth. As Isgar struggled in the bottom of the ditch, Monroe scooped more cinders and planted them in Sam's face. Realizing his right knee was square in Sam's solar plexus, Monroe stabbed all his weight into Sam's stomach. Sam belched food and water all over his face. Then, with both hands, Monroe massaged the sharp mixture of snow, ash, and vomit into Sam's eyes and nose.

Although aware of Sam's desperate wriggling, Monroe heard only Sam's arms and legs thrashing the snow. Thinking his knee had stopped Sam's breathing; he pressed his elbow under Sam's chin and pushed down, while listening for a snapping sound. Hearing nothing, he assumed Sam's neck and Adam's apple remained uncrushed. Moments' later, Sam's body seemed to relax. Holding steady for a moment, Monroe began backing off. Monroe grabbed Sam by the lapels, lifted his head and shoulders off the ground and watched his head fall backward. Sam proved he was still alive because his body convulsed with a choking sound. Monroe dropped him and moved in the direction he'd last seen Charlie.

Charlie stood motionless, a short distance from the only other man in the alley. This other fellow had tilted his head to the sky and was staring into the night while Charlie stood poised to strike. Both dark figures remained motionless between the white snows underfoot and the dim electric light overhead.

Monroe thrust his face close to the stoic newcomer. "Who are you?"

"Carméllo Basíllo," answered the swarthy man. His wide set eyes, his wispy beard and upturned face, never moved.

"Where'd you come from?"

"In there."

"What were you doing?"

"Cleaning up."

"You work here?"

"Yes, Sir."

Monroe pointed at Sam. "Know him?" Sam sputtered and coughed while he struggled to right himself. His hands were working feverishly about his eyes and nose, trying to clear his vision and unblock his nose. Carméllo remained non-committal.

"Well, Carméllo. You'd better help your friend back to his hotel." Then a question crossed Monroe's mind. "Were you having a Ku Klux Klan meeting in there?"

"He was." Carméllo jammed his thumb in Sam's direction and walked toward the ditch. Carméllo moved as if sleepwalking, but he still indicated a willingness to help the snorting Isgar. Bending over, Carméllo thrust his hands beneath Sam's arms, urging him to his feet. Sam staggered up and the two edged their way from the ditch and into the alley. Silently, they moved toward the Strater.

Monroe turned to Charlie: "I owe you one. He surprised me with the dammed blackjack and knucks."

"Don't mention it. Fair's fair."

Monroe began to pace. Things hadn't gone as he'd expected. "We let Isgar know he isn't welcome at Cascade, but other than that, we didn't accomplish a damn thing. He might try to over-power Bonnie when I'm gone. And I've got to be gone sometime. The Sheriff still can't pin anything on Bob and Earl. We do know, however, that Bob and Earl are part of Sam's Klan. But that's not against the law.

"I feel bad, Amigo," Charlie said. "Want to go inside?"

"Inside the store?"

"Yeah. The door's unlocked."

Monroe thought a moment. "No. We could be charged with burglary. It's tempting though."

"Let's get our horses." Charlie headed to the public stalls behind the Strater.

"I'll call Bonnie before we go home. She'll be worried."

Charlie put a hand on Monroe's arm. "I think we should talk to the Sheriff, before Sam does."

"Oh, hell," Monroe exploded, "you're absolutely right. I'll call Bonnie from his office. If he's not in his office, we'll try his home."

CHAPTER NINE

January 1923

As Sam, with Carméllo's help, struggled to move down the snow-packed alleyway, he wiped his hand across his face, and then squinted at the hand to see if blood appeared. He couldn't be sure in the dim light. It seemed as if his blood oozed from every pore about his face and head. No one had ever rammed a knee so deep into his belly that his stomach, intestines, and kidneys were shoved clear up into his lungs. His heart and lungs had never been forced into his neck. He felt as though his brains were plastered to the top of his head. He wanted to vomit—again.

Believing that he and Carméllo were out of earshot, Sam coughed, spit, and glanced over his shoulder, then asked, "Did you see him attack me?"

"You were already fightin' when I came out," answered Carméllo.

Sam seized on Carméllo's words. Evidently, no one had seen him attack Monroe. Therefore, he concluded that he could tell the story any way he chose. It would be his word against Morgan's. Well, there was that dammed Indian—One-armed Charlie they called him—but he sure as hell didn't count. Sam decided to tell everybody that Morgan had laid for him and attacked him without provocation.

"The sonuvabitch came at me like a mad man, Carméllo. And you didn't help. You let that goddamn Indian knock me into the ditch when I was trying to recover from Morgan's surprise attack. They set me up." Sam wiped his hand across his mouth and looked for blood again. He tried to relieve the pain around his Adam's apple by massaging his throat. The liquid that dribbled down his chin turned out to be saliva.

"I'm sorry, Mr. Isgar. I didn't know you wanted me to take a hand. You were swinging your blackjack, cussin' and chargin', when I saw you. I thought maybe you had him."

"You said we were already fighting when you came out."

"You were. But I couldn't tell how long."

This sonuvabitch is no help, thought Sam. He's a goddamned rattlesnake.

Carméllo continued. "But anyway, I wasn't too keen about fightin' that dammed Indian. He's got a reputation that causes a man to think twice." Sam maintained his silence. "Once I saw him work over a guy, and I'm tellin' ya', that fuckin' Indian is fast as hell. He may be one of the meanest bastards you'll ever meet."

Sam felt tired. He couldn't stand much more of this. "You've got to learn who your friends are, Mr. Basíllo. Letting me down in favor of a dammed Indian is a bad beginning. Now, take me to the hotel and get Bob Stout over here."

Sam started thinking about getting rid of Carméllo, all together. He didn't like Carméllo's lackadaisical attitude and Carméllo looked entirely <u>too</u> Mexican to be a Klansman. He concluded that Bob Stout had a recruiting problem. Maybe he'd have to teach Bob to find the kind of people the Klan needed and wanted.

As Sam and Carméllo neared the Strater, Sam began to worry about people seeing him with a Mexican, but he knew he couldn't get to his room by himself. If he passed-out in the lobby or hallway, and somebody had to help him, it could get in the Durango Herald. Pictures! Everybody'd see him beat-up. Ask questions. Oh, God!

Sam glanced around the lobby. It was empty! "The stairs! The stairs, man!" Sam gestured to the door on the right. "Third floor."

Going up stairs was painful. Laborious. On two occasions, Sam felt as though he might lose consciousness. He'd been smart to keep Carméllo with him. If he could just lie down, stretch out … maybe he'd feel better.

Finally, Carméllo pushed the door open to the third floor.

"Here's the key. Room 323. When I'm in, you take off. Don't waste time."

"Sure thing." Carméllo was gawking at the lush hallway.

"Straight ahead, man. Straight ahead."

At room 323, Sam struggled to be patient while Carméllo unlocked the door and pushed it open.

"Get me onto the bed. Let me lay down." Sam began to relax when he felt a bed under him. "I'll just lay here for a second, then get up and wash. Get Bob and get back as soon as you can."

"Sure, boss. Sure." Carméllo bowed, nodded and backed away. Sam concentrated on a spot in the ceiling. He wanted the room to stop spinning.

Sam drowsed. Suddenly, he opened his eyes. The room had slowed its revolving and its tilting motions. He had to get up. He was losing time. The Sheriff should be hearing his story about the fight.

A knock on the door caused Sam to leap off the bed. He felt disoriented, nauseous. He must have fallen asleep, or passed out. Momentarily gripping a chair, he steadied himself. The knock repeated. Must be Bob. Starting for the door, a sharp pain shot through his head. He felt dizzy, but he opened the door.

Bob Stout looked anxious. "I got here as soon as I could." Carméllo peeked over Bob's shoulder.

"Come on in," Sam ordered, stepping aside, and sticking his head into the hall for a quick look before ducking back. "Sit on the bed."

Sam closed the door. "Now, I don't want a long discussion. But we've had Morgan running from us until now. I want him running again."

Sam had no idea how to accomplish his desires, and he knew he needed more time. He just hoped Bob, or even Carméllo, would have an idea.

"For openers," Sam continued, just to keep the dialogue going, "you boys have to make money for the Klan. I like the idea of a whiskey still, and I like Basíllo handling it. Could be a moneymaker. But don't take forever starting. Get customers now."

Sam knew he was repeating what he'd said earlier in the day, but he had to keep talking until he had a plan for handling Monroe.

Carméllo fidgeted in silence. "Well, I've got the place. On the Florida Mesa. Like I said. I've got most of the equipment. I need a condenser. I need money to make one, or buy one. An old man in Ignacio knows all about stills and stuff, but he won't do anything without money."

Sam walked to the bay window overlooking Main Avenue. "Well. Get to it, man. Earn some money. Print and pass out handbills. Ask for donations. Advertise your Klan." Sam stood looking down Main. "Got any ideas?"

"About money?" asked Carméllo, while Bob stared at the floor.

Aggravated, Sam whirled. "No! About Morgan."

Bob dropped his hat and turned to pick it up, then said: "Well, I did hear something interesting."

"Hold it, Bob. I want to tell you about Reverend Davis, and then we'll let Carméllo go home. He's had enough today." Sam patted Carméllo's shoulder and feigned a grateful smile. "I've imposed too much." Carméllo smiled his gratitude for the recognition.

Sam continued: "I've recruited Reverend Davis. You know, the Pastor presiding over the Evangelical Church of God on Fourth Avenue. He's now a Klan member. He's willing to allow Klan meetings at his church. That's important because Morgan has compromised your place in back of Ambold's Grocery. I want you to meet me at the church tomorrow, 2 P.M." Both men looked surprised and then nodded their agreement.

"Okay. That's all. You can go, Carméllo. And thanks for your help." Sam smiled and shook Carméllo's hand while ushering him out the door.

Sam turned quietly back to Bob. "Let him get down the hall—away from the door." He stood still, waiting, for several seconds, and then yanked the door open. He lunged into the hall. Looked both ways. He stepped back into the room and closed the door. "I don't trust that man. I'll check again in a minute. But, Goddamn Bob, I find it hard to think of him as Italian. He looks like a fuckin' Mex. The more I see him, the worse he looks. And I know damn well, Reverend Davis wont take to him. You say he's Italian and Indian. Shit!

"He is Italian and Indian. I knew his father and I know his mother. She's Indian. Still living in Ignacio."

"Well, maybe he is." Sam shook his head. "You think he can make whiskey?"

"He says he can."

Sam shook his head. "Okay. We'll introduce him to the preacher tomorrow. Then lets try to keep him on the mesa making booze. Away from Davis. As much as possible. Davis is joining the Klan because he needs help with the Mexican population in south Durango. His whole congregation hates Mexicans."

Sam opened the door and stepped into the hall. The hall was empty.

"I guess he left. What did you learn about Morgan?"

"Well you know Anna Morgan, Monroe's mother? She just died, right?"

"Yes."

"She left the ranch to Monroe—and it's mortgaged. The First National Bank almost foreclosed on it, a month or so ago."

The information intrigued Sam. "Who told you this?"

"My sister works in the bank."

Exciting thoughts filled Sam's head. This information he could use. "What does he owe?"

"I don't know, but I told her to learn everything she could."

"Why would she give you confidential bank information? Maybe lose her job."

"She hates Morgan."

"Oh, yeah. How come?"

"She had a heavy crush on him when they were in school. He wouldn't give her the time of day."

"And you kicked the shit out of him, right?"

"No."

"You mean: he whipped you?'"

"That's what everybody says." Bob flushed red and turned away.

Sam knew how Bob felt. "Well. We have a score to settle, don't we? If he hadn't had that damned Indian with him, I'd have had his ass this afternoon. Carméllo told you, I bet?"

"No, not much. When I saw your puffy face, I knew it was worse than Carméllo made out. He said you're blaming him."

"I am. The sonuvabitch! He stood there and watched that goddamned Indian knock me into the ditch and he didn't turn a hand. Then, when Morgan jumped on me, rammed his knee in my gut and practically broke my neck with his elbow, your Italian-Indian just stood there. The sonuvabitch!"

Bob smiled. "He probably didn't want to tangle with Charlie."

"He made noises like that. What's so special about that fuckin' Indian?"

"He's always been mean, but since he lost his arm he's gotten meaner." Bob struggled for words. "He fights with his mouth now. He'll rip your fuckin' throat out with his teeth, if you don't watch him. He'll bite your ears off—your nose—your fingers—anything he can get his mouth on. Nobody wants to cross him. He's quicker than greased lightning and stronger than a sonuvabitch with that right hand of his. The best thing to do with either Morgan or that Indian is to shoot 'em."

Sam looked hard at Bob. "Is that why you shot Charlie after you burned the barn?"

"Exactly."

Sam continued staring at Bob. "I don't think we need to go that far, Bob. They toss you in prison for shootin' folks, Bob—even hang you. No. We can find better ways of handling people like that. Think along the lines of poison— or accidents. Something that can be done when you're not even in the vicinity."

Bob seemed to calm down. "Well. I'll tell you—I'm open minded where Morgan and that Indian are concerned."

Sam's mind wandered to chokecherries. He dreamed of the poison that could be made from the leaves and the bark of chokecherries. Getting Monroe to drink, however, might be a problem.

"Now, let's get back to the issue at hand. I'll have to think of something to take care of Mr. Morgan," Sam said. "I've got to convince the Sheriff that Morgan attacked me in the alley behind the grocery store this evening."

Bob answered, "We probably can't see the Sheriff until tomorrow, but since you're telling me that you want something done about Morgan, we might say that you reported an unwarranted attack to me, today. We'll say Monroe attacked you for no reason—we <u>can</u> say that, <u>can't</u> we? We don't have to tell Sheriff Harvey that you attacked Morgan with a blackjack then tried to maim him with brass knuckles, do we?" Bob was smiling.

"Wait a minute. Who said I attacked him with a blackjack and brass knuckles? Did that goddamned Carméllo say that?"

"I got it from somewhere. He must have said something like that. Did you do it?"

"Did I what?"

"Did you attack Morgan with a blackjack and brass knuckles?"

Sam hesitated. "Well, yes. But, that's not my story to the Sheriff—or anyone else, for that matter. We've got to shut that Mexican up.

"He's not Mexican," corrected Bob.

"Well, I don't give a shit <u>what</u> he is, he's got to realize whose side he's on."

"I'll take care of it," said Bob.

"Okay, then." Sam tried to settle his jangled nerves. "Where were we?"

"How about I meet you at the Sheriff's office at nine o'clock in the morning? Harvey gets there about that time. In the meantime, you try to get some rest," suggested Bob.

"I feel all right now," Sam said. "I'm just pissed-off."

"What did Morgan want, anyway?"

"Oh, he warned me about coming out to his ranch to see my wife and kid. I told him I'd see them whenever I damned well pleased."

Suddenly, Sam felt tired. He was hungry. He hurt all over. "I'm going to bed ... get some rest. See you in the morning."

Bob let himself out, and Sam decided to pour himself a drink.

* * *

At eight forty-five the next morning, Sam arrived at Sheriff Harvey Howe's office. He could see the Sheriff's private office through the large plate glass window in the south wall of the room. The place seemed empty. Evidently, the Sheriff hadn't come in yet. The entire building was quiet except for someone snoring behind the long counter that stretched across the entire room. Sam looked for the noisemaker in the desk area behind the counter. Bob hadn't arrived, but Sam discovered Earl Mills on a cot in the southwest corner. Mills was probably working the night shift. Even though Sam made no effort to be quiet, Earl continued to snore.

Sam decided against waking Earl. He didn't want to converse with the pint-sized deputy while he waited for Bob or Sheriff Howe to came in, because he couldn't remember Earl ever saying anything interesting. He leaned against the counter, winced from the pain in his shoulder and chest, and then extended his arms over his head and cussed Morgan under his breath.

On the way over, he had passed the First National Bank and cupped his hands between his forehead and the front windowpane of the bank to get a look inside. The bank wasn't open, but he was wondering how much it would cost to buy Morgan's loan. He didn't know why he should wait for word from Bob's sister when he could just go into the bank and ask to buy some loans.

Sam heard the front door open. He turned as Bob Stout bustled his way into the office. The noise Bob made would have awakened any normal person, but when Sam glanced at Earl, the little fellow simply smacked his lips as though he were eating a sumptuous meal, rolled his face toward the wall and continued to snore.

Bob strode to the gate in the counter and said in cheery tones, "Good morning. How're you doin'?"

"Stiff and sore," said Sam, watching Bob occupy the office.

"Get up, Earl! Make the bed and wash your face before Harvey gets here." Earl flopped onto his back, let his head hang partially off the cot, opened his eyes, closed them again, and then popped his eyes wide when he realized the Western Slope's Kleagle was standing at the booking counter.

Earl jerked to a sitting position on the edge of the cot. "What's up?" Since Earl's demeanor and facial expression hadn't changed, Sam assumed he was still asleep. Sam watched in stunned silence as the two most important Klansmen in Durango stumbled around in front of him. He'd been trying to recruit a higher class of Klan personnel for La Plata County, and now, the need had never been more apparent.

Sam felt bad that he hadn't seen the Sheriff last night, and he would have, if he'd been physically able. "Will the Sheriff be along shortly?"

"I don't know why not," Bob responded. "Did he say he'd be in this morning, Earl?"

"I don't know. Can't remember."

"What do you mean? You don't know whether he said he was coming in or you can't remember what he said?"

"I don't know. I think he's coming in."

Sam walked to a front window and peered up and down the avenue. "Well, he's nowhere to be seen and it's after nine o'clock." Sam glanced from one deputy to the other.

Bob fell into his chair behind the counter. "Give him time. He'll be here."

The door opened. Sheriff Howe rushed into the office. He huffed and puffed as though he'd been running.

"I want to see you men in my office, right now." Sheriff Howe pushed through the counter gate.

"Yes, Sir," Bob and Earl chorused. The Sheriff barely glanced at Sam.

As anxious as Sam was to tell his story, there was no way he could intercept the Sheriff. Sam moved a few feet down the counter as the Sheriff's office door closed. Sam arranged himself to get a better view of the happenings inside the Sheriff's office. He leaned closer to hear what was said. He turned his face away to avoid looking directly through the window, but continued to glance furtively when he felt it safe or heard something he thought needed further interpretation.

Sheriff Howe hung his hat on a rack and dropped a note pad on his desk. "Are either of you men members of the Ku Klux Klan?" Sam glanced quickly at the scene inside the office. A significant period of time passed as Sheriff Howe stood behind his desk and stared at his two Deputies. "Well. Speak up. 'Yes' or 'no'."

Neither man responded. Earl acted as though he hadn't heard the question. He shifted his weight from one foot to the other. Bob just stared back at the Sheriff. Seemed to be trying to determine what would be the best thing to say.

"Don't lie to me." Howe gazed at the men after taking one of their options away.

Finally, Bob spoke. "We're both members, Sir."

"Well. What took you so god dammed long to answer? Ashamed of it?"

Bob's eyes shifted back and forth. "No, Sir. We just didn't know what you'd think."

"You do what you do—on your own time." Harvey Howe shuffled some papers on his desk. "There's no law against the Klan organizing. It's what you do as a policeman that counts with me. And you better not break the law, whether you're on my time or yours. Do you understand?"

"Yes, Sir," Bob and Earl chorused.

"In that regard, I'm told you two were seen burning a barn and wounding people in the north valley. Is that true?"

"No, it ain't!" Bob's answer was quick and emphatic.

"You two were riding black horses, wearing white robes and pointy hoods with eye holes cut out. Is that true?"

No, it ain't!" The emotional stress heard in his two Klansmen set Sam's teeth on edge. He suddenly experienced an urge to relieve his bladder. He looked for a toilet. Seeing no sign for "men" or "women," he decided to hold it. He had to listen to the Sheriff. His need to urinate increased exponentially with time, but he refused to miss the Sheriff's interrogation. "Who said we burned the barn?" Bob interjected.

"Never mind that. I've been told that you two looked like the people who wounded Charlie Eagle, killed two of Morgan's favorite horses and hurt Mrs. Morgan. Did you or didn't you?" The Sheriff raised his voice.

Bob squirmed. "We didn't. We weren't even there. Ain't that true, Earl?"

"Yeah. Yeah. That's true, Sheriff. Why would we? Who'd wanna burn Morgan's old barn?" Earl was batting his eyes and shaking his head.

"Maybe you were carrying out an order issued by someone in the Ku Klux Klan." Sheriff Howe continued to talk loud. "It looked like a Klan raid ... the way it was described to me. If you two were dressed in bed sheets and wore pointy-hooded-hats, you'd look just like the men described. I know everybody in Durango and when I get a picture painted by people who where there, you two fit right in." The Sheriff moved to the window. "One more chance. Are either one of you mixed up in this?"

Without hesitation, Bob answered, "Trust me Sheriff, we weren't there."

Harvey Howe turned slowly from the window and shook his head. "Okay. I'm going to trust you. But, I think it's only fair to tell you that I'm going to look into this, and if I find you're lying ... well, there'll be hell to pay."

Bob and Earl remained silent. Sam watched his recruits shifting uneasily on their feet and giving quick sidelong glances to each other. Finally, Bob asked: "Who told you we were out there, Sheriff?"

The Sheriff didn't give a straight answer when he said, "Charlie Eagle and Anna Morgan were both there, you know."

Sam thought both Bob and Earl looked guilty as hell. Goddamn the two of 'em! He wished he'd never recruited them. The stupid bastards! He'd have to get different people for future missions and keep these two out of the field. They couldn't be disguised.

"You're not going to take the word of a dammed Indian, are you," Bob bristled.

"Well, Monroe Morgan was with him when he told me. They got me out of bed last night. Talked my leg off," remembered Sheriff Howe about the visit paid by Monroe and Charlie last night.

"Oh, my God!" Bob scoffed. "Morgan's just making things up since Sam Isgar kicked the shit out of 'em in the alley behind Ambold's Grocery last night."

"They talked about that, too, last night. Told me they went there to see Isgar and tell him to keep away from Cascade. Their story didn't sound like Isgar did the kickin'—just the reverse. But I don't care who kicked who, I want to know whether my deputies are doing something illegal or not. Get it?" The Sheriff leaned halfway across his desk.

Bob pointed to the waiting room. "Well, Mr. Isgar's out there to see you. Why don't you ask him?"

When Sam realized he might be called at any moment, he felt a warm stream of watered flush down his left leg. The shock and the shame of his condition stung him in a way that brought instant fright to every nerve in his body. The struggle to control the flow of urine succeeded partly, but not before he had stained the front of his pants and much of the left leg. Staring down, panic seized him. He couldn't think of anything except "escape!" Like a wild man, he charged into the hall and out the front door. Leaping recklessly down the steep front steps, he ran straight into the street. Fear, anger, and pain wracked his body as he sprinted toward the Strater Hotel. "Oh, God!" Sam cried, again and again, as he ran.

* * *

Sam spent two hours bathing and dressing. Through the process, he determined to forego his meeting with the

Sheriff, altogether. He'd let Bob Stout and Earl Mills fend for themselves. He'd let the fight with Monroe ride. It was too late anyway, and his entry into the Sheriff's investigation of Cascade would only complicate things. He'd see Bob and Earl at the Evangelical Church this afternoon and capitalize on their introduction to Reverend Davis. Now, he'd go directly to the First National Bank of Durango.

* * *

"By way of introduction, Mr. McGovern: my name is Sam Isgar. I'm in business in Grand Junction, and I'm here looking for business opportunities in Durango. I want to meet folks and I want to consider investing where I can."

"Good of you to stop in, Mr. Isgar. What do you do in Grand Junction?"

"I own and operate a fine restaurant in the middle of town and I share interest in several enterprises including a produce packing and shipping company. We're looking to expand our produce interests to the Durango area. We want to know more about coal and cattle. Maybe ranching."

"Well, I'm sure a number of people will be happy to meet you. Are you a club member?"

"Odd Fellows, Elks and Lions, Sir. I intend to run for political office in the Republican Party.

"Odd Fellows meet tomorrow night. Why don't you come? I'll introduce you around. Give you a chance to meet some of our men."

"I'd appreciate that. Is the address in the telephone book?"

"Sure is. Make it 7 o'clock."

"I was wondering about loans on property. Loans on ranches in the Animas Valley. Something you might consider selling."

"Oh, we've got lots of those. However, we've always prided ourselves on being a partner with our debtors. Do you have something in mind?"

"Well, yes I do. There's a ranch called 'Cascade' about five miles out on East Animas Road. I hear there's a loan against it. Is that true?"

"We just negotiated a contract with the owner. He inherited the property from his mother."

"I liked the looks of the place when I chanced by the other day. My guide said it might be heavily in debt. Is that right?"

"I don't know about 'heavy'. We arranged a rather liberal agreement. He'll pay interest each month for two-and-a-half-years, and then pay the balance in full. If he misses a payment, or if he can't make the final payment, we foreclose. In which case, we'd be interested in selling the property."

"Would you like to sell the loan? I'd make it worth your while." Sam observed McGovern closely.

"Well. I don't know. He's made two or three payments now, all early. Can't fault that."

Sam edged forward in his chair: slowly, like a cat trapping a mouse. "Maybe I could give you all those interest and principle payments at the time you turn the loan over to me. Would that work?"

"I don't know. That'd be quite a sum. Could you do that?" asked McGovern.

Sam grabbed a pencil and pad from the Vice-president's desk. "Name a figure."

"About $4,000," said McGovern.

The figure was well within the amount Sam had previously planned to pay for the axe he wanted over Morgan's head. "Sounds good."

"You'd be gambling that the owner would default in some way," said McGovern. "You'd have to sell the ranch or you'd have to renegotiate the contract. Would you want to do that?"

"Renegotiate with an already failed borrower, you mean?"

"Why, yes Maybe you just want Morgan under your thumb?"

"Morgan. Is that the owner's name? Well, let's just say: I like the property very much. I'd like to have it," said Sam.

"Your offer is a good one, Mr. Isgar. There's no law against our selling the loan. You'd relieve the bank of one worry. Believe me, we could use the relief. We've got other property in Animas Valley … in the same or worse shape." McGovern shook his head and smiled thoughtfully. "I'd like to think about it for a while. I don't want to damage our reputation. We've never contemplated selling our people's loans to outsiders."

"I might see my way clear to up the ante some, if that would help?"

"No. No. It's a fair deal." McGovern seemed to cogitate. "I wonder what Morgan would say?"

Sam shifted in his seat. "I'd like to keep this between you and me, until you make up your mind. I think bringing the owner into it before we resolve our own concerns would be a mistake."

"Oh, I fully agree. I was just wondering."

"Well. In the meantime, I'll look forward to meeting you tonight." Sam rose from his chair and extended his hand. "I'd like to have Morgan's property."

CHAPTER TEN

February 1923

When Monroe and Charlie finished watching Sam Isgar and Carméllo stagger down the alley toward the Strater, they both knew it was mandatory for them to get to Sheriff Howe before Sam Isgar did. They also knew the sheriff wouldn't be in his office at this time of night. So, without a word, they turned toward their horses. Still silent, they mounted their horses and rode to Sheriff Howe's home in Animas City. They had to tell the sheriff about the fight before Sam Isgar got to him.

Now, outside the sheriff's house, with the story told, Monroe threw his leg over the saddle and felt the freezing night wind strike his face. He glanced back at Sheriff Howe's house, and then, he and Charlie headed north toward Cascade.

"It's eight-thirty, Charlie. We've been talking to the Sheriff for an hour. I'm dammed glad, though, that we forced ourselves on him—rather than waiting for tomorrow and trying to beat Sam Isgar to it. I think the Sheriff is pretty straight. Don't you?"

"Yeah, I think so, but who knows?" Charlie tugged his collar over the back of his neck and ducked his head into wind. "I don't trust politicians."

"Well, I know one thing. We've got to stay one jump ahead of Sam Isgar—until this thing's over. We've got to do it by whatever means available. I've been running all over the country like a scared rabbit trying to keep Bonnie out of Sam's reach. Now, I'm going to stop and fight. If he thinks this afternoon was the end of it, he's got another think coming. I can see he's playin' for keeps, and I'm gonna do the same."

179

"We need about three foot of snow to make everything real sweet," said Charlie, as he leaned forward in his saddle.

Monroe nudged Chukaluks. "We got to Howe before Isgar did. That's good."

"Isgar won't be going anywhere or calling anyone, tonight. You had your knee too deep in his gut. He's probably still gaggin'," Charlie chuckled.

Monroe felt a chill run up his spine. He wished he'd removed his sheepskin while he was in the house, but the meeting hadn't been social. "Let's stay on this side of the river and across over at Trimble Lane. Okay?"

"Okay, but damn it—it's snowing," commented Charlie.

"Nah," said Monroe, attempting levity.

"Hell, it isn't. What's that hitting your face … sunshine?"

"No! Ice," shouted Monroe.

"Okay. Have it your way, but let's move out." Charlie chuckled and kicked Nakaii into a trot. "I need shut-eye."

"Don't challenge Chuky. He'll think you wanna race." Monroe tightened Chukaluks' reins.

The trot was short-lived, but the satisfied feeling inside Monroe continued. He scrunched down in his saddle, huddling against the storm.

Immediately, Bonnie filled Monroe's mind. He could see her naked. Her bright blue eyes dazzled him. The nipples of her breasts protruded and her hips swayed invitingly. Suddenly, a surge of passion swept over him. He wanted her. It had been more than a week since they'd made love, maybe longer. He wanted to feel her soft, yet firm body tight against him. The hunger increased while he squinted into the night. He shifted the bulge in his pants to a more comfortable position. He squeezed his legs tight against Chukaluks sides, leaned forward and whispered in the horse's ear, "Hurry, every chance you get, Buster Brown. I can't wait much longer."

No matter how urgent his desires, Monroe resolved to take it slow and easy when he got home. One of Bonnie's complaints spoke of Sam's lack of technique. Maybe the kids would be asleep … that would help.

Although he wanted to be alone with Bonnie, he thought he'd better have a bite of supper with Charlie, then bathe—get cleaned up—even shave. Of course, he'd answer all Bonnie's questions—satisfy her curiosity about what happened in town today. He might even tell her how much he wanted her to go with him when he went to Grand Junction for brandy. Anyway, when everything was just right, he'd suggest that they get some rest. Hopefully, she'd agree, and they could go to bed. Maybe that whole waiting period wouldn't take too long. Oh, God! He loved her body! Everything, from the top of her head to the tip of her toes; her dark red hair, all soft and wavy; her deep-blue eyes, bright with intellect; the tiny freckles flung everywhere; her full mouth; her luscious breasts; her slender waist; her rounding hips. Oh, God!

Monroe jabbed his heels into Chukaluks sides. "Know what I mean, Chuky?" Chukaluks raised his head, quickened his pace, passed Nakaii, and remained in front the rest of the way.

When the saddles were hung and the horses fed, Charlie headed for the bunkhouse. Monroe quickened his pace toward the female form that flitted from window to window as Charlie and he eagerly finished the day.

"Want a bite to eat, Charlie?"

"Mañana," said Charlie.

"Mañana then, my friend." Monroe yanked open the screen door and crashed into the house. He hung his hat on a peg, ripped off his coat, and swept Bonnie into his arms.

Tightly, she clung to him, kissing every inch of his face. The smell of steaming raisins, cinnamon rolls and coffee filled the air, and when he ducked his face into the hollow of her neck he smelled lilac, almond and the natural sweetness of Bonnie's delicate skin. He didn't know how long he'd held her—he didn't care—she felt so good!

"I don't mind how cold you are," Bonnie whispered, unbuttoning his shirt. She extended her left hand to dim the light and pull the window blinds. She left the kitchen in semi-darkness while a small, dim light in the living room continued to burn.

Blinding passion seized Monroe when he realized Bonnie wore nothing except that thin silk dress she'd worn … the first summer night they made love by the Colorado River. He couldn't remember having seen the dress since, but it was definitely a part of their beginning. She seemed to be re-inventing the start of their love affair. The body she gave beside the rolling Colorado River, she offered again, and he wanted her now, more than he'd wanted her then!

"Let me take off my boots." He eased himself toward a chair while burying his face in the sweet, soft smell of her abundant breasts. Then, sliding lower to the chair, he kissed her belly and slipped his hands beneath her dress, caressing the back of her legs and feeling the tightness of her soft and yielding flesh. She stepped forward, lifting her hips to his touch. "Let me untie my boots." He kissed her thigh as he bent to the task.

As he leaned over, his cold head and neck extended horizontal to the floor, and the temptation was too much for Bonnie. She had to feel his cold skin between her warm thighs. She stepped forward placing her crotch above his neckline and lowered herself to close about his chilly flesh. The sensation was electrifying for her while she warmed his ears, his head, and his neck with her legs.

"Hurry," she said, swaying in ecstasy. "I've waited for you all day."

He slowly raised his head and gently lifted her body from the floor. She squeezed her legs tight about his neck, rolled to her right, and allowed her body to slide into his eager arms.

"Oh, that was fun! Let's do it again," she said as she set her feet on the floor and pushed him into his chair.

She straddled his right leg and grabbed the heel and toe of his right boot. "Here. I'll start pulling the boots." She tugged as he tensed his leg. "Now. Push in and pull back—slowly," she instructed.

He lurched forward, took cheeks of her butt in either hand and kissed with all his might. "The only reason I'm undressing is because I can't think of any way around it." Lurching back, he nearly missed the chair, but finally crashed astride the seat.

Bonnie still gripped the boot and as he retracted his leg, the boot slipped off. "Now. Give me the other foot."

"I will if you'll take that dress off."

She smiled, knowing he remembered the dress. "Why? Don't you like this dress?"

"I love that dress," he said. "I remember the first time you wore it. Didn't know you still had it. But I really love seeing you with nothing on. I want to see every bit of you."

Her fingers flashed over the bodice buttons. Her hands grabbed the skirt. She and the dress landed on the floor. Then, stretching back and placing her hands palm down on the floor, she uncurled her legs from beneath her body and posed as she'd seen nude women poise in artistic paintings. "Like this?"

"Oh, Honey. If you only knew how much I love you." He leaned back in his straight-backed chair, mesmerized. "Every lovely curve of you. Every shade of pink and cream. Every auburn hair. Every glint of gold. You are my perfect love. Forever."

Her thoughts remained fixed on the bulge at the front of his pants. The protrusion appeared greater and more defined as the minutes passed. She felt a flush of desire crowd her own body and noticed the increased wetness between her legs.

Tearing herself away from his breathless gaze, she stood and said, "Let me have the other boot."

Bonnie gripped the offending garment and yanked back in near frenzy. She was surprised when the boot left the foot with ridiculous ease. The momentum of her tug carried her sideways into a roll that turned her body over twice and landed her face down on the floor.

Instantly, Monroe pounced to a position near her side. "If you're going to roll around on the floor, I'm going to roll with you!" He chuckled and gathered her into his arms. "Wherever thou goest, I will follow."

She was all business as she struggled free. "Come on, Honey. Let's get your clothes off and make love right here. The house is warm and everything."

"It better stay warm all night because we're going to make love until the sun comes up. Then we'll start all over again."

Bonnie fumbled with Monroe's belt buckle. "You unbutton your shirt. I'll undo your pants," she said, smiling. Bonnie struggled to her knees while tugging his belt.

Monroe leaned back with both hands working the shirt buttons. Bonnie opened Monroe's pants at the waist, and then grabbed the cuffs, yanked hard and released his body from the inhibiting trousers. His manhood throbbed, lengthened, and sprang to attention.

Bonnie gasped. "I love to see it bloom!"

Monroe braced his feet and bridged his back. Bonnie positioned herself between his legs, grabbed the waistband, kissed him and tugged at his clothes. All of him displayed before her. Her eyes shone like diamonds, and her cheeks turned rosy red.

Bonnie walked on her knees to move her body closer. "There can't be more than this. And it's all mine."

"Sit on it," he whispered, moving his legs together as she spread herself above him.

As if her wet female parts had eyes, they searched for, found him, and covered him in one delicious thrust. Instantly, he was inside her, filling and stretching her with his need.

"Oh, my God, at last you're home," she said.

"And I intend to stay right here, forever." The delicate touch of her hard nipples brushed against his skin. "Come, lay your head on my chest and remain still." He held her tight. "Don't move."

Her mind sailed into outer space. Now that she had him completely surrounded—buried deep inside herself—she felt complete control. She strove to remain perfectly still, but the muscles between her legs and inside her body began to spasm deliciously.

He felt the sensation of a hundred silky-wet fingers griping him, holding him, and pulled him toward her. The fingers stroked, they munched, they released, and they sucked. This passionate, convulsive movement continued involuntarily and unendingly.

She'd had inklings of this searing delight, but she'd never experienced this quantity or this magnitude. The sensation was electric. Intuitively, she knew Monroe was receiving all the love she had to give. Her body and soul made themselves available. She was a young girl dreaming again of how she'd make her husband happy. She was, now, all she'd ever hoped to be.

"Oh, my darling," Monroe gasped, gnashing his teeth. He'd been transported to another realm. And when he exploded, he lost consciousness among the stars and the firmament that swirled about him. He hadn't any idea how long she'd stroked him. But, time was unimportant. And as his senses slowly returned, he found their bodies clinging together and falling endlessly through space. Panic seized him. He must not lose her now. He couldn't travel through space forever without her. Please God. Help! He desperately clung to her until the cyclone passed. Then, like the dawning of another day, they lay breathlessly still— wedded by the experience.

Finally, she nibbled his nipples. "I love you, so."

"Our love is very special, sweetheart," he said, languidly. "Except us, no one can know what we have. What we think. What we do."

"I know," said she. "That's why I'm confident we will prevail. Marriage would certainly help us with the church and with God, but everything will come out right. It has to." Bonnie moved ever so slightly and gasped. "You're still hard."

"I'm still in love with you. That won't go away."

"Aren't you hungry? I thought you'd be starved."

Monroe encircled her waist with his arms and held her tight. "I'm hungry for you, my love."

"But you need food."

"I'll take a bite of you. That'll nourish me."

"Let me feed you. Then, we'll have the rest of tonight— and all day tomorrow, if you wish."

"If that's a promise, I'll let you go. We do have to talk, sometime."

Gently, she released him. With a wiggle and a kiss, she slowly lifted her body from its nesting place. He rose to his knees, kissed each breast, and then lovingly held her tight as they knelt on the floor facing each other kissing long and deeply. "I love you," he said.

Bonnie rose, scooped up her dress, sheathed her body in it, grabbed a nearby robe and plunged her feet into a pair of slippers. She handed him his robe and slippers.

"Why do I get the feeling you were ready when I came home?" he asked.

"Because I was." Bonnie smiled and glanced at him over her shoulder as she moved toward the stove: "You've got hardboiled eggs, cinnamon rolls, coffee and marmalade. How about that?"

"Mom's marmalade?"

"I found it in the cellar." She poured two cups of coffee. "Did Charlie or you eat today?"

"While we were searching for Sam, we ordered sandwiches to-go. That's all. We ate in a boxcar. I intended to eat something when I first came home."

Bonnie smiled. "It didn't work out that way, did it?"

Monroe gazed at Bonnie. "You had another idea, and it worked out better. Even the boys cooperated."

While he ate, he broached the subjects that needed discussion. "Honey, I've got to go to Grand Junction. I hope you can go with me." Monroe sipped his coffee, waiting for her reaction.

"February's a bad time to go anywhere, isn't it?" she asked.

"Yes, but February's about over. We're pressed for time." Monroe cradled his cup in his hands. "We wouldn't go through Silverton and Ouray, or up through Telluride, if that's what's worrying you—snow's too deep. I love that Dallas Divide between Placerville and Ridgeway, but you need to give it a little respect in the wintertime. We'd go around by Dove Creek and Slick Rock—Naturita and Gateway—up the Unaweep and down the Unaweep—from Gateway to Whitewater. We've had good weather since the heavy rains last fall. If winter continues mild, we shouldn't have any trouble."

"You want to drive—the Ford, I mean?" Bonnie placed a plate of sliced hardboiled eggs, a large cinnamon roll and marmalade in front of Monroe. "The marmalade is wonderful."

"I know. Mom was always good at marmalade." He pulled a strip of cinnamon roll and reached for the butter. "We're going to need a trailer, or something, to tie onto the back of the car if we haul all the brandy I've got made-up in Grand Junction—and especially if we bring more peach wine to start our still."

187

"I don't understand." Bonnie took her place at the table.

"Peach wine is fermented peach juice."

"Oh. Is that what you use ... for ... brandy?"

"Yes," said Monroe. "They said they wanted peach brandy—at Trimble Springs. But, Honey, what about the boys—what about Wade? Can he do without you for a couple weeks?"

"I don't see why not," said Bonnie, sipping her coffee. "I started weaning him before your mother died. He's eating cereal. Fruit. Vegetables. No problem. He'll be fine with his bottle." Bonnie poured more coffee. "But who do you think should have them? Mrs. Jackson or Mabel Laurence?"

"Ask Mabel," answered Monroe, relishing a mouthful of cinnamon roll spread heavy with butter and marmalade. "She'd be best, I think. We want to see Douglas Downey, of course, because we want to coordinate his activities with James here in Durango. If Mabel has the kids, we can talk to James when we call about the kids. If Mabel can't take the boys, try Mrs. Jackson."

"I wouldn't want to leave them with anyone else, would you?"

"No. But, I really want you to go. I think you need a little rest from the boys, don't you?"

Bonnie smiled. "I think—you're a very thoughtful man. I think—I love you more each day." She reached for his left hand and held it tight while she gazed deep into his eyes. Seconds ticked by. "How much peach juice do you need?" she asked, quietly.

"About a hundred gallons. Four twenty-five-gallon barrels. Maybe I can rent a trailer in Grand Junction."

Monroe wiped his hands on his napkin. He swallowed the last of his coffee, rose from the table, leaned over, and kissed her upturned mouth. "Let's go to bed."

Bonnie gasped and gestured at the floor. "What? Not here?"

"No—but, I'll never forget how wonderful it was. I want us to remember every room of this house." He reached for her hand and headed for the stairs.

* * *

Three days later, Monroe and Bonnie sat in their "practically new" Ford while they crossed the Graden Bridge on their way out of Durango. Bonnie's face beamed with happy smiles. But then, why shouldn't they both be happy, Monroe thought. After all, Mabel Laurence had the children, Charlie had the ranch, the First National Bank had the March mortgage payment, the sky was clear, and a great adventure lay before them, i.e., an automobile trip across the Western Slope of Colorado.

"The Flour Mill's on your right, Mrs. Morgan. The Smelter's on your left. Say goodbye, because you won't be seeing them very soon. Thank God, the smelter and mill are still working. People need the jobs. There'd be fewer strikes, though, if the men were paid better."

"With all we've got to do," said Bonnie, "I hope we can be back in two weeks." Bonnie lit her pipe by ducking near the dashboard where she shielded her match from the wind and steadied herself against the rough road. Even though Monroe had the Ford's top up and its side-curtains snapped, wind had no trouble filtering in. "You said it'll take two, maybe three days to get there, and another two or three days to get back. If we stay three or four days—that's ten days for sure."

"Yes, my love, that's about it—if we don't have any problems." Monroe yanked the steering wheel to the right to avoid a deep chuckhole. "Our goal is to get our business done, have some fun, and get back home as soon as possible."

Perins Peak caught Monroe's attention. He gazed at the towering mountain and watched the sun blaze bright on the snow accumulated there. "We're not going to feel the sun until we reach Red Mesa."

Monroe fished into his pocket retrieving his pipe. "Light mine, too, will you?"

Behind them, the roundhouse clanked and wheezed its metallic sounds through the morning air. The smelter growled and groaned. The electric lights that lit these giants were still shining.

Monroe turned the wheel to the right and stepped on the gas. The black Ford hissed and purred as it made its way up Lightner Creek Canyon. Bonnie and Monroe embraced the future—a future that appeared as uncertain as the road ahead.

The road was damp from the light rain last night. It wound its way through cottonwood, box elder and willow while it paralleled Lightner Creek and the Denver and Rio Grande Southern Railroad tracks.

After traveling about three miles west of the Graden Bridge, Monroe and Bonnie turned south up Wildcat Canyon. The road was wetter—chuckholes deeper—canyon darker.

Monroe's heart leaped exuberantly as the canyon widened and the day brightened. Porter, Colorado lay just ahead. A new spirit of wonder and happiness enveloped him. He admired the aspen trees and the silver spruce that engulfed either side of the road. The sun wouldn't reach this dell for hours yet.

Bonnie perked up when she saw the sign "PORTER." "How many people live here?"

"Not many—if any. The mine closed about fourteen years ago." Monroe stared at the surrounding hills—the engine house—the giant trestle. He watched the trestle extend some two hundred and fifty yards from the west tunnel, all the way across the canyon, to the east tunnel.

"The whole place is a beautiful setting—but a little remote. None of the houses have electricity. All have outhouses. The water comes from the creek in buckets. You do the carrying."

The busy Model T entered the little town by crashing its way under the bridge/viaduct and through a grove of scrub-oak. Porter Coal Mine and its out buildings dominated the canyon. The dirt road, a narrow gully running wet from spring rains, and the Rio Grande Southern Railroad tracks marked the way through the canyon, across Red Mesa, to Hesperus and beyond. An old coal car remained parked on the siding that ran under the mine's tipple.

"Did they haul coal from the mine into Durango by using those railroad cars and tracks over there?" Bonnie asked.

"That, plus they could get more coal cars off the main tracks and let the train run from Durango to Hesperus and on up to Placerville." Monroe pointed to the large building on the right. "I've seen as many as eight coal cars dumped into that tipple—one after the other. Folks say the trestle is strong enough to handle more cars than you can get up there." Monroe gawked at the magnificent truss work that supported the structure. "You know coal is king here, don't you? Some might think it's gold or silver.

And some think the railroad built Durango. I've also heard: ranchin'. But it's really the coal that built the town. All other minerals were just gravy."

Monroe sobered while passing through the ghost town, and then while going up Old Blue Hill, just south of town, he removed the pipe from his mouth, knocked the ashes out, and stuffed the thing away in his pocket.

The moisture in the ground had frozen, and even though the clay-shale wasn't quite as slick as it could be, the ruts left from yesterday's thaw forced a slippery, bumpy ride. When the car wasn't leaping into or out of a rut, it was slipping into and out of the ditch that ran between the embankment and the side of the road. Bonnie was so busy hanging on, her hat slipped over her ear and down the side of her face and head.

Monroe laughed. "Straighten your hat. You've got over two hundred miles to go."

The sun's penetrating rays struck Monroe's chilly back. He snuggled in his seat and welcomed the bright beams as they lit patches of brilliant snow clinging to the ground under giant pine trees and scrub oak.

The day warmed considerably as Monroe and Bonnie made their way to Hesperus. The Porter Coal Company's whistle rent the air as they arrived in Hesperus.

"Why the whistle?" Bonnie asked.

"Change of shift, I expect. They blow it for start times, noontime and closing time. That's the long blasts. If they blow short anxious toots, you have to believe there's a cave-in or an emergency of some kind."

"It's a busy place, isn't it?"

"Still thriving. Three general stores, two pool halls— probably four hundred people, all in all. Serves the mines in La Plata Canyon, north of here, and the farms on Red Mesa, to the south. It's a busy place."

Bonnie saw a gas station on the corner. "When do we have to get gas again?"

"I've got five gallons in a can in the back seat, but that's just for emergencies. We'll definitely gas-up in Dove Creek before we start for Slick Rock and Naturita. We should get two hundred miles from every tank, but we won't take any chances. If we get stuck, we might burn several gallons in one place."

They made their way through the bustling town of Hesperus and turned left toward Mancos. Hesperus faded into the forest behind them.

Bonnie gasped at the mighty San Juan Mountains on her right and the rolling foothills on her left. "I think this is the most beautiful country I've ever seen. This part right here."

"Wait 'til you see my special valley. I call it Cherry Creek Valley. But it's really Thompson Park—or a piece of it. I guess it's the TXT Ranch. Anyway, you'll see a great meadow completely surrounded by mountains."

Suddenly, Bonnie exclaimed. "Look! Deer—three—no, ten of them! Oh, Honey! They're all over the place. Look! They're jumping everywhere!

"Elk."

"Elk?"

"Uh huh."

"Oh my! How beautiful! Let's stop."

"Another time, Honey. We've got to keep moving."

As the elk faded from view, the heavy growth—pine and bare aspen—opened to reveal a vast meadow of sparkling snow: a picturesque valley surrounded by forest-covered hills. The land curved into the shape of a shallow bowl some four miles in diameter. Far to the south, a tiny black line scribed northward across the pasture until it vanished in the northern forest. On the western side sat a ranch house with corrals, haystacks, horses, cows and a tall column of smoke twisting from the chimney. Bonnie's mouth gaped. Monroe said, "That black line is Cherry Creek. You should see this in the summer, when everything is green and the hay is tall enough to brush a horse's belly."

Bonnie marveled. "It's like Animas Valley, only smaller."

"Isn't it wonderful?" asked Monroe.

"It is that," Bonnie answered.

The road circled north along the rim of the bowl, keeping touch with the forest and climbing a long, steep hill. Monroe turned right at the top of the hill. "I'm going to show you something you'll never forget."

"Are we getting near Mancos?" asked Bonnie.

"Yes, but I want you to see something else. Each day we seem to learn more about the ancient Indians who once lived here." He pointed west to a mesa that formed the western skyline. "That mesa over there is where two cowboys were looking for stray cattle and discovered an Indian Cliff Dwelling in 1888. We call it Mesa Verde." He directed his finger slightly north to a range of mountains standing stark against the cloudless sky. "But look over there across the valley, on the horizon. That's the Sleeping Ute! See him?"

"A Ute is an Indian, right?" asked Bonnie.

"Yeah, yeah. See him? See him?"

"No," she said.

Monroe stopped the car. "This is too important to miss. You'll see him better when we get further down the road, but it's important to see him now." Monroe leapt from the car.

Coming around to Bonnie's side of the car, Monroe said, "Get out. Get out." Monroe helped Bonnie to the ground. "Now look," he said. "See that blue mountain range making up the entire horizon?"

"Yes."

"Look at the north end of the range. See how it slopes down. Well. Just imagine a giant lying on his back. He has a feathered headdress, his war bonnet, falling away to the north. See his face, looking into the sky? The nose, the mouth, the chin, the neck, and then his arms folded over his chest?"

"Oh, yes! I see him!" Bonnie jumped up and down.

"And look down toward the feet. Can you see his knees, his feet, even his toes?"

"No … "

Monroe smiled. "At least you're honest. You can't see all of him from here. But, get in the car and keep your eye on him. You can't see his feet from here, because Mesa Verde is blocking your view. We'll see his entire body, all stretched out, when we head into Cortez. Legend says he's a great warrior god who came to fight against evil people. During the battle he was wounded, so he laid down to rest and fell asleep."

The Ford rounded curves, climbed hills and flew over the countryside. Checking his watch, Monroe noted his schedule was being kept. They'd make Cortez by noon. As they climbed the hill that would reveal Bonnie's first view of Cortez and the entire Sleeping Ute, he gave her a warning.

"See the road turning off to the left? That goes to the cliff dwellings? When we start down the other side of this hill, I want you to keep looking to your left. You'll see the magnificent, the wonderful, the marvelous … "

"Sleeping Ute!" Bonnie shouted, laughing.

"And?" Monroe's finger jabbed a hole in the sky.

"Cortez!" shouted Bonnie.

"Right on, Mrs. Morgan! You must have been here before."

"No. I've just got a wonderful guide."

"Oh. I suppose you're right," he agreed. "Now, look to your left." Monroe held his breath.

"Oh! My God! He is breathtaking! And I see every bit of him. His feet are sticking straight up. His entire body is stretched out, forming the horizon. He's marvelous!"

"I thought you'd like him—and there's Cortez in front of you. Wherever you go in the Four Corners area, you need to look for the Sleeping Ute because he's visible from nearly every point. But if you don't see him like this, you'll never know what you're looking at."

"I'll be looking for him—always," said Bonnie, dreamily.

A few minutes later, Bonnie watched Cortez bustling under warm sun and dry winds. They didn't stop. "Why did people settle here? It's as dry as Kansas in August. There's no grass, no trees."

"Well, now Honey. There's lots of real good stuff here. They grow peaches, apples, wheat, alfalfa, cattle, and now they're even saying they're 'pumping black gold.' "

"Oil?"

"You betcha!"

Monroe watched Bonnie turn her head and gawk until the town began to disappear. "When do we stop for gas?" she asked.

"Oh boy! Wait 'til you see that place. Its called 'Dove Creek' and it's the Pinto Bean capital of the world!"

"Do we have to wait 'til Dove Creek to use the facilities?"

"Oh, I'm sorry, Honey. We'll start looking for a place near the road. Can you wait a minute?"

"Don't you have to go?" she asked.

"I guess so. But, we want to make Slick Rock, or beyond, before we sleep, and we'll need all the daylight we can get."

After the stop, Bonnie reached into the back seat and brought forward her lunch basket. "Are you hungry?" she asked.

"Getting that way." Monroe said. "Let's eat a sandwich. Okay?"

"That'll be swell," she answered, enthusiastically.

Bonnie busied herself with lunch as vast stretches of developed fields—alfalfa and bean—unfolded mile after mile on either side of the road. The Sleeping Ute was still visible.

At three-thirty, Bonnie and Monroe pulled into Dove Creek. Monroe drove directly to the only store in town. General Mercantile and Gas. The street was deeply rutted after a period of thawing and rain. Some of the ruts appeared to be twelve inches deep.

Monroe stepped from the car when a young man came out to the pump. "Fill it up, please."

"Well, that didn't take long," said Monroe, as they passed the last building on their way out of town. Bonnie turned in her seat, stuck her head out the window and squinted at the sun. "How far is Slick Rock?" she asked.

"About twenty-two miles, I suppose, but our problems, if we have any, will come before we get that far."

"What kind of problems?"

"Stair steps," answered Monroe.

"You mean we might drop down from one level to another, or step up from one level to another?"

"That's about it," said Monroe. "The whole countryside is formed by layers of rock—one on top of the other. Clay and shale separate each layer. When we have a lot of moisture, like recently, the dirt washes away and the stair steps are left. A wagon, or a car, going down hill, might have to drop from one layer to another."

The sun seemed to linger in the sky. A warm breeze pushed through the little black Ford as it chugged along. While the shadows lengthened noticeably, a benevolent sun granted additional time for traveling.

Inspired, Bonnie turned to Monroe. "Why don't you buy a truck?"

"I've been thinking of that," answered Monroe. "It'd solve a lot of problems—like hauling brandy and peach juice. Also, a truck would be a big help delivering booze and starting a homestead on the Florida."

"When might that be available—the property on Florida Mesa?" asked Bonnie.

"Anytime, now."

"Do we need money?"

"For the truck or the land?" he asked.

"Both," she said.

"I'm not sure, but I might be able to trade this Ford and pay the difference," said Monroe. "Probably about $800 dollars."

"That's a lot."

"I know," agreed Monroe. "But we've got a little, too. I've saved for two years—all the time I supervised the Vinegar Works and sold booze in Grand Junction. When I started selling whiskey, I didn't have an overhead. I simply used the produce and the equipment owned by the vinegar works." Monroe pointed to a coyote racing across the road. "I plan to take all our money from Grand Junction and deposit it in Durango, and then prepay several interest payments on the Cascade mortgage—just in case. We have almost $4,000 dollars in Grand Junction."

"Oh, Honey," smiled Bonnie. "I didn't know that! Why not pay the mortgage off?"

"Then we wouldn't have any money in the bank and none coming in," said Monroe. "No, Honey. I've worked too long and too hard for a little independence. Don't worry, though, I'll be earning money in a few weeks and we'll start saving money to pay off the mortgage."

Monroe had never purposely avoided telling Bonnie about the $4,000 in the Grand Junction bank. The subject just hadn't come up. He and Bonnie had been so busy covering their tracks and working where they could, they'd been able to earn what they needed as they went place to place.

"Which bank will you use in Durango?" asked Bonnie.

"First National Bank of Durango. Wouldn't consider any other bank. They've been good people all through these years."

The road smoothed out. Not many ruts. Monroe peered into the distance looking for a farmhouse, a cabin—anything. He seemed to remember traveling downhill for six to eight miles before you get to Slick Rock. He saw a cattle guard with a fence running away from each side of the road. That fence was there to keep cattle from going down into the valley," he thought.

After the cattle guard, they encountered one sharp curve after another, and they were definitely dropping down to Disappointment Creek and the town of Slick Rock.

He glanced at Bonnie. Her eyes held steady on the road. "Looking for stair steps?" he asked.

Bonnie nodded.

"Whoops. Here they come," heralded Monroe, his voice rising. The steps didn't appear too bad, but they would require considerable slowing. And when he hit the brakes, he felt the hind wheels skid.

Bonnie grabbed the dash. "Ouch!"

"What's the matter?" Monroe divided his attention between the expressions on Bonnie's face and the bouncing car.

"Nothing. Just making noise. I'll get used to slipping around, I guess."

"Okay," said Monroe, gradually applied the brakes. "Get ready for a bump. We're about to take a step down. The road's straight, now, and the drops aren't so bad, but when we drop on a curve, it's a bitch. You always drop one wheel at a time. That's four bumps per step."

Monroe tightened his grip on the steering wheel. Bonnie clutched the passenger door while bracing herself with a hand on the dashboard. The car had slowed to a walk. Surprisingly, the bumps seemed quite mild. "That was easier than I thought," he said.

Monroe stared ahead, anxiously looking for the next encounter. "I hope no one else comes up while we're going down."

They approached the next bend. A curve to the left. Shadows extended far across the road to the east.

"Roe. Look at the coyote!" shouted Bonnie.

"Look at both coyotes." Monroe pointed with two fingers.

"Oh yes! One on each side of the road."

"Looking for supper, I expect."

As Monroe rounded a hillock to he left, a team of horses and a loaded hayrack blocked the road. He slammed on his brakes. The car slid dangerously close to the road's outer edge. Bonnie gasped.

"Hold her, Knute!" Monroe smiled. "It's a good thing we weren't going any faster."

Bonnie leaned forward in her seat, and asked. "Where'd he come from?" Then, after searching the scene: "No one's here…just a stack of alfalfa piled on a wagon."

From behind the wagon came a clean-shaven man dressed in bib overalls. He wore a white Stetson and a red-checked coat. His face carried a worried expression that bordered on desperation. He seemed surprised to see a touring car with passengers.

Monroe backed to the nearest wide spot in the road and parked near the outer edge. He noticed Bonnie hold her breath while she clutched the dashboard. Stepping from the car, Monroe motioned Bonnie to the driver's side. When Bonnie stepped to the ground, Monroe reached into the back seat for his shovel and grubbing-hoe. "Honey, you stay near the car. Sit on the running board, or whatever, just don't sit in the car. If for some reason that edge gives way ... "

"Why can't I come with you?" asked Bonnie.

"You can. I just thought you'd rather sit and watch rather than tromp around on the wet ground. You'll get your boots muddy."

Her sidelong glance told him he was mistaken. "Okay. Come on, you get to carry the shovel."

As they walked hand in hand toward the stalled rig, the man lifted his hand in the air. "Howdy."

Monroe waved. "Need some help?" A boy, about twelve, came from behind the wagon. "Oh, I see you got a helper."

"Yep. That's my son. We're trying to get home tonight. Sorry for holdin' ya' up."

"Don't give it another thought. We're in no hurry. My name's Monroe Morgan—my wife, Bonnie. From Durango."

"Howdy, Mam." The man tipped his hat. "I'm Todd Hunter. This is my boy, Dick. From north of Dove Creek. Got a mess here."

Monroe moved slowly along side the wagon, sizing up the problem. He saw a good team confronted with an impossible job. The wagon's front wheels were jam up against a rock step while the back wheels were doing the same thing at another step back down the hill. The front step was at least twelve inches high and the back step was about nine inches high. If the team moved the wagon, they'd have to lift the whole load straight up in the air … and that was impossible.

Monroe turned to Todd. "You don't have enough horsepower to move it. We'll have to build a ramp."

"You're right, but, like a damn fool, I didn't bring a shovel. Glad you have one."

"Well. Back your wagon away from those ledges and I'll get a tarp to help us move the dirt and rock."

Bonnie extended her hand to the boy. "Come over here by me."

When Todd Hunter had backed his rig to a spot that allowed ample room for work, he spoke to the boy. "Dick, you get over here and hold this team. Keep 'em where they are. I'll put a big rock behind each wheel."

Bonnie stepped forward. "How about me. I want to do something?"

"Honey. In addition to dirt, we'll need flat rocks—pieces of wood—sagebrush or anything else you can find—to hold the dirt and gravel." Turning to Todd Hunter, Monroe suggested, "Maybe she could hold the team while Dick helps you look for filler?"

"Okay. We'll gather filler and start forming ramps. We'll help throw dirt and gravel, later. Mrs. Morgan holding the team'll be a great help."

Soon ramps began to take shape. If a stick or a stone didn't fit, it was tossed aside.

"When was the last time you and Dick had anything to eat?" Bonnie interjected.

"We've got beans on the rack there." Todd hurried away.

After working hard for three quarters of an hour, Monroe began feeling the evening chill. He glanced east across the country. Saw the long shadows streaking the land. The sun was falling fast. Less than two hours of daylight. "Dick, tell your Dad, I think he can give it a try."

"Yes, Sir."

Todd Hunter arrived with an armload of brush. "Think I should try it, huh?"

"Yeah. Let's tromp it down one more time." Monroe handed his shovel to Dick and picked up his grubbing-hoe. "It looks good to me."

Todd Hunter clambered onto the hayrack, gathered up his reins and raised his voice to his team. "Okay, boys. Let's do it. Giddy-up!" The team strained against the traces. The traces tightened. Muscles bulged. The load began to move.

"Yeah-ha!" Hunter yelled, snapping the reins with a quick up-and-down flick of his wrists and arms.

The wagon groaned. The front wheels wrenched to the right, straightened in a direct line, and moved up the ramp. "Yeah-ha, Buster! Keep goin'." The wheels creaked as they crashed against rocks and slipped off. As if by magic, what had been an impossible task seemed like child's play.

When Hunter had cleared the offending steps, he stopped the hayrack in the middle of the road. He climbed down from his wagon and extended a hand to Monroe. "Can't thank you folks enough for your help and the loan of your tools. But I won't keep you 'cause I know you're anxious to be on your way. Come on, Dick. Get up here. Let's go home."

"We'll be using the same ramp, so we should be thanking you."

"You've got some rough spots ahead, but none as bad as this."

Bonnie waved. "Good luck."

Monroe carefully adjusted the spark and the gas levers at the Fords steering wheel. After helping Bonnie into the car, he walked around front and cranked while Bonnie helped with gas and/or spark adjustments. The load of alfalfa continued to roll up the hill. His engine began to purr. Monroe jumped into the drivers seat, turned on the headlights, carefully pulled to the center of the road, and headed for the newly constructed ramps.

Throughout the slow and laborious trip to the bottom of the hill, the little Ford encountered chuck-holes, drop-offs and slippery mud, but Monroe and Bonnie had already successfully overcome the most difficult challenge they'd face on Slick Rock Hill.

When they arrived in the town of Slick Rock, the sun had set. Before them stretched the sagebrush, the juniper, the rolling inclines of Disappointment Valley, as well as Gypsum Gap.

"Honey, we might as well keep right on traveling until we find a wide spot in the road, then we'll pull out for the night."

"Can you sleep in the front seat, Roe?"

"Sure. I'd want my head up anyway. See what's going on."

"How about another sandwich?" Bonnie asked.

"No thanks. I'll have a drink of water when we stop. That'll be enough. You go ahead."

"I'm not hungry," Bonnie said. "But it's getting kinda' cold."

"Get a blanket and wrap it around you." Monroe searched the road ahead. No place to stop.

* * *

The next morning Monroe calculated that they'd gone about 115 miles. Less than half the distance from Durango to Grand Junction. But, they got an early start, and when the sun came up, the Model T had passed Naturita. "From here on, Honey, you're going to see some of the most startling country in the world. We'll be deep in vertical red-rock canyons, where the canyon walls seem to trap you in a box. When you come to the end of one box and you think the red wall will keep you from going farther, the roadway will open up and you'll find yourself in another box. After you've entered and exited several box canyons, you'll just put your trust in God for complete deliverance. The canyons follow the Dolores River all the way to Gateway."

"This is already the most exciting trip I've ever taken," said Bonnie. " Well, that's not counting the road between Durango and Ouray." Monroe slapped the steering wheel and laughed out loud.

"And we'll add the wonders of Rico, to Telluride, to Placerville, to Ridgeway, some day. Then, you'll have a feel for the Western Slope of the Colorado Rockies," bragged Monroe.

At a quarter past two, they pulled into Gateway.

"I don't know how much more of this excitement I can stand," Bonnie said, feasting her eyes on the palisades just north of Gateway. "Everyone in the world should have this experience, at least once."

"Well, Honey, there's more ahead. We're going through Unaweep Canyon next."

"Oh! Good Lord! What's that?"

"Why, you're going to see our dream house and a truly unique canyon." Monroe honked his horn at chickens crossing the road.

"Our dream house?"

"Driggs Mansion. Everyone's dream house, really. Sits near the Divide. Between East Creek and West Creek."

"You know, I don't know what you're talking about, don't you?" Bonnie asked.

Monroe smiled. "Well, bear with me, my dear. You're going to love it, I promise. The Ute Indians called the canyon 'Unaweep,' their word for 'canyon with two mouths.' The West Creek flows out the west end of the canyon, and the

East Creek flows out of the east end of the canyon. Mr. Driggs built a mansion for his wife at the top of the Divide, but she, being an easterner, couldn't stand the country so the Driggs never lived there. But the house is near a huge lake and I thought we might stay there tonight. We can drive on to Grand Junction tomorrow."

"Oh! I love it already. Hurry!"

"Okay," said Monroe. "But I've got to fill the water bags."

Monroe drove into a schoolyard across the road from the Post Office in downtown Gateway. He filled both water bags at the yard's hand pump and gazed at the towering Cottonwood trees that nestled near the bottom of vertical sandstone canyon walls that stood hundreds of feet high. The sun still warmed his shoulders.

Back in the car, Monroe found Bonnie enthralled. "I want to see our mansion."

"<u>Our</u> mansion?" Monroe questioned, with a smile.

The road made a gradual climb from Gateway to the Divide east of town. It wound through sparse sagebrush, piñon and pine, but always buttressed by the red-sandstone mountains on either side.

"How far to the Mansion?" asked Bonnie.

"About seventeen miles, I think. We should be there pretty soon."

"It'll still be daylight, won't it?" asked Bonnie.

"Yeah," Monroe said, swerving to miss a pothole.

"Want to eat and drive?"

"Might as well," said Monroe. "Eating now would give us more time to look around."

Just before sunset, Monroe left the road toward the Mansion and stopped to view the scene. He had forgotten some of the magnificent scenery surrounding the yellow stone house. Looking across the valley, which stretched in every direction, his eyes immediately caught and held Thimble Rock. Unmistakably, the likeness a seamstress' thimble was visible to the south, and the sun's last rays flooded the fertile valley with a warm, golden glow that softened the craggy sharpness of the cliffs beyond. No winter snow accumulations remained anywhere. Only a deep blue lake that sparkled like a huge diamond lost in a thick carpet of young, green grass. Cattle grazed east and south of the lagoon.

"What a lovely place." Bonnie shaded her eyes, breathlessly devouring the land.

"His wife didn't think so," Monroe said, leaned forward onto his steering wheel.

"Is that one of the creeks down there?" Bonnie pointed to an obvious waterway running west from the lake.

"I think that's West Creek. It joins the Dolores River down by Gateway."

Bonnie shook her head, incredulously. "This is amazing. I suppose somewhere east of here it starts flowing east. Is that right?"

"Well, not quite, my love. We'll find Unaweep Divide about two or three miles east of here. The creeks start at the Divide." Monroe let the car move forward until they were in the yard around the house. There, he applied the brakes. "Let's look at the house," he said.

As they walked toward the house, Bonnie observed, "It looks empty." The large, graceful arched windows, the massive strength of its walls, the great entry way and the peculiar light-yellow color seemed to fascinate her. "I can't wait to get inside."

Monroe pressed his face against a windowpane and jumped back. He quickly extended his hand to block Bonnie from coming closer. Frowning, he returned to the window for a second look.

"What's the matter, Roe?" asked Bonnie.

"There's someone staying here." Monroe placed both hands on Bonnie's shoulders. "We better get out of here."

"Who's here?" Bonnie sounded as though foreigners had occupied her house.

"Just campers. They don't live here. That's for sure. It's a hunting party or something. They're probably out there right now watching us." Monroe curled Bonnie in the crook of his arm to guide her away from the house. "Their bedrolls, cooking utensils and camping equipment is all strewn around."

"But, I want to see inside." Bonnie twisted in his grasp to gaze back toward the house.

"Well, go look," he said, sympathizing. "But don't go in."

Bonnie ran to the window while Monroe scanned the countryside for people. She stood on tiptoes, cupped her hands about her face and peered through the window. Scrubbing her gloved hand back and forth across the window, she attempted to see more clearly. "Damn, I can't see anything but the chandelier. Isn't it beautiful!" She ran around the corner in search of another window.

"Come on, now!" admonished Monroe. "Don't get carried away. They may be watching us, right now."

"Oh damn. Damn. Damn. Damn. Damn." Bonnie turned toward the car and continued directly into the passenger seat.

Monroe climbed into the Ford. "We'll have to come back...sometime. Maybe on our way home."

"Didn't they know we were coming? Didn't they know we planned to spend the night here?" asked Bonnie.

"It's okay, now," Monroe assured. "We'll show 'em by staying in Grand Junction tonight."

"But I planned to put our two bed rolls together and snuggle," complained Bonnie. "I'm not comfortable with you in the front seat and me in the back." Bonnie threw her arms around Monroe's neck and kissed him long and hard.

Finally, Monroe moved his head gently. "I'll take you to a hotel and make love to you on a hardwood floor. How'd you like that?"

Bonnie pushed him at arms length. "What is it with you and wood floors, lately?"

"Just something <u>you</u> started, I guess." Monroe opened his door to get out.

"Where you going?"

"Forgot to crank the car."

Bonnie smiled and while Monroe cranked, Bonnie continued to gaze at the house and the valley. "Where'd they get that beautiful stone in the walls? It's bright yellow and all the other rock around here is red."

Monroe jumped in, whirled the car around and headed north. "See right up there?" He pointed straight ahead.

"Yes."

"Mayflower Stone Quarry is over there about two miles. It's the only place in the country you can find that yellow stone."

"And his wife didn't think this was a beautiful place?" asked Bonnie, incredulously.

"They both were easterners. But Mr. Driggs came out here, fell in love with the country, built the house and brought her out. She didn't like the west and wouldn't live here," said Monroe.

"It looks like someone has," said Bonnie.

"Yes, it looks like it. But, it's only five or six years old and everyone uses it for whatever. But, I don't believe anyone has actually lived here."

Monroe turned west on the road to Whitewater and Grand Junction. "We're going up here a few miles and cross the Divide. Then, the road's pretty much all down hill until we get to Whitewater. The last nine miles are a bitch. Very narrow, very curvy. Impossible to pass another vehicle if you meet one. They call it Ninemile Hill."

"Will we be on it in the dark?" asked Bonnie.

"Not if I can help it. I want to get there in one piece. I think I'll pull off at the top of the Divide and go into town tomorrow."

"Fine with me. We can eat apples, okay?"

"Sounds good."

* * *

The next morning, near the top of Ninemile Hill, warm sunshine awakened Monroe. He struggled from under the steering wheel.

Bonnie spoke from the back seat. "Are you awake, Roe?"

Monroe sat up straight and grabbed his hat. "Just waiting for you, Honey."

"Maybe—but I doubt it," smiled Bonnie.

Purring down the road ten-minutes later, Bonnie said, "I don't know why I'm so anxious to get back to Grand Junction. I've been running away for two years. This is Isgar country, you know. Makes me wish I'd left the show in Salt Lake City."

"Yeah, but you wouldn't have met me," Monroe reminded.

"When you put it that way, I'm glad I stopped in Grand Junction."

Monroe sat silent for a moment, then reflected: "A year-and-a-half ago I had a good job—a booze business—and no end in sight."

"I've been a problem, haven't I?" said Bonnie.

"One I wouldn't trade for anything," said Monroe, squeezing her hand in her lap.

"Well, you've still got your friend in the vinegar works. You've got money in the bank and you've got enough brandy to start a business in Durango. That's not all bad, is it?"

"No it isn't." Monroe peered as far as he could see down the canyon. "I sometimes wonder if we shouldn't pull up stakes and start again someplace else."

209

"I'll tell you why we shouldn't," Bonnie said. "You love Cascade, and now that it's yours, you'll never leave.

Monroe thought a moment. "Yes. I guess you're right. I want us to have our life there. We'll get rid of Sam, pay-off the mortgage and live happy ever after." Monroe felt confident. "Sam has political clout, but we don't care. We'll win in the end."

Monroe slammed on the brakes. The car slid to a stop in the middle of the road. "Honey, I've got to see something."

"What?"

"The road." Monroe shut off the engine. "Now, be quiet. Look as far ahead as you can." Monroe leaped from the car. "We have to see if anyone's on the hill." He reached for his 30-30 behind the seat.

"Oh yes! I see," Bonnie said. "You said there's no room to pass."

Monroe stepped as close to the embankment as he dared, raised his rifle and fired two quick shots. The shots reverberated through the hills. "Hope no one's between here and the bottom. If there is, we'll have to decide what to do. Be quiet."

A slight breeze created a sound: a whisper that vibrated the rabbit brush, the sagebrush, the pine and the hollows of the rocks. It seemed to say: the race he'd been running was about to end … that the vastness of the earth had swallowed him … and he was alone with Bonnie. Monroe couldn't be sure … but then … it seemed he'd never been sure about anything. Not even the breath of wind he heard. He waited. Finally, he spoke. "Hear anything?"

"No. Did you?"

"Nope." Monroe replaced his rifle, climbed behind the wheel and said: "Next stop: Grand Junction."

* * *

Grand Junction's posh La Court Hotel had been on Monroe's mind since including Bonnie in his trip plans. He hadn't said anything because he wanted to surprise her. But, during all their months of hiding and running, he'd steered her from one hovel to another. Now, there was no reason to hide. He wanted Bonnie to live in the best places he could find. In addition, the La Court fit several of their needs. Bonnie's lawyer would be impressed when he learned she was staying in Grand Junctions finest. Sam's people wouldn't expect them there. No one would believe they would be brazen enough to stay in that fine hotel! No automobile dealer would think twice about a cash sale from a La Court resident. It was an easy walk to places where they had business, i.e., the Vinegar Works, the bank, the lawyer, the automobile dealers, the church, and the courthouse. Bonnie could go one-way and he another, if they wished.

When Monroe stopped in front of the La Court, Bonnie's startled look pleased him. Her surprise increased as he stepped from the car and headed for the door.

"Where are you going?"

Monroe smiled happily. "Well, it's a nice morning, I thought we'd stay here."

"Here?" Bonnie's eyes widened.

"Why not?"

"Well, I … . Well I … ."

When Monroe returned from the lobby, Bonnie leaned from the passenger window excitedly. "Did you register?"

"Yes. We'll park in back."

The parking lot allowed complete seclusion from Main Avenue and Second Street traffic, as well as, Colorado Avenue (the first street south of Main). Anyone seeing their car would have to be traveling the alley in an east or west direction.

"You want to clean-up and eat, or eat now and clean-up later?"

Bonnie's response came back like a shot. "Clean-up! Let's take in a few clothes and bathe."

"Then, we'll eat and shop for a truck, okay?"

"Okay. You shop for your truck while I go to church. We'll meet back in the room and decide what's next."

By the time breakfast was over, Monroe had decided to withdraw his money from the bank and then shop for the truck. Bonnie had decided to call her lawyer and make an appointment for the two of them tomorrow. They agreed to call James Laurence and Charlie as soon as they both got back to the room.

* * *

Monroe saw a truck standing on what appeared to be a used car lot. The truck looked new. This truck had crowded his dreams for several days: a shinny, staked, flatbed, with a cab. A one-ton-platform-truck with a starter ... probably? Looked like a 1923 Buick ... maybe a Chevrolet ... he couldn't tell. His step quickened.

Before the salesman arrived, Monroe knew the truck was perfect for him. The tires were brand new. The stakes around the bed weren't even scratched. The odometer indicated 493 miles.

"It's a green Chevrolet—olive-green trimmed in black. It's got a starter and seats like an overstuffed rocking chair," the salesman said, coming up behind Monroe.

"Oh yeah!" said Monroe. "Does the cab leak?"

"Not a drop. Want to drive it?"

"No. Not now. Can I trade my car for it?"

"Sure. What've you got?"

"Enclosed Model T Ford—two seater. Low mileage. I need a truck. How much difference?"

"What year's your Ford?"

"1922."

"Well, if she's nice—five-hundred to a thousand. Bring it in."

"Okay, I will. Around two or three this afternoon. How's that?"

"Fine with me, but don't blame me if this baby ain't here. It won't last long."

* * *

Monroe returned to the hotel. Bonnie announced: "I made an appointment with Downey tomorrow, okay?"

"Sure, and I found a truck. I'm going to trade if the money is right?"

Bonnie reached for her hat and gloves. "Then, I might as well go to church … see if I can talk to Father Conway."

Monroe spent the next hour cleaning and polishing the Model T and when the Ford was spick and span, Monroe returned to the room for some personal cleaning and straightening.

Bonnie was in the room. "I saw Father Conway, but let's talk about it later when we have more time. Are you going to get your truck?"

Monroe thought a second. "I've got to go to the bank first, but let's call home. The Laurences and Charlie."

They went to the lobby and asked to make a long-distance call. The hotel operator called Grand Junction's operator who called Durango's operator and Durango's operator got Mabel on the line. After a short talk with Mabel, Monroe turned over the phone to Bonnie. "Nothing important has happened."

When Bonnie finished talking to Mabel, Bonnie's eyes were brimming with tears. "What's the matter?" Monroe asked.

"Oh, those boys are so precious. I miss them so much."

"But everything's okay, isn't it?" pressed Monroe.

"Oh, yes. She's wonderful."

Relieved, Monroe said, "Well, let's try Charlie. He may be out, but it won't hurt to try."

Monroe stipulated to the hotel operator that they'd be making a rural call to a ranch outside Durango. After the Durango operator went through Animas Valley's Central operator, Charlie answered immediately. "This is my lucky day," Monroe said into the phone. "I thought you might be out of the house this time of day." No response. "Charlie it's me, Roe. Don't you recognize me?"

"Sure. Just lettin' you talk."

"How are you? What's happening—anything?"

"Sheriff Howe was here, yesterday," said Charlie.

"Yeah. What'd he say?"

"He said you were in Grand Junction."

"Damn! How'd he know that?"

"Didn't say," responded Charlie. "But everybody knows, probably. You best be careful."

"I will. Is that all that happened?" asked Monroe.

"I think so. Call me before you leave, okay?"

"I'll do it. Now, write this down. Got a pencil?"

Monroe heard a scramble at the other end of the wire. "Okay, Roe. Shoot."

"Phone number: Grand Junction 348. We're at the La Court Hotel, Room 119. Call anytime you need to, okay?"

"Sure," said Charlie. "See you later." Monroe heard a click and Charlie was gone.

"What did he say?"

"He said that Sheriff Howe knows we're in Grand Junction. That could mean that Sam knows, and if so, his cronies may be looking for us right now. Dammit! We've only been here a few hours."

"So?" asked Bonnie.

"We're going to have to be careful—more careful than I originally thought. Lets stay together wherever we go, okay?"

"Whatever you say," said Bonnie with a frown.

"I'm going to call the vinegar works and tell Dave I want to pick up my brandy and some of his peach wine. I'll get the money from the bank and trade for the truck this afternoon. We'll see your lawyer tomorrow, pick up the booze and get out of here early the next day. What do you think?"

"I'm ready." Bonnie reached for her hat.

* * *

As planned, Monroe and Bonnie accomplish all their plans during the one full day and two nights at the La Court. The following day, they headed north toward Fruita on their return trip to Durango.

The stay in Grand Junction had been hectic, but profitable. They had changed but one plan. Instead of returning by way of Unaweep Canyon, Monroe decided to return via Moab and Monticello. He believed that Sam's potential knowledge of their whereabouts made the longer trip necessary. They'd miss their stay at Driggs Mansion, but traveling would be easier and they might throw a kink in any plans Sam may have hatched.

There had been no incidences involving Sam Isgar's men. Monroe felt good—felt rested. Bonnie had the La Court prepare two breakfasts, two lunches and one dinner for the return trip.

As they passed through Fruita, Monroe noticed that Bonnie seemed reflective. Since he couldn't fathom her mood, he decided to ask. "What's the matter, Honey? Don't you like Fruita?"

Bonnie hesitated a moment. "I was just thinking about what Father Conway said." She remained silent.

"And what did Father Conway say?"

Bonnie turned her face to the passenger window and gazed at a large Cottonwood tree passing from view. "He said I should go back to Sam."

Tears sprang to her eyes and rolled down her cheeks. Monroe's first impulse was to stop the truck. Grab her. Hold her close. But confusion and anger stunned his mind. He drove on.

The little town of Fruita faded away behind them. Sunshine streamed through the cab's rear window striking warmth to Monroe's right shoulder. Darkness shrouded his mind. Finally, he drove the truck to a shaded spot beneath a huge Cottonwood tree that leaned heavily toward the south bank of Salt Creek.

Monroe placed his right arm around Bonnie and cupped his hand over her shoulder. He reached his left arm to her waist and drew her to his chest. Bonnie wept as Monroe held her.

When the passage of time had stopped the crying and the tender silence could do no more, Monroe lifted Bonnie's chin. "What did the good Father say about our son—Wade?"

"I don't know." Bonnie sobbed again. "He didn't say anything."

Monroe sought excuses for the priest, but found none. "Maybe he thought you'd return to Sam with Wade and Sam would accept Wade as his very own." Then, doubting his own statement: "Does Father Conway know Sam Isgar? The kind of man he is? What he's capable of? What Sam really wants?"

"He doesn't know Sam at all," answered Bonnie.

"Then, how-in-the-hell does he deliver such an edict? Go back to Sam! My God! That's a little simplistic, isn't it? We know the church doesn't condone our living as we are. We'd change it if we could. We're caught between State Law on one hand and Church Law on the other. What law made us fall in love? You weren't looking for me. I wasn't looking for you. What law governs that? Nature's Law?" Monroe could have continued, but misery clutched at his throat.

Monroe stepped from the truck, walked around to Bonnie and opened the door. He helped her step from the running board to the ground. Enclosing her in his arms, he kissed her eyes, her cheeks, and her mouth. He picked her up, carried her to the stream's edge, and stood holding her tight against his chest. When, finally, he released her to her feet, he stared at the yellow bluffs beyond. "Honey, we're not bad people. We knew...what we were doing. Is the alternative better? Who can say, with certainty that we should live apart. I only know I love you. I only know: I want you to be my wife. And I promise you: I'll make it right with the Church and with the State ... if you'll give me time. Until then, I'll take care of you and protect you." Monroe kissed both her hands and looked deep into her eyes, hoping to find happiness.

Bonnie looked up, questioningly. "Wade is special, isn't he? He deserves to be treated in a special way, doesn't he? He can be a monument to us."

"Honey, I want us to just go about our business and become the family we want to be." Monroe released her.

Bonnie smiled, turned quickly and dashed happily toward the truck. Suddenly, she whirled and faced Monroe. "Can we have a taste of your brandy to seal the bargain?"

"I don't see why not." Monroe reached for the rope that tied the tarp to the truck bed. "I knew you'd want to taste my brandy somewhere on the way back. You see, I knocked the bung from this barrel and replaced it with your own private spigot." He smiled and turned a twenty-five gallon keg so the spigot could be seen.

"Just a little," said Bonnie. "Let me get a spoon." Bonnie reach into the long box she'd placed on the floor between her feet. "Here's a tablespoon. We'll eat breakfast as we go down the road."

CHAPTER ELEVEN

(March 1923)

Monroe drove through Loma and on toward Mack, Colorado. Bonnie appeared to be her happy self. In fact, she set to singing. Some of the songs she'd sung in the Chautauqua, no doubt. Her singing continued as they passed through Mack. But they hadn't gone two miles when Monroe noticed a black Model T Ford pulling closer and closer. The Ford had a convertible top. The top was up. He couldn't see the passengers, but something told him that this automobile was trouble.

The road widened a bit, and it became obvious that the driver of the black car wanted to pass. Monroe pulled to the right to oblige.

The car pulled even. Monroe heard Bonnie's gasp. Her expression registered horror and disbelief. He quickly glanced to his left. Fear clutched him.

"What the hell!" Monroe grated, when he saw the four men in the black car dressed in white robs and white pointy hoods that covered their faces. A spasm struck his arms. The steering wheel jerked back and forth. "The sonzabitches. Get my rifle from behind the seat."

Bonnie reached for the rifle and banged her arm into the back of the cab. "Dammit!" Monroe exploded. "I left the rifle in the Ford!" Confusion gripped his mind.

"Oh no!" Bonnie exclaimed, with fear constricting her throat.

"You better go back, you wife stealin' sonuvabitch," yelled the man in the Fords passenger seat. "Leave Mrs. Isgar in Grand Junction, if you think anything of her."

Bonnie leaned around Monroe and shouted: "I'll walk to Durango, if I have to."

"Don't worry, Honey. We're not going back!" growled Monroe. To emphasize his point, Monroe stomped the gas pedal hard to the floor.

The truck responded with a forward lunge. A roar from the bigger engine preceded the increased speed, and the truck pulled slightly ahead of the challenging car. Suddenly, Monroe yanked the truck's steering wheel to the left. The truck jumped directly in front of the Ford. Reacting to avoid a crash, the driver of the Klan car jerked his vehicle to the left and plunged deep into the roadside ditch. The black Ford struggled, recovered, climbed back onto the road, and charged toward the loaded truck. The determined Klan driver obviously wanted to pull along side. Seeing a culvert and a bridge ahead, Monroe hogged both sides of the road.

The bridge loomed. Monroe pulled slightly to the right offering a chance to pass. The Klansman took the bait and saw the disasters too late! He stomped his brakes, his rear wheels slipped and dipped into the soft embankment. His car twisted sideways, bounced and flopped over on its side. In a cloud of steam, the wreck remained half in the ditch and half on the road.

Monroe pulled smoothly back to the center of the road, aligned himself with the bridge and passed over East Salt Creek. As he cleared the bridge, he glanced into his rearview mirror, smiled and watched four men in bed sheets wave their arms excitedly as they tumbled from the car while the spooked wheels spun.

In the chase, Bonnie had leaped to her knees in the passenger's seat, and now, sat gawking through the back window of the cab. Monroe wanted to laugh, but realizing the seriousness of the situation, he contented himself with a smile.

"Look at them! They're wrecked!" Bonnie clapped her hands in glee.

"Not bad enough, I'm afraid. There are enough of them to put it back on the road again. They'll be after us." Monroe stuck his head out the left side of his truck, hoping to better see the extent of damage to the Ford. He couldn't. "We'll be quite a ways down the road, when and if, they recover. Wish I had my rifle."

* * *

As the sun edged ever higher in the sky, Monroe noted how the warm weather continued to suck moisture from the ground. The countryside was dry.

Soon, the Olive-Green-and-Black Chevrolet truck passed from Colorado into Utah. There, the Book Cliffs loomed and Crescent City offered a road south to Moab, Utah. The pale-green sagebrush seemed to extend its color forever into the reds and yellows of the spectacular rocks that thrust themselves into the blue sky and twisted human imagination into shapes never before dreamed of.

The road lengthened on to the middle of the day and the truck hummed along like a true champion. "Look at those hills on your right, Honey. Aren't they something? They look like gigantic shelves of books."

Bonnie nodded, enthusiastically … but her mind seemed to be miles back on the road.

"What do you think of this country?" Monroe hoped to take Bonnie's mind off their attackers, if possible.

"We had a line in one of the shows—it seems appropriate." Bonnie smiled and spoke the line: "It's stunning!"

"Isn't it, though?" agreed Monroe. "Well, from here to Monticello, you're going to be stunned."

The breath-taking scenery continued, before and after, they passed through Crescent Junction. It stayed on both sides of the road all the way down to the Colorado River, just north of Moab. When Monroe neared the river, he turned the truck off the road. He saw Tamarack and Cottonwood trees in the distance. It was getting hot. He felt the need for a nap. If the hooded men were following, might they not overshoot this location? He and Bonnie had been traveling about nine hours. A pretty good day's work, he told himself. They couldn't be more than twelve or thirteen hours from Durango. They might just slip the Klan by ducking into the trees—especially if the Klan intended to travel all the way into Durango.

Other vehicles had turned off the road at the same place he did. Their tracks would help obscure his. He drove around a heavy stand of Tamarack and into a Cottonwood clearing where the sand slopped gently down to the edge of the Colorado River.

"Oh!" Bonnie said. "At first, I thought you were crazy. But, this is wonderful. Can we stay here?"

"I hope we can spend the night. We both deserve a nap, especially if we have to run all the way to Durango tomorrow. Our friends may not notice that we've left the road. If they come down here, I'll use my revolver." Monroe said.

"Do you think they might—find us, I mean?"

"No, I don't. But I've been wrong before."

Monroe released the tie-downs on the tarpaulin and threw the tarp back revealing eight twenty-five-gallon barrels. Four on each side of the truck. Between the barrels, a space wide enough to sleep two had been arranged. Blankets and a mattress were already in place. "This isn't the La Court Hotel, but we should be comfortable enough."

"We'll enjoy it. Trust me," Bonnie said, confidently.

Monroe smiled. "Let's walk around our camp and become familiar with our surroundings. Look at the road— then back at the camp. Get an idea about whether someone traveling the road might see us." He reached for her hand. "We may need to know the lay of the land in case we have to move around during the night."

When they completed their "walk-around," Monroe gathered the tarpaulin and spread it on a flat piece of ground that slowly inclined toward the water. He brought two pillows and a blanket from their bed and laid the bedclothes on the canvas. He removed his derby hat, lay back on one of the pillows and covered his eyes with his hat.

"Well, I like that, Mr. Lazy. I suppose you went to all that trouble just so you could take a nap in the sun!"

"No. I thought you might take a nap with me. We've been working pretty hard, you know."

"I grant you that." Bonnie looked across the river's clear waters to a towering monument of red sandstone with a sculpted window at its very top. "These red cathedrals—this multitude of arches—simply stunning."

"Everything is 'stunning' don't you think?"

"It truly is, Roe! I'm not kidding." Bonnie sat quietly surveying the water, the sun and the deep-red rocks. "I want to go swimming. Can I?"

"I don't see why not. Just stay in this cove. Don't go out too far." Monroe thought again. "Maybe, I'll go with you."

He watched from a tiny peephole between the bridge of his nose and the brim of his hat. Bonnie sat on the blanket, removed her shoes, her silk hose, and slipped her one-piece dress over her head, leaving her petticoat, bloomers and brassiere. He marveled at the pink-whiteness of her skin and the wonderful contrast between her auburn hair and that soft whiteness.

She stood removing the petticoat. The smooth, symmetrical curves of her breasts and hips sent a thrill through his body. He felt aroused.

Monroe rose to his elbow and watched her advance toward the river. "Not too far, now."

He sat up, removed his boots, his socks, his pants, his shirt, his hat, and stood in his underwear. "Watch out, here I come." Running, he splashed his way beyond Bonnie and dived into the cold water.

Bonnie screamed as the splash of water hit her. "No fair! I wanted to be first!"

"Who said life is fair. Come on in!"

Monroe saw Bonnie dive for him and rolled to his right as they both floundered in the current. Both came up snorting and wiping water from their eyes. "How'd you like that, big boy?" Bonnie chided.

"Fun!" he said. "Now watch this." Monroe scooped her up in his arms, tried to run down stream and throw her into the water. But his struggle with the swift current unbalanced him and he fell on top of her. He came up gasping for air while reaching to rescue her. "Are you all right? I lost my balance."

Bonnie laughed. "Likely story. You could have lost more than your balance. What if a big fish got me?"

"The world doesn't have a fish big enough to take you from me." Monroe stepped closer, circled her waist with his arms, and kissed her as the cold water circled their waists.

"Let's go dry in the sun," said Bonnie, tugging gently toward the shore.

"Can you swim?"

"Not much," she said. "They tried to teach us at the orphanage, but I didn't quite get it."

"Then let's dry off. I don't want to loose you—for any reason." Monroe gazed up and down the river. Nothing moved except the water. "It's certainly refreshing, don't you think?" he asked.

"Glad I suggested it?" Bonnie ran her fingers through her naturally wavy hair.

"I'm glad for everything you do. And you know why, don't you?"

"I think I do, but I like to hear you say it."

"Because I love you. That's why." Monroe drew her to him and gently kissed her upturned mouth. "Now, you've heard it again. I'll be saying the same thing for the rest of my life."

"I know it. You must always remember how happy and proud you've made me these short months."

On the blanket, Monroe lay flat on his stomach, with his crossed arms under his head. His eyes closed as he felt the warm sun on his bare back and legs. Barely opening one eye, he saw Bonnie lie down beside him.

* * *

When Monroe awakened, the moon hung high in the night sky. Bonnie, curled in a fetal position, pressed tight against his chest. A blanket had been pulled over their partially clad bodies. It took a minute for Monroe to realize it was early morning. They must have fallen into a deep sleep and kept right on sleeping.

Gently, he began to extricate himself from Bonnie. He didn't want to waken her, but he had to learn the time. He reached for his clothes and fumbled into his watch pocket. He'd need a light.

Finding the watch and the match was easy, but lighting the match without waking Bonnie was impossible. When the match lit, Bonnie said, "What's the matter, Honey?

"Trying to see what time it is." He squinted. "Oh, my god! It's five minutes after four." He looked again. "It's morning!" He jumped up grabbing his pants.

"You mean we slept the afternoon and the night?" Bonnie sounded incredulous.

"I guess so. We've got to get moving."

"Why?"

"It's tomorrow, already."

"So."

"We've got to get home."

"I know. And we will, but ... "

"Come on, Honey. Let's get moving," said Monroe.

Bonnie jumped up. Started dressing.

Monroe headed into the bushes near their bed. When he returned, he pulled the blankets from the tarp. "Here. You stand on the blanket. I'll take the tarp to the truck and begin to cover the barrels. Do you remember waking up and covering us?"

"No. I thought you did it."

Monroe realized how lucky they'd been through the night and how tired they must have been when he drove off the road yesterday. "Well, if we start now, we may be able to get gas and get out of Moab before Isgar's friends know we're in town. Assuming they're still following us."

Bonnie threw the bedclothes onto the truck in the space Monroe had arranged for their bed. "Maybe we won't get to use that neat spot between the barrels. We'll probably be home before we sleep again."

Monroe came around to the barrel with the spigot. "Want a spot of brandy before we go?"

"No, thanks. I'll go pee and I'm ready."

When Bonnie climbed into the truck, the engine was running and Monroe was ready to go. "Let's eat in the truck after we get gas and leave Moab. It'll be daylight by that time. Okay?" Monroe raised his voice so Bonnie could hear him.

"Okay," Bonnie said, longing to stay.

Monroe moved the truck slowly away from the river. He tried to follow the path he'd come in on, but the moonlight wasn't quiet bright enough. He'd keep his headlights off in case someone chanced by.

When they reached the road, Monroe turned left and headed for Moab. The town must be about three miles away, he thought. They'd take their time. Cross the Colorado River slowly. It might be a long time before they passed this way again.

In Moab, Monroe pulled into the only service station available. He noticed a restaurant about and eighth of a mile to the south—nothing else seemed awake. Ever on the alert, however, he scanned the entire area for movement or recognition. He thought he might see a black ford, a group of four men huddled together, or suspicious looking men having breakfast inside the restaurant.

He glanced at his watch as the station attendant approached. "Fill'er up." His watch read 5:08. Daylight was coming. "Glad to see you're open. Ready for business."

"We know folks like to get an early start," said the attendant. "Where ya' goin'?"

"Durango. Seen anybody else—going there?"

"No. Not yet." The attendant pumped more gas into the tall glass cylindrical tank at the top of his pump. "Four fellows came in from Fruita last night. Got gas just after dark. Didn't say where they're goin'."

"Just stayed here last night, huh?"

"Down at the Red Arches, I guess," answered the station attendant.

Monroe drank from his water bag and handed the bag to Bonnie. "How much do I owe you?

"That'll be two dollars and ten cents. Want me to check the radiator and the tires?"

"No, thanks. They should be alright." Monroe handed the man exact change.

Back in the truck, while passing the restaurant, Monroe saw the suspect Model T Ford parked on the south side of the building. The car was dirty. The right side was damaged from its roll in the ditch. There was no one around the car. However, Monroe made a conscious effort to eliminate as much noise as possible by throttling back, finding smooth lanes, and avoiding anything else that might disturb the quiet as he passed on his way to the highway. He hit the road with ever-increasing acceleration and glanced alternately between the rear view mirror and the windshield.

"Well, Honey, they're still on our tail. I don't know exactly where they are or whether they've seen us, but we've got a full tank of gas and I'm not going to stop between here and Cortez. Let them do their damnedest. We'll see what good it does." Monroe continued to glance back. "Are you okay?"

"Don't worry about me. I'll do whatever is necessary," said Bonnie resolutely.

"Maybe they haven't seen us? Maybe we can get a long way down the road before they wise up?" said Monroe.

"I hope your 'maybes' are right, and I hope they go back to Fruita or wherever they came from," said Bonnie, clasping her hands tight and pushing them into her lap.

While the little Chevrolet rolled down the road toward Monticello, Monroe and Bonnie rode in silence, glancing back every moment or two … hoping the black Model T would not appear. But, between Moab and Monticello, they rounded a slow curve that put them on a long straight piece of highway south. After a short distance on the straight road, they climbed a low hill and saw a black speck rounding the curve.

"Dammit, here they come!" Monroe, striving not to frighten Bonnie, continued: "I can't really tell if it's them … and I sure can't tell how fast they're coming … or even whether they are trying to catch us. But I'm not slowing down and I <u>am</u> going to keep tract of that little speck back there."

"Can they catch us—I mean, if it's them?"

"Well, Honey. I don't see how they can miss." Monroe checked the temperature gage at the radiator cap. It was normal. "You see—we're loaded. Got a ton of fruit juice on here. I doubt we could outrun 'um even if we were empty. And I know we'll slow down going up hills. So, it's only a matter of time, if that's them."

Monroe and Bonnie continued at about twenty miles an hour or less—depending on the slope of the road. Monroe glanced at Bonnie starring back. "Are they closing the gap?"

Bonnie turned, stuck her head out the window and concentrated. "I can't tell," she said.

The better part of an hour went by. Now, it was obvious that the car was black, and that it <u>was</u> a Ford. The distance between the two vehicles had definitely shortened.

"When we get to Monticello, we'll have to slow down, you know," Monroe said. "We can't speed through the town. If we do, we could be stopped by the police."

"Will the men catch us in Monticello?"

"I don't think so, Honey. They'll get closer, though. Probably catch us before we get to the Colorado border."

"Then what are we going to do?" Bonnie asked, calmly.

"I put the revolver on the floorboards this morning. Think you can shoot it?"

"Oh, Roe! I don't know? I'll try."

Bonnie and Monroe drove carefully through Monticello and headed for the Colorado border. The black Model T was a short distance behind, now. There was no doubt about the occupants, either. A short distance south of Monticello, a long climbing hill rose in front of the Chevrolet.

"Oh, Oh! Here we go, Honey. Get my 45 up here. We'll shoot someone, if we have to. You stay down."

The tension built inside the Chevrolet as the Ford pulled close to the back end. Monroe, looking through his rearview mirror, saw a man leave his place in the passenger seat and step onto the running board with his left hand gripping the top of the car.

Monroe couldn't believe his eyes. "What's the crazy sonuvabitch trying to do, kill himself?"

Only a few seconds passed before Monroe had his answer. He saw the fellow throw something at the back of the truck. A loud explosion split the air. Monroe felt his truck swerve and glimpsed a white puff of smoke fill the air. He glanced back and saw the Model T steer desperately to the right as the fellow on the right running board hurled another stick-like projectile. The object had a fuse in it! The fuse spewed fire as it flew through the air. Almost instantly, dynamite exploded near the truck bed. Monroe felt the concussion and watched the Model T swerve. The dynamite seemed to affect the attacking Ford more than it did his loaded truck.

"The stupid sonzabitches. They're trying to hit us with sticks of dynamite! But, it's hurting them worse than us. I hope they keep missing us—or the dynamite keeps rolling off before it explodes." Another blast rocked the truck.

As a desperate and thoughtless reaction, Monroe purposely applied his brakes, hard and suddenly. The truck, moving up hill, slowed markedly and without warning. The surprised driver of the Ford, found himself rushing headlong into the back of the truck, and swerved sharply to the left. This jarring maneuver was too much for the dynamite thrower. He lost his grip and fell tumbling into the sagebrush and rock that lined the road. "Hope there was some cactus down there," Monroe shouted, with glee.

Pandemonium seemed to erupt in the Ford. Bodies hung out both sides of the car. Arms waved excitedly. Voices screamed as the Ford receded in the distance. The men shook their fists in the air, as the truck proceeded on its way.

Bonnie, enthralled, sat backwards, on her knees, in the seat, gripping the revolver and smiling, as she stared out the truck's back window. The confused scene of frantic men faded from sight as the truck roared around another slow curve to the right. Monroe slacked off on the accelerator and the truck continued to climb.

"That may have done it," Monroe said, believing in his sense of finality. "Surely they'll take their wounded back to Monticello for treatment. That should free us for the rest of our trip!"

CHAPTER TWELVE

(March and April 1923)

The one-ton Chevrolet truck purred through Durango with its load of brandy and fermented mash. The streets were silent. Monroe caught himself staring at the stores as though he expected them to burst forth with throngs of people. He noticed a speechless Bonnie gazing through her window in a non-committal manner. Evidently, they both were so tired of sitting, so exhausted from worry, so relieved of fear, and so pleased to be back in Durango; that the only activity left for them was the gazing, the senselessness, and the comfort of a silent night.

Monroe looked at his watch as he passed under the light at Ninth and Main. The bright streetlight flooded inside the cab. "10:04." They'd be home in 15 or 20 minutes.

"Won't be long now, sweetie," Bonnie said. "Wish I could drive."

"You can. We just haven't put you behind the wheel, yet."

They fell silent again. Monroe turned east on Fifteenth Street and drove toward East Animas Road. He looked north, across the river to the lights in the hospital windows, and remembered his mother.

As he traveled along East Animas Road, he couldn't explain the sense of foreboding, the feeling of loss that came over him. When he neared Cascade, the depressing feeling became a premonition, and as he drove into the yard a stifling fear of the unknown attacked him.

"Well … we're home, and it's dammed cold!" Monroe said, distractedly, while looking suspiciously at the bunkhouse. The door was wide open. *That wasn't like Charlie.* "Bonnie, why don't you go into the house and turn on the lights. I want to let Charlie know we're home." *Why wasn't Charlie greeting them? No lights!*

Monroe stepped onto the bunkhouse stoop. *Something was terribly wrong!* Pieces of glass littered the stoop. Monroe hesitated. He tried to see inside … into the blackness beyond the open door … into the silence.

"Charlie?" Monroe questioned, tentatively. There was no response.

"Monroe!" Bonnie screamed, in horror.

Monroe whirled toward Bonnie's scream. He could see her standing with a lit match held high above her head. He ran toward the house. On the porch, he stumbled over a cream can and crunched into Bonnie.

"It's all blown up!" Bonnie cried, turning and gripping his shoulders.

"What do you mean?" Confusion reined supreme in Monroe's mind.

"The lights won't work." Bonnie pointed to the kitchen door.

Monroe smelled an acrid odor. It was familiar. Dynamite! After hesitating momentarily, Monroe whirled, banged the screen door open, and ran for the truck. He grabbed the lantern, lit it, and returned to the house holding the lantern high above his head. Bonnie hadn't moved. She appeared to be attached to the porch, as though the shock had nailed her feet to the floor. Monroe, still holding the light high, stared into the illumination beyond, and then entered the kitchen door.

The entire back wall of the house had been blown into the room. The kitchen sink lay mutilated on the living room floor. Ice, snow and rocks littered the kitchen floor. The blast had shattered the back window and thrown the kitchen stove, the firewood, and the logs that formed the back wall—everything—into the kitchen—into odd places. "The sonzabitches!" Monroe rasped. Then, peering as far as his eyes and the lit lantern would allow, "They've destroyed our water system!"

Monroe began to move. He crashed his way through kitchen rubble, tore his way to the back wall, struggled to get outside of the house, and wadded through ice that had formed on long blades of grass. The grass crackled and clacked as his feet pushed angrily along. The slippery surface caused him to fall. There on the ground, among the beams that had supported the large water tank, he raised his light and looked hopelessly around. He sniffed again. This time, he caught ... a bitter stench ... a more pronounced whiff ... of exploded dynamite! He stifled a scream—wanted to cry out, but his anger forbid it.

A structure he'd loved and admired—even taken for granted until now—had been destroyed. His father, with his own hands, had developed the water system, as he built the house. It was one of his mothers most prized possessions. He wanted it for Bonnie.

Scrambling to his feet, he gazed at other damage. No wonder Bonnie couldn't turn on the lights; the electrical power-entrance had been destroyed. Open electrical wires stabbed into the night. He struggled, through the rubble and back into the kitchen. Bonnie had not moved.

"Honey. Come with me," said Monroe. "We've got to find Charlie." Monroe took Bonnie's arm and moved her toward the bunkhouse.

"Charlie," Monroe called, hoping hopelessly that Charlie would answer. There was no response.

They passed through the broken glass on the porch. The brittle sound crackled in the cold night air. Monroe put out a hand and stopped Bonnie. "Just stay here, Honey." He moved through the door.

The bunkhouse was empty. Charlie's bed was torn apart. Blankets had been dragged from the bed and lay strewn across the floor. It looked as though Charlie had been dragged from bed. *They must have been awful damn quiet. Nobody sneaks up on Charlie!* Lowering the lantern,

Monroe saw patches of frozen blood on the floor. A spent cartridge under the small table caught his eye. *Charlie's 30-30?* "God damn!" he said. "It looks like it happened tonight—or last night … maybe the night before? I wonder if he's still here?"

Finding Bonnie on the stoop where he'd left her, Monroe said. "Come on, Honey. Stay with me. I've gotta find Charlie and check the stock."

Swinging the lantern, they crossed the road. Monroe heard a whinny. Sounded like Chukaluks. Then, standing by a gate, open to the pasture, he saw Chukaluks. Two cows, sheltering from the wind, were standing between the haystacks.

Satisfied that Charlie wasn't in the yard, he took Bonnie's arm and hurried toward the house. "Let's see if the phone works. We'll call the Laurences. We've got to learn as much as possible, as soon as possible. They need to know we're home. Maybe they know about Charlie."

In the kitchen, Monroe lifted the receiver and listened, then turned the crank for Central. "Number, Please," said the operator.

"Number 232, please." Monroe struggled to be calm.

"Just a moment, please," said the operator.

Monroe listened to the clicks and hums on the wire. Finally, he heard a drowsy John Laurence say, "Hello."

"John, this is Monroe. Can you talk?"

"Oh, thank God! Let me get James." Monroe could hear John struggle out of bed. "It's best you talk to him." John Laurence was gone.

Bonnie looked anxiously at Monroe, reached out her hand and laid it on his shoulder. Her tense facial expressions asked question after question—about the children—the Laurences— any information they might have about Charlie …

Monroe whispered to Bonnie. "It sounds like everything is all right there. He's getting James." She raised tear-filled eyes and wiped both hands across her cheeks.

Monroe heard scuffling at the other end of the line. "Where are you?" James asked.

"We're at Cascade. How are the boys?"

"They're all right. Real good, as a matter of fact. Don't worry on that score. Are you in the house?"

"Yes."

"Then, you know?"

"I don't know anything," Monroe exploded. "Where's Charlie?"

"He's in the hospital. The Jacksons brought him in." James paused. "And, Roe. He's not good. They nearly killed him. May die yet. Burned him on a cross."

"What cross? Where?"

"On your front lawn."

"Goddamn! When?"

"Last night."

"What is it?" Bonnie asked. "Are the children, okay?"

Monroe nodded his head vigorously, up and down. His heart twisted and writhed in pain as he imagined his dear friend dragged from bed, beaten, tied to a cross, and burned. "Damn!"

"Come over here, Roe. Stay with us. We need to talk. The Sheriff knows about everything. Hear?"

"Okay. We're on our way." Monroe pushed the receiver hook down with his left hand and moved slowly to hang up the receiver.

* * *

When Monroe entered the Laurence driveway, he thought every light in the house was on. It was after midnight. He saw Mabel Laurence through the living room window carrying coffee cups. A sense of urgency existed everywhere. James came into the room with a notebook in hand.

Monroe turned off the engine. "You all right, Bonnie?"

"I'm fine. I want to see the boys," she said.

Monroe unlatched the door on the driver's side and heard Bonnie opening her door. "Be careful. The snow is packed," he said, hurrying to help her down.

"Thank God we have friends, Roe. What would we do without them?"

At the front door, the nightlight flashed on. The door opened and John Laurence stood in robe and house slippers. His nightcap tilted to the left. The tassel swung like a pendulum across his ear.

John said, "Forgive me. I didn't bother to dress." He swung wide the screen door and smiled a welcoming smile. "Get in here before you freeze."

Mabel grabbed Monroe, hugged him, and turned to Bonnie. "I know you're worried about the boys, but they're all right. In fact, they couldn't be better, so put all your concerns aside. We're glad to help."

"I didn't worry at all until I saw Cascade. Then everything just fell apart." Bonnie embraced Mabel. "You folks are the only good thoughts we have."

"Well, bless you child! Come back here and take a peek." Mabel put an index finger to her lips.

Mabel led Bonnie and Monroe down the hall to a door on the right. She turned quietly, pursed her lips, and then gripped the knob. She whispered. "There's a night light. No need to wake them."

Bonnie nodded her agreement. She leaned against the wall and glanced at Monroe. "I'm not sure what we're going to do."

"You're going to stay in that room across the hall. It's all made up," said Mabel. "We won't take 'no' for an answer." She opened the door half way. "Look at those angels."

Gazing into the dimly lit room, Harold and Wade could be seen sleeping in a large bed bounded by the bedroom wall on one side and straight-backed chairs on the other. Harold lay with his arm draped over Wade's shoulder as though he intended to protect his little brother from whatever harm might befall. Wade's right hand balled into a tender fist.

Monroe placed his hand on Bonnie's arm. "You stay here with Mabel and the kids. Get some rest. I want to see Charlie before I sleep and I've got to do something with the load we brought back from Grand Junction." He turned to Mabel. "We'll talk a minute. Get up to date on what's going on. Then I'll leave."

Mabel pursed her lips, pulled the door shut, and shooed her guests' toward the living room. They all tippy-toed over the hardwood floors.

"Sit down, both of you," John said, as they entered the living room. "I know you're tired of sitting, but just relax a minute while you talk." He directed Bonnie to a large, overstuffed chair in the corner. "Mabel and I are going to bed. You don't need us. We'll let James fill you in."

"Please, John," Monroe said. "We can't thank you enough for all you've done."

"Now, now. There'll be plenty of time for 'thanks.'" John said. "Come on, Mabel."

Monroe stepped to the sofa that squared with Bonnie's chair leaving a large end table between. The table lamp burned low and gave the room a warm, comfortable glow. Bonnie leaned back, rested her head against the comfortable chair, yawned, and then moved forward to pour hot coffee from the large pot Mabel had placed on the table.

Monroe touched her arm. "Why don't you go to bed, Honey?"

"I want to hear about Charlie and the house, then I'll go."

James returned from the dining room with a straight-backed chair, which he placed cross the coffee table from Monroe and Bonnie. He moved into the chair and laid a notebook on the table before them. Monroe leaned forward.

"I've tried to make notes about things, in the sequence they occurred. Thought they might come in handy if you need information for court." James turned the first page. "Barbara Jackson called me Sunday night, at 11:34 P.M., saying she and everyone in her family had heard loud explosions that woke them. Then, from their upstairs bedroom, they looked down the valley, in the direction of the noise, and saw what they described as a 'glow' in the night-sky. The light seemed to be coming from the vicinity of your house." Monroe and Bonnie sat motionless.

James continued. "The Jackson boys dressed quickly, bridled their horses and rode bareback toward your place while Mr. Jackson called the Sheriff."

"Jackson called the Sheriff?" Monroe repeated.

"Yes."

"What'd the Sheriff say?"

"He said—well—wait a minute. I'll get to that." James waved a protesting hand and returned to his notes. "When the Jackson boys came from their barn—before they left for your place—Mr. Jackson instructed the boys not to run head-on into something they didn't know anything about. He told them not take a hand until the Sheriff arrived— unless something was life threatening. Mr. Jackson told the boys he'd be along later."

"Did he? Did he go over to Cascade, I mean."

"Yes, but let me tell you," insisted James

"Did the Sheriff get there?" Monroe wanted to know.

"Yes—but wait," James pleaded.

Monroe swallowed in an effort to control himself. "Okay. I'm sorry. I won't interrupt again."

"When the boys arrived at Cascade, they approached slowly and looked things over pretty good before they showed themselves. They could smell the smoke and they could see the burning cross before they got there. They waited in that clump of oak trees at the north side of your front yard. They didn't move until they made sure no one was around. As they rode into your yard, they thought they saw somebody hanging on the burning cross."

"God Damn!" Monroe exploded.

"I know," James said, "but listen. The boys rode closer. They could smell burning pine tar. They heard a man groaning. He was writhing on the cross. The devils had wired his left wrist to the transverse, wired his body to the upright by stringing wire under his arms and around his chest. Then, they wired his ankles to the post. They lit the cross around the middle of his body. The upper part of his body is burned black."

Monroe couldn't speak. He turned to Bonnie. Her eyes had filled with tears. She stared horrified.

"You said on the phone that he's still alive," reminded Monroe.

"He's in terrible bad shape, Roe. The Sheriff got in touch with his family. They arrived at the hospital today."

"What are his chances? Do we know?" asked Monroe.

"I don't think anyone knows."

"Can we see him?" Bonnie asked.

"Oh sure. But he won't see you," James said. "He's blind. His good arm is gone, I think. The pine tar burned longest and hardest up and down his spine."

"I want to see him," Monroe said, "as soon as we get through here." He turned to Bonnie. "I'm going to ask you to stay here. Get some sleep for tomorrow. I'll unload the booze tonight so the Sheriff doesn't see it. I can't keep it at Cascade."

"What are you going to do?" Bonnie asked.

"I'm still thinking, Honey. I have some ideas. By the time I'm through at the hospital, I'll probably know."

"Shall I tell you the rest?" asked James.

"There's more?" Monroe asked, incredulously.

James consulted his notes and continued. "The Jackson boys carried water from the creek and doused the cross. They got towels and blankets from the house, pulled the cross to the ground, laid everything on a blanket, and cut Charlie loose. The wires had burned their way into Charlie's body. The hospital had a terrible time getting pieces of wire out of his body."

"Oh Jesus, Mary and Joseph! I don't want to hear any more," Bonnie cried. "If you don't mind, I'd like to go to bed. I think I understand."

"I'm sorry. I probably made it too graphic," James apologized. "Take the room on your left. You know where the bathroom is."

"I'll get my small suitcase." Bonnie headed for the door.

"Let me go, Honey," Monroe said, hurrying to beat Bonnie to the door. "I'll bring mine in, too."

When Monroe came back from the truck, Bonnie had gone. He carried their cases to the bedroom, put them on the bed, and returned to find James sitting in the living room with more coffee poured.

"Thought you could use another cup. If I heard you right, we're going to need more than coffee tonight. I'll put some in a thermos before we go."

"It'll take both of us to unload the brandy," said Monroe.

"How'd you get it over here?"

"Twenty-five gallon barrels—on a truck." Monroe smiled. "Each barrel weighs around two hundred pounds."

"Well, I need the exercise," said James.

"Remind me to tell you about our trip, sometime," said Monroe.

"Okay. But first, you want to hear about the Sheriff, don't you?"

"Sure," Monroe said, as James picked up his notebook.

"Well, when the Jackson boys unhooked Charlie from the cross, they thought they'd vomit—the smell

239

and all. When their dad arrived, they covered Charlie with blankets and waited for Sheriff Howe. Howe got out right away because he was on duty—he just called for the ambulance, grabbed his 30-30, and drove out. Anyway, when the Sheriff got to your place, Jackson and the boys walked with him though the house. They saw the back wall. They saw the water tank. And the ambulance was there by the time they were through looking in the bunkhouse.

"God! Let's go see Charlie, James. Tell me the rest as we go."

"Okay," said James. "It's here in the book. A hell of a mess." James went to the hall closet and grabbed his winter coat.

"Does the Sheriff know who did it?" asked Monroe.

"No. But you do, don't you?"

"We all know," responded Monroe. "They left their calling card." Monroe headed for the door. "Does anyone know where Bob Stout and Earl Mills were—when it happened?"

"I hear they got air-tight alibis." James closed the front door quietly, then said: "I've been cultivating old friends at the hospital, but I still can't get in to see Charlie."

* * *

The hospital was quiet. Their heels clicking on the hard floor created a hollow sound that seemed louder as they went. 1: 30 A.M. appeared on the clock inside the door. Monroe walked directly to Sister Agnes' office.

Sister Agnes was on duty. The single lamp on her small desk lit her surprised face when he peeked through the door. "Yes," she said. "Can I help you?" She stood up.

"Hello, Sister. I'm Monroe Morgan."

"I remember you. How are you?"

"I'm fine. It's my friend Charlie Eagle I'm here for." He turned to James. "This is James Laurence?"

"How do you do?" said Sister Agnes, nodding to James.

"My pleasure, Sister."

"We were hoping to see Charlie. I've just arrived from Grand Junction."

"We don't allow visitors after nine o'clock. You know that, Monroe."

"But Sister, his injury is probably my fault. I couldn't stand it if something terrible happened before I saw him." Monroe felt tears well in his eyes as he contemplated the unthinkable.

"Mr. Morgan, you've had so much trouble … " Sister Agnes seemed ready to make an exception. "Mr. Eagle left the hospital such a short time ago, now he's back." She went to her desk. Leafed through a notebook. After a short review, she looked up. "He's never regained consciousness. He's so badly burned, Dr. Miller says he doesn't understand what's sustaining him."

"Sister … " Monroe paused a long moment while gazing deep into her eyes. He was arguing with himself as much as he was arguing with Sister Agnes. "He'll know I'm here. I have to let him know."

Without further conversation, Sister Agnes scooted sideways through the door and lead the way down the hall. On the way upstairs, Monroe recalled the several times he'd visited Charlie when his mother and Charlie were on the same floor a few months ago. At the top of the stairs, Sister Agnes suddenly stopped. "I doubt Mr. Eagle will know you, and for all good intent and purpose, you'll not recognize him. Your visit must be very brief. Do you understand?"

"Yes, Sister."

Sister Agnes reached inside the room on her left and flipped the switch. She stepped aside. Monroe stopped the scream in his throat. This grotesque mass of quivering human flesh couldn't be his friend. James turned away. The head lying on the white pillow had no hair. No eyebrows. No eyelashes. The skin—burned black. The whole body was too small! All charred—except the feet. And there, a liquid dripped onto a soggy pad that protected the sheet. A shriveled ash corresponded to his good right arm. The finger bones were showing—the nails gone.

Monroe swallowed hard and gripped the door. "Is this Charlie?"

"I'm sorry," answered Sister Agnes.

James stepped into the hall. The sister followed.

Monroe struggled to move. Finally, he stepped to the foot of the bed, put out his hand and touched Charlie's bare feet. "I'm here, Charlie." He choked back tears and fought helplessly to find words. "I'll miss you every day of my life."

Monroe found Sister Agnes and James waiting for him in the hall. "I want to get in touch with his family. Do you know how I can do that? They visited, I understand."

"They come here early in the morning, about six o'clock. You might want to meet them, then," said the Sister.

"Thank you, Sister. Thanks for everything." Monroe motioned to James and turned toward the stairs.

* * *

In the truck, Monroe and James drove in silence, staring straight ahead. They passed through the middle of town, crossed the Graden Bridge and chugged up Lightner Creek.

James couldn't contain his curiosity. "Where are we going, Roe?"

"To Porter."

"Porter! Why Porter? There hasn't been anyone there for fifteen years."

"Exactly. That's why we're going. It'll be tough for Bonnie and the kids, but I can use the Superintendent's

House, the tipple, everything. We'll be right there at the west tunnel. It's above the road out of Durango. We can see everyone, coming or going, long before they get to us."

"Is there a road up there?"

"How do you think Old Mister Wright and his Misses got there? The whole idea occurred to me when Bonnie and I went through Porter on our way to Grand Junction. But it didn't sink in, I guess, because I didn't think I'd ever want to use it. Bonnie'll be surprised."

Moments later, Monroe turned south into Wildcat Canyon. It was pitch dark. They passed under the great bridge/trestle, which extended from one side of the canyon to the other. "Aren't we supposed to have a moon sometime tonight?"

"I don't know. Maybe," James said. "Where's the road to the Superintendent's House?"

"You have to go into the town itself. At the old General Mercantile Store, you switch back." Monroe squinted into the night.

"Have you been here, recently? Looked at the house?" James was sitting on the edge of his seat with his face near the windshield.

"No. But I bet it's okay. If not, Bonnie and I'll have to find a place in town and I'll run my booze business out'a here."

"What if some old mucker's still living in one of these shacks and doesn't like you for a neighbor? Is he going to report you?" asked James.

Monroe thought it over. "Let's wait and see if there's an 'old mucker' living here. On our way to Grand Junction, we came through Porter early in the morning and I didn't see a breath of smoke from any of the chimneys. The whole settlement looked completely dead."

Monroe jerked the steering wheel to his right, darted over a wooden bridge, crossed railroad tracks, and turned hard right again. "Well, the bridge held up. Glad they built it strong. I'll take a look at it in the daylight."

"What do you mean?" asked James.

"That bridge," Monroe answered. "My load weighs almost a ton, and when you add the weight of the truck and you and I, I bet we are close to two tons."

"You mean you drove over a bridge you didn't know would hold up?" exclaimed James.

"James, you've got to learn to trust your fellow man." Monroe made the sign of a cross over his chest, stopped the truck, shifted to compound low, lit a match, and squinted at the gas gauge. "I'm glad I filled up in Cortez. It figured to be to late to buy gas when we got to Durango. Now, with all this running around, I've still got half a tank."

Monroe stepped out of the truck and lit another match. The wind blew it out.

"What are you doing?" ask James.

"I'm going to light a lantern and walk this road to the mouth of the tunnel. There may be deep holes or washouts. I doubt anyone's been up here recently."

James got out. "Okay. I'll help."

Monroe found the lantern and lit it. They made their way up a steep grade to a point where the road leveled off and then ran straight north to the mouth of the west tunnel. There they found the tipple buildings and the Superintendent's House.

Monroe turned to James. "I'm surprised the road's as good as it is. They must have graded and graveled it so much when they were working the mine that very little water has been able to penetrate it."

"Me, too," said James.

"Let's look at the house." Monroe walked forward. "Let's keep our eyes on the shacks. We might see lights come on while we're here."

"I've been doing just that," responded James.

They crossed the coal car tracks that ran east out of the west tunnel and through the tipple. The Superintendent's House loomed large up ahead. The house had a yard, surrounded by what had been a white picket fence, and the whole place sat more than two hundred feet north of the tipple. There were no weeds, or other growth, cluttering the yard. Two giant silver spruce stood guard on either side of the path leading up to the front door.

"Old Mister Wright must have planted these spruce trees when he built the house."

"Probably," agreed James.

They made their way around the house observing what they could with the limited light they had. James said, "No windows broken."

Once they'd entered the Superintendent's home, Monroe concluded that no one had been in the house since the family closed the door years ago. The place was dusty and cold, but remarkably well preserved. As a rental in Durango, it would fetch a pretty penny. The outhouse would be an inconvenience, and he'd have to haul water from the creek, but otherwise, everything was in good shape—the fireplace—the large kitchen stove.

Monroe liked it. "I think it's going to be fine. If you folks can put up with us for one more day, I think we can clean tomorrow and move in the next day."

"I'm surprised it's in good condition," said James. "But, don't be in a hurry to move in. You've got to get furniture and everything else up here. You don't even know who you can rent from?"

"I thought maybe I'd ask McGovern at the bank, when I take my Cascade money in," said Monroe. "He'll probably know the right people. Union Pacific had it, last I heard."

"You know who I'd ask, Roe?"

"Who?"

245

"Sheriff Harvey Howe. You've got his attention. I think he's in your corner. He knows about the destruction at Cascade."

Monroe immediately recognized James's wisdom. He'd confide in the Sheriff. Well, he'd confide about everything but the booze. With the right approach, the Sheriff might condone his using Porter as a temporary hideout and forget paying anyone—for the time being. He couldn't imagine staying there more than three months. Certainly, Bonnie would have her divorce in three months and they might be able to move to their new homestead on Florida Mesa, soon.

"You know, James, I think you may be right. It's a good idea. Let's get the truck unloaded."

The unloading of the truck proved surprisingly simple. They just arranged two mine timbers to fit at the truck bed and rolled the barrels down. When all eight containers were off the truck, Monroe found a dolly and placed the brandy in a shed. He'd rearrange things tomorrow or the next day. Everything had to go underground.

"What time is it, James?

"I don't know. Look at your watch."

Monroe fished for his watch while he walked to the lantern. "Getting late. 4:10 A.M. I want to see Charlie and his folks at 6:00. Would you stay with me to see that I don't go to sleep before I see them?"

"Sure. I'll keep watch while you take a nap, Roe. You've got about two hours, maybe more, if Charlie's folks arrive late."

Monroe thought a moment. "Let's go to the hospital now and you wake me when the Eagles show. Okay?"

"Sure."

* * *

At the hospital, Monroe assured that James would stay awake, and then he leaned back in his seat and dropped immediately into a sound sleep.

Monroe thought he was at Porter. He stuck his head into a crawl space while cleaning the Superintendent's House. Suddenly, something huge and furry struck the back of his neck—a spider. The limited space didn't allow him to grab the furry spider and it sank its fangs into his neck. As he writhed in pain and fright, he kicked the ladder from under his feet and fell headlong to the floor.

"Wake up! Wakeup! You're having a nightmare."

It was James voice, high pitched—excited. James' hands were reaching to subdue Monroe's flailing arms and thrashing legs. "It's a nightmare, man!"

"Oh! I'm sorry, buddy!" Monroe said. "I got bit by a big spider on the back of my neck at Porter."

"Well, anyway, it's getting about 6 o'clock," said James.

"What time?"

"Time for the Eagles to get here. Charlie's parents, remember."

"Oh yeah. Damn!" Monroe rubbed his eyes. "That spider was big and black."

"How'd you know it was black?"

"I saw it flying through the air with me, when I fell off the ladder." Monroe got out of the truck and walked away, then came back. "Boy! It's cold. I wonder if I could borrow their wash room."

"I don't see why not. Go ahead. I'll watch."

Monroe glanced toward the street. "What time is it?"

"6:10," said James.

When Monroe came back, he asked: "Is the coast clear?"

"No."

"Are they here?"

"Yep."

"Oh." Monroe looked at the hospital door. "How long ago?"

"Maybe five, six minutes."

"Okay. Let's go in." Monroe started toward the door. He stopped, waited for James to catch up. "Just Charlie's mother and father?"

"No. Four people," said James. "I assume two were Charlie's parents."

"Let's go see," said Monroe.

When Monroe peeked into Sister Agnes' office, he found the office vacant. "Let's wait," said he.

They stood by the door. Minutes passed. Daylight tore at the darkness. Finally, they heard a rustle at the top of the stairs. Seconds later, Monroe saw a tall, young Indian carrying a bundle wrapped in that beautiful Navajo blanket he'd seen folded on a chair in Charlie's room. The black, red, white and gray blanket caught his eye because of its size and singular beauty. The long fringe, finishing each end, waved silently as the barer stepped down the stairs. Charlie was in that blanket! Tears flooded Monroe's eyes. The scene became distorted. He wiped his eyes, but the flood would not stop. The procession came closer and silently, walked on by. Charlie's mother, being last in line, stopped at the door. She returned to Monroe, put her arms around him and said: "You were his friend. Don't cry. Now, you are my boy." Monroe wanted to cradle her in his arms, but she turned away and passed through the door. Monroe followed after her, feeling useless and hopeless.

James grabbed Monroe's arm to hold him. He took the truck keys from Monroe's hand and guided him out the door and to the truck.

As the Eagle family laid their beloved son in their wagon and drove their team away, James opened the door to the trucks passenger's seat. Monroe climbed in burying his face in his hands. He could not control his emotions.

CHAPTER THIRTEEN

(April 1923)

James's mother came to the window when James drove the Morgan's truck into the driveway. The living room lights were on. Monroe evidently felt the truck stop, because he raised his head from his hands and sat up straight.

James didn't move to get out. He'd let Monroe make the first move. Sitting quietly, he watched the sun brighten the morning sky.

Mabel left the living room, returned to the window, stood and peered quizzically at the truck. She left the room and returned to the window with John. John motioned them to come in.

"We better go in," Monroe said.

"When you're ready," said James. James had held his peace for hours, it seemed, but his curiosity would wait no longer. "What did Charlie's mother say to you—there at the end, I mean?"

"She said I was her son, now." Monroe gazed through the passenger's window. "And, you know what, James? I'm proud to be her son."

James watched his father leave the house and walk toward the truck. John Laurence stepped up to James's window and rapped.

"What are you doing?" John Laurence asked, quietly.

James lowered the window. "Charlie died."

John looked down, disconsolate. He started to return to the house, then stopped and gazed at Monroe. "Well, come in where it's warm. We'll talk."

Monroe opened his door, got out, and headed for the house with John and James following. Mabel met them at the door. She turned away and went directly to the kitchen. "I'll get some coffee."

"Dad, I want a truck like Roe's."

"You got the money?" answered John, then, said: "I haven't seen any thing like this around here, yet. I think Grand Junction gets things before we do."

Monroe stood in the middle of the living room. He seemed unable to decide what to do next. Mabel came in with the coffee. "Sit down, Roe. Both of you look like you've been dragged through a knothole. I'm going to give you some ham and eggs, and then you're both going to bed."

Monroe sat in the corner chair. "Where's Bonnie?" he asked.

"She's sleeping. Don't wake her."

"I've got to see the Sheriff," said Monroe.

"You've got to get some rest is what you've got to do," Mabel said, pouring coffee.

James sipped his coffee. "I've been thinking you should let your lawyer do that for you. I could see the Sheriff for you while you get some rest, and then, you and I can haul furniture this afternoon—or even tonight."

"Maybe he needs to see me. Know I'm in town. Answer some of my questions about Charlie."

"Both of you get in here and eat something, and then, make up your minds." Mabel turned back into the kitchen.

James glanced at the clock as he entered the kitchen.

James heard the bathroom door open and close again. It had to be Bonnie. Why couldn't Bonnie go with him to see the Sheriff? Her being there would give good evidence that Monroe was in town, and Monroe would have a chance to sleep.

Monroe glanced toward the hallway. "Was that Bonnie?"

"I think so," said James. "Mom and Dad are in the living room."

Just as he and Monroe finished their meal, the bathroom door opened again. Bonnie stepped into the kitchen wearing one of Mabel's housecoats. "How's Charlie?" she said.

James waited for Monroe. Finally, Monroe swallowed, moved a chair for her, and said: "Sit down, Honey."

Bonnie's face clouded with apprehension. She moved stiffly to the chair and stared searchingly at Monroe, as his eyes filled with tears. "Oh, Roe!" exclaimed Bonnie, jumping to her feet and cradling Monroe in her arms.

Monroe grasped her hand. "He's gone. They killed him."

Bonnie's shoulders slumped. "Is it our fault, Roe?" Her eyes grew misty. "Oh, how could they?"

Monroe pushed himself away from the table and stood beside Bonnie. "I don't know whose fault it is?" he said. He shook his head—confused. "I hope it's not totally ours. There's plenty of fault to go around. Maybe it's God's will? I don't know."

James saw mitigating circumstances for everyone except the Ku Klux Klan. "These are difficult times with complex problems and prejudices," he said. "Labor unrest. Religious bigotry. I think people are struggling to improve their lives, but while they are battling their own problems, they lash out and hurt each other."

"Well, James, if it's every man for himself," Monroe said. "I can tell you this: I'm going to do my best to protect my own. And, I'll tell you straight up, I'm going to need your council."

Mabel entered the kitchen. "I've got the day to give to the boys, so you folks make plans and don't worry about the children." Monroe looked gratefully at Mabel and returned to his chair. Mabel walked down the hall.

Bonnie gazed at Monroe. "You look terribly tired, my husband."

"I am. But I've got to see the Sheriff."

"I've been suggesting that he let me visit the Sheriff for him—while he gets some sleep," James said.

"You haven't slept for two days, Roe. Let him go to the Sheriff for you." Bonnie's eyes were pleading.

"The Sheriff needs to see me. He needs to know I'm in town."

"I can tell him that," James said. "He needs to know you have an attorney—that you're not alone."

"If I went with James, he'd know you were in town, wouldn't he?"

"Oh yes, Honey."

"Then let me go with James. We could do what needs to be done and you could get some rest."

Monroe seemed to recognize that the idea was a good one. "How about the house in Porter, James. Do you think you could manage that?"

"I don't see why not. You want to hide your wife and kids from whoever is out to get you. You think Isgar and the Klan, because a cross was burned at Cascade. You don't have your place on Florida Mesa, yet, and you don't feel safe in town. We'll explain Bonnie's divorce process and how Sam's fighting it. We won't mention the booze. Okay?"

Monroe looked at Bonnie. "Feel like going, Honey? You haven't had much rest, either."

"I feel fine. I'll feel better knowing you're resting."

"Okay, then. Do it your way."

* * *

Bonnie had never been in La Plata County's Courthouse. She didn't know why, but she thought it strange to have a jail in a courthouse. She thought courts and trials and records, all belonged in one building, while jails and Sheriffs and police and prisoners, all fit in a separate building. James said the main jail was in the basement, under the Sheriff's office, and that the barred windows she saw above ground were jail windows. When she and James climbed the stone steps, she searched the barred windows for prisoners.

Inside, Bonnie found a wide and long lobby that led to a wide set of stairs going up to a second story. The wide stairway parted into two additional hallways—one going north and the other south. More offices and/or courtrooms on the second floor, she surmised.

The first door on her right had a big sign above it: "Police Station". James opened the door and stood aside while Bonnie entered. She saw chairs and a long counter. The counter divided the room, but the whole office appeared empty.

She saw James crane his neck to peek into a large plate-glass window in the back wall. "Sheriff Howe isn't in, I guess," he said. Bonnie heard the disappointment in his voice. "At least he's not in his office right now," continued James, shoving his hands into his pockets, grinning sheepishly, and raising a finger to indicate a chair. "Maybe we should have called, before we came."

Bonnie took the chair. "I don't think so, James. We can wait."

"It needs to get done," he agreed.

As they waited, Bonnie noticed that each little noise caused a hollow sound that reverberated around the room. Also, the unmistakable smell of floor-sweep filled her nostrils. Huge amounts of daylight crashed into the room through windows facing south and west. She wondered how long it had been since the windows were washed.

The green door behind the counter burst open. A huge man in a Stetson hat lumbered into the room. His boots slapped the floor as he stopped dead in his tracks. A surprised look remained on his face as he tried to glance over his right shoulder at another large man with brown eyes, brown hair, and a flowing mustache.

"What the hell? What are you stopping for?" The huge man with the flowing mustache nearly bumped into the giant in the white Stetson

"Sorry, sir," said the first arrival. "We've got visitors. Surprised me, I guess."

When the big fellow had cleared the doorway and the mustached man could be seen more clearly, Bonnie noticed a Silver Star pinned to his buckskin vest and she knew she was looking at Sheriff Harvey Howe, Sheriff of La Plata County. She presented her brightest most pleasant smile.

"Good morning," said the Sheriff, moving a chair aside and walking to the counter opposite James. "I'm Sheriff Howe and this is Deputy Bob Stout. We've been checking cells. What can we do for you?"

"I'm James Laurence." James extended his hand and turned to Bonnie. "This is Mrs. Monroe Morgan from Cascade Ranch up the valley. We want to talk to you, if we may."

Sheriff Howe hadn't taken his eyes off Bonnie. His attention became riveted when he heard "Morgan" and "Cascade." Bonnie also noticed Bob Stout jerk his eyes back and forth between James and her.

"Of course. Of course." The Sheriff seemed a bit flustered. He literally jumped to the flap-door in the middle of the counter top, raised it and invited them behind the counter. "Let's go to my office." He gestured to the office door by the window in the back wall. "Bob, you go on downtown and take care of that call from Graden's Mercantile."

Bob looked disappointed but neither could he take his eyes off Bonnie. He stumbled over a chair. "Yes, sir."

"Just go right in the office, folks, and make yourself comfortable."

Once in his office, Sheriff Howe seemed reluctant to remove his eyes from Bonnie. So intent was his stare that Bonnie began to feel self-conscious. She felt as though she might be blushing. She sat in a chair indicated by James and continued to gaze at James while she prepared herself to look at the Sheriff again.

"Well, I must tell you right off the bat Mrs. Morgan," Sheriff Howe said, "you're the prettiest woman I've ever seen in my whole life." Bonnie definitely felt the blush now. "Now, I don't mean to embarrass you, but you've been advertised as a 'real looker' and I've always thought it was just so much talk—until right now—and if anything, the facts have been understated."

Bonnie smiled her appreciation. "Thank you for your kindness, sir."

The Sheriff stared unashamed until he seemed to realize his actions were unmannerly. He then cleared his throat, wriggled in his seat, shuffled his hands and feet, and looked away—through his window. "Well, I'm sorry to stare, but that's not what you wanted to see me about, is it? As a matter of fact, I've been anxious to talk to <u>you</u>. Where is Mr. Morgan?"

Bonnie wanted to say: 'Well, your honor'—but she caught herself. "Monroe Morgan is my intended, Sir. I'm suing for divorce in Grand Junction and as soon as it is final, Mr. Morgan and I plan to marry."

"I see," said Sheriff Howe, smiling self-consciously. The Sheriff paused and gazed, first at Bonnie and then at James.

"Mr. Douglas Downey is my lawyer in Grand Junction and Mr. Laurence, here, is my lawyer in Durango."

"And where is Monroe Morgan, now?"

Bonnie straightened in her chair. "Sir, we just got back from Grand Junction and he drove all day yesterday and last night just to get here. When we got home, he found our house destroyed and one of Monroe's best friends in the hospital, near death. I'm referring to Charlie Eagle, who has since died. Did you know about Mr. Eagle?"

"Well, I knew he was in desperate straights, but that's all. Did he pass away last night?"

"Early this morning. Monroe spent the night with Charlie. He wanted to see you this morning, but while waiting for daylight, he sat down and simply went to sleep. James and I let him sleep while we came to visit with you. We thought we would speak for Roe, if you don't mind?"

Sheriff Howe nodded his agreement. "Well, there's certainly a lot to talk about. I've been to Cascade."

The conversation continued with James covering the need to hide Bonnie and the kids. In detail, they discussed Monroe's suspicions about Sam Isgar and the Ku Klux Klan, i.e., the burning cross, the death of Charlie Eagle, the pending divorce, the two divorce attorneys, and Monroe's intention to move to a homestead on Florida Mesa. They resolved each question as the question arose. The Sheriff didn't know who to see about renting the house in Porter, but he recognized the need for secrecy and agreed that Monroe and Bonnie should move to Porter, on the "QT", until they had Florida Mesa available to them. He promised to say nothing to anyone—including his own department personnel.

Bonnie believed the interview had gone quite well, until the Sheriff asked one more question. At first the question seemed innocuous.

"But, even though, Sam Isgar is a significant figure in the Ku Klux Klan, and even though, you have irrevocably decided to divorce him; why do you suppose Klan members would be willing to break the law—both here and in Grand Junction—just to satisfy Sam's desire to hurt an incorrigible wife? According to you, Sam may have even murdered a man, who, from what we know, never harmed anyone in the Klan. Charlie wasn't even a Catholic, was he?"

Bonnie considered the question. "Catholics are high on the Klan's list of prejudices. But no, Charlie was not Catholic. Of course, both Monroe and I are. Maybe, it's part of an extreme vendetta against us."

"Do you feel you are living in sin?" Sheriff Howe's concern seemed friendly.

"Somehow, I don't think so," Bonnie said. "I'm happier than I've ever been." She contemplated her gloved hands. "I haven't been beaten since I left Sam Isgar. And I haven't been thrown from a house, either."

When Bonnie looked up, the Sheriff seemed confused. She waited. "I find it difficult to believe that anyone would beat you, or throw you from a house." Finally, he continued. "But, from what I'm told, the Catholic Church would frown on a married woman who gives birth to a child which is not her husbands."

"At first it worried me a great deal, because I've tried to be honest with myself and I've tried to be faithful to my church, but now, I believe it depends a lot on circumstances."

"How so." asked the Sheriff?

"Let's take it from your point of view." Bonnie was anxious to discuss the situation with someone outside the church. "I haven't broken any laws, have I? You don't want to arrest me for what I've done, do you?"

"No."

"That's a legal point of view, isn't it?"

"But, you're a Christian, right?" asked the Sheriff.

"I've been a practicing Catholic—one of several different kinds of Christians. I think I may have evolved into a person who has her own personal religion. I feel comfortable praying to God. Like Abraham, David, or Moses." She gazed through the window and watched the wind move the branches of a large tree. "If He doesn't answer my prayers, I still find it easy to maintain my faith in Him—perhaps, the things I understand He stands for? I think it's possible to have a personal religion, don't you?" Bonnie turned her attention back to the Sheriff. "Kinda' like a Lutheran, or a Baptist or a Methodist. They all believe in God the Father, God the Son, and God the Holy

Ghost. My church taught me that I couldn't understand the Blessed Trinity. But when I was younger, I used to think I could. Now, I don't know. Maybe the Sisters were right. The Blessed Trinity is difficult to understand." She gazed at the tree again. "When I danced and sang in the tent Chautauqua, I met and had long discussions with three wonderful ladies. We were all pretty much in the same boat. Each had grown up in a different religious environment. Each of our religions was based on love and each religious organization was different. One, a Moslem, was taught to believe in one God, Allah. She followed the teachings of Mohammed. Another was Hindu. She believes in a supreme and absolute power, which embodies three other Gods: a Creator, a Destroyer and a Preserver. The third person was Jewish. She believes in One God. We all came to care for each other, and we seemed to understand each other."

"Religion always gets too deep for me," said the Sheriff, turning to James. "How about you?"

"I'm going to stay out of it—except to say that both Monroe and Bonnie are fine people. They both want to finalize Bonnie's divorce, get married and make their peace with the Church. Anything you can do to protect them from illegal attacks by Isgar and/or the Klan will be greatly appreciated, I'm sure."

Bonnie smiled. "I just wanted to suggest that there are differing points of view where religion is concerned."

The Sheriff nodded and started to move from his desk. "How's your divorce progressing? When will it be final?"

"I saw Mr. Downey last week. He said he needed to see the Judge one more time. His best guess is the end of May."

"Well, let me know when you've moved to Porter. I don't think you'll find anyone there, but you should be on guard, just in case." Then as an after thought: "Oh, tell your husband that I have Charlie Eagle's rifle—his

30-30 Winchester. Monroe can have it, if he wants it. I picked it up outside the bunkhouse at Cascade. I also picked up sixteen spent cartridges, all from that gun. I think Charlie was raising hell with whoever blew up the house. That may be why they wired him to the cross and burned him."

CHAPTER FOURTEEN

(April 1923)

Monroe stood in the spacious yard behind the Superintendent's House at Porter Coal Mine, and looked north out of the canyon. The mine was only about four and a-half miles from downtown Durango. That bit of knowledge caused him to smile. He gazed east and realized that Durango lay on the other side of the hill in front of him. He noticed that there wasn't much snow left. We might have an early spring, he thought. He let his eyes browse under the tall pines, through the black and white barked aspen, and beyond the bristling oak. The clean, fresh air of the hills—the Rockies—had a flavor to it—a tasty, sweet, hint of summer. The beauty from every quarter seemed to seep into his bones. God, how he loved his mountains!

Feeling warmth on his left shoulder, Monroe turned and followed the late afternoon sun to the west side of the house. Reaching his destination, he leaned his tall frame against the heated wall, and searched in his pocket for his jackknife. He cleaned his fingernails and calculated. With the blade open, his conscious gaze searched the hillside in front of him. He looked for broken branches, for signs of unjustified traffic—anything—anything at all that would indicate that he had been traveling up and down that hillside to get to the slope tunnel through which he'd been traveling to his still inside the mine. Seeing nothing out of the ordinary, he re-thought his entire process of entering and exiting the mine.

He put his knife away, and walked toward the West Mine entrance. At the west tunnel, he stood facing east and studied the distance through the tipple, across the trestle—some 400 yards to the other side of the canyon, he thought—and at the end of the 400 yards, he saw the east tunnel of the Porter Mine. He studied the tipple and the bridge. He admired the entire structure. The bridge appeared to be about 150 feet above the Denver & Rio Grande Southern Railroad tracks, the wagon road, the narrow ravine, and the creek. All of which ran parallel to each other and under the bridge. The tipple was 75 to 80 feet above the siding tracks that accommodated the coal cars while they received their loads from the tipple. Giant timbers formed the trestle-truss members and imbedded themselves in the ground to provide support for the entire structure. The coalmine tunnels, at either end of the bridge, had been barricaded and locked by the Union Pacific Coal Company when the mines petered-out in 1908.

Now, Monroe had carefully devised an undetectable way to remove and replace the lock on the gate to the western drift. When he needed to, he unlocked the gate and entered or left the western drift at his own will. That was very rare, however. He'd only opened the hinged barricade once and that was when he moved his fermented peach juice, his brandy and his still paraphernalia into the mine. That was about three and a half weeks ago. Since then, he'd left the tunnel locked. He accomplished all his whiskey making by entering and exiting through the slope tunnel.

The slope tunnel was a gradually sloping hole in the ground that ran on a slant down to the main drift level from an entrance high on the hillside above the Superintendent's House. The slope tunnel connected to a large room located about 100 yards into the mountain from the western entrance. The Porter Company had excavated the slope tunnel along with the large room in order to funnel air into the various drifts that followed the several veins of coal they found in the mountain. When the company found the main vein of coal, they continued to use the room as a holding and switching room for coal cars. Now, the room provided a perfect place for a still, and the slope tunnel gave Monroe a secret entrance and exit. In addition, the room served as a chimney to vent smokes and fumes when he cooked fermented peach juice.

When Monroe left the house to go to the still, he was careful to travel a route that had not been used recently. And then, once he'd made his way into the bushes and trees on the hillside, he'd ascend to the slope tunnel by various circuitous paths that eventually allowed him to reach the opening to the mine. From the opening, he'd slip down the slope to his still. He exited the same way: always careful to assure the complete secrecy of the still.

Periodically, Monroe walked about the deserted village to search for other life that might be there. He had no reason to believe that anyone other than he and Bonnie had moved in, but he checked anyway.

One day, while touring the camp, he purposely forced his way into the old Power Plant that still nestled among the beams supporting the trestle on the eastern side of the canyon. Inside the power plant, the huge steam engines and the great drums of three-quarter inch steel cable looked as though they were ready to fire up and pull the strings of coal cars from the depths of their respective tunnels at either side of the canyon. As Monroe gawked, he imagined the roar and the smell of the power plant in action. He recalled a fellow from his youth that said he could remember as many as fifteen coal cars being dumped, at one time, from the bridge into the tipple. "That was a lot of coal to sort and size," he breathed, as he turned to leave. Walking toward the door, he touched the layer of heavy dust accumulated on the silent cable drum and felt the loneliness of the aging buildings and the silent machines. "Fifteen years is a long time," he said, aloud.

Now, as Monroe moseyed, he recognized that it was Sunday, April 29th. Two weeks ago, he'd delivered 100 quarts of Peach Brandy to Trimble Springs Resort. He'd also taken an order for 100 more. That brandy delivery had been comparatively simple and he'd used up the contents of only one 25-gallon keg brought from Grand Junction. Effectively, he'd now transferred his Grand Junction booze business to Durango.

In addition, he'd deposited his Grand Junction savings into the First National Bank of Durango and paid Cascades monthly mortgage interest, in advance, for one year. The money from Trimble Springs had gone to Bonnie for family use and safekeeping. Another piece of luck: on April 11th, last Friday, he'd gone to the Homestead Claim Office and, lo and behold, his claim on Florida Mesa had been granted.

Staying in the booze business for the rest of his life was not part of his overall plan. Just a temporary means to an end.

Back at the west mine entrance, Monroe watched dark shadows stretch across Wildcat Canyon while bright sunlight glowed on the tops of the eastern hills. Monroe heard a rustle on his left. Little Harold came running around the tool shed as though someone were chasing him. The toddler stopped in his tracks when he saw Monroe. His face brightened. He stretched his arms and ran to Monroe expecting to be picked up. Monroe obliged by bending down, scooping him up, swinging him around and pulling him into his arms.

Following the young escapee, more deliberate steps revealed Bonnie with the look of a concerned mother.

"Oh! There you are. Both of you." Bonnie halted her determined pace. "I guess I lost track of you, for a second."

"We're right here." Monroe detached a small hand that grabbed his cheek.

"As long as he's running around inside the fence, I'm not worried. It's level and clear of weeds. But it scares me, when he gets out and runs over here by the buildings."

Monroe smiled. "How does he get out? Is there a break in the fence?"

"I don't know. We'll have to look." Bonnie stepped closer to Monroe and put out her arms to take Harold. "What are you doing?"

"Getting ready to come into the house." Monroe pulled Harold back. "I'll carry him. I've been touring the camp and nosing around."

"Me, too." Bonnie fell in step. "Let's talk."

"Okay, but have you noticed a change in the weather."

Bonnie glanced at the hills. "Well, I'm sure you know a lot better than me, but hasn't this been a nice spring?"

"Spring is always a wonderful time here."

Monroe shifted Harold to his left arm and reached for Bonnie's hand. They walked to the gate where Bonnie lifted the latch and swung the gate wide. Monroe walked through and waited. Bonnie latched the gate. When she'd completed her task, they joined hands and walked to the house.

"Want to sit outside?"

"No. It's getting dark and it's a little too cold."

"Yeah. I expect."

"I'll get the boys ready for bed while you pull shades and light the lamp."

When the lamp was lit, Monroe turned the wick low. "Can you see what you're doing?"

"Hold the light over here—I dropped a pin. If I don't pick it up someone may get stuck."

Monroe, with the lamp elevated, entered the room. "Gets dark quick around here." He leaned against the door jam. "Want me to turn the lamp up?"

"No. Living like this is a pain in the you-know-what. But you never know who may be going by or watching." Bonnie squinted, found the pin, and placed it in her pincushion near the large basting pan she used to bathe the boys. Turning to Wade, now dressed in a long flannel nightgown, she pulled the covers up about his neck, tucked him in, kissed him and said, "Good night, big boy." Wade kicked his stubby legs and gurgled at something he thought he saw on the ceiling. Next to him, on the bed, Harold lay motionless. His eyes were closed. His chest rose and fell steadily.

Bonnie hesitated over the boys. "We've got a pair of beautiful boys," she said, and placed three straight-backed chairs beside the bed. She then walked to the window to pull the drapes aside. "Take the light into the other room, Honey. I want to see the night."

Monroe left the room drawing the door after him. He stood in the living room waiting. Moments later the bedroom door opened.

"Boy, it's blacker than the hubs of Hades out there," Bonnie said. "Unless the moon's out, you can't see a damn thing in this canyon."

"I know. That's why I like to go out just before we go to bed. I get a confidence about the night."

They walked to the kitchen. Monroe scooted the salt, the pepper, and the sugar bowl aside and sat the kerosene lamp on the table. Bonnie sank into a chair. Monroe gazed at Bonnie in the soft light. Stepping forward and extending his hand, he touched her chin, raised her face, and kissed her gently on the mouth. "I love you, Honey. Now, what were you saying?"

Bonnie reached for both his hands. "I said: lets talk."

Monroe took the chair opposite her. "About what?"

"About us, naturally."

"I've been thinking about us for the last hour or so," said Monroe. "Would you like to start?

"Okay. My first question is: how long are we going to stay here?"

"Don't you just love it?" said Monroe, jokingly.

"It's fine. I'm happy. It's just not our home. I want <u>our</u> home, Roe."

Monroe searched deep within himself. The whole hurtful business of postponing their lives swept through him like a tidal wave. The wave seemed to scald his soul with frustration. He had tried to rush things along but he'd been blocked at every turn. He finally found a word ... a single word.

"Soon," he said.

"I know. And I'm being patient. But you talked to James today. Did he say anything?"

"He said 'sometime this month'. He said he thought the divorce would be final sometime this month."

"Is that all? The month is half over," reminded Bonnie.

"He said he talked to Downey yesterday and that that was his best guess. Downey doesn't want to press anything for fear the Judge or the County Clerk or somebody might get uppity and delay things just for spite. Sam's friends are everywhere. Downey thinks things will go smoother if he doesn't push."

Bonnie looked quietly away—and moments later, returned. "Do you think Sam will back off when the divorce is final?"

"Gosh. I don't know, Honey. I go almost every day to feed the stock at Cascade, and every time I see our destroyed house, I wonder about the kind of man who could do that. Last Friday, I went to see the Jacksons. I wanted to see how much trouble we were causing as a result of the Jackson's taking our milking chores off our hands. Anyway, we were all wondering how far the man would go before he gives up. I think he'll go pretty far—as long as he has someone else to do the dirty work. If he didn't have Klan members to do the sneaky deeds: I think he'd shrivel up and blow away."

"Think he's still in Durango?" asked Bonnie.

"I know he is. I checked the Strater today."

"You didn't go in there, did you?" Bonnie asked, alarmed.

"No," said Monroe. "I just checked with the clerk. He said Mr. Isgar wasn't in, and asked if I'd like to leave a message." Bonnie gasped and held her breath. "I said 'no' and left."

"Monroe! You promised you wouldn't start anything."

"And I've kept my promise. I just checked to see if he's in town."

"Oh, Roe! What would I do without you?"

"Probably find a nice guy and settle down."

Bonnie walked to their temporary cupboard. "I'm going to have a glass of brandy and smoke my pipe. You want a brandy?"

"Don't mind if I do." He watched her as she moved about the kitchen preparing her pipe and pouring the brandy. Reaching into his jacket pocket, he hauled out his own pipe. Soon they were smoking and sipping.

"I love your brandy," Bonnie said.

"You just like Peach Brandy."

"No. I really like bourbon—for real drinking. Something about the taste, I guess. And I've had various grape brandies, too—but I think your peach brandy is the best brandy I've ever tasted."

"Most people like it. And for those kind words, I'll make you a promise: we'll always have Morgan Brandy in the house. How's that?"

"That'd be wonderful, Roe. I'm so happy with you. I want to marry you so you won't leave me. You won't, will you?"

"Are you kidding? Leave the only woman, for me, in the whole world? You must be out of your mind, lady."

Monroe sat his drink down, rose from the table and bowed deeply while waving his right arm across his body. "May I have this dance, my queen?"

Bonnie laughed. "I can't resist the music." She floated from her chair.

They moved quietly and rhythmically as the night tightened about the remote mining site. The dance continued until both were lost in time. Neither wanted the interlude to end. They swayed, shuffled and kissed. The hour grew late.

Suddenly, out of the silence burst a fearful sound. It crashed through the night air like a huge hammer striking flint. The house shook. The windows rattled. Thunder roared up and down the canyon. Outside, blackness glared into brightness, died, and dazzled again.

Monroe knew the sound. He'd heard it before. Just recently, on the road home from Grand Junction. "That's dynamite! They're dynamiting the trestle across the canyon!" The sound of his voice grew louder as he spoke.

In the dim lamplight, Monroe saw the fear, the surprise, on Bonnie's face. "Grab the kids. Get as many blankets as you can. We're getting out of here."

Monroe charged in front of Bonnie. They both made their way to the boy's room where darkness hindered every move. Monroe, on his knees in the middle of the bed, scooped Wade into Bonnie's arms, then grabbed Harold for himself. "Get every blanket you can carry and follow me!"

More salvos erupted. Monroe noted that all bombardments were coming from the east side of the canyon. He ran to the master bedroom. Stripped the bedclothes from the bed, and tossed the blankets, one by one, over Harold who lay asleep on his shoulder. When he entered the living room, he saw Bonnie gathering blankets for Wade.

Monroe, with his right arm free, headed for the door. He jerked the door open, grabbed a rifle nearby, and cautiously peeked outside. The dynamite continued to detonate across the canyon. Coming closer with each blast.

Since no gunfire greeted him at the door, and since the only light came from the dynamite, he yelled, "Follow me!" Throwing his arm and the rifle over Harold in the blankets, he ran out the door and around the house. He raced toward the northwest corner of the yard. There, two strong bracing logs angled down to the ground from a vertical cedar post in the corner of the wire fence. He stopped, stretched himself over the fence, and dumped the bundled child on the other side. Turning to Bonnie, Monroe quickly collected Wade and all the blankets Bonnie carried. He dropped one blanket on the ground, wrapped Wade in the remaining blankets, moved the baby over the fence and placed him gently on the ground. Picking up the dropped blanket, Monroe stepped to the corner post, draped the blanket over the fence and knelt on all fours. "Climb over," he said to Bonnie. Bonnie grasped the fence post in her left hand, placed a firm left foot in the small of Monroe's back, tossed her right leg over the fence, found a toe hold on the corner brace, and lowered herself to the ground outside the fence.

"Take them to that big pine tree, and all of you get behind it. Stay warm." Monroe glanced over his shoulder as yet another barrage rent the air. "I'm going back for coats."

Monroe ran to the house and leaped inside as still another explosion cracked somewhere near the middle of the canyon. It seemed the detonations were getting closer to the tipple now. He streaked through the house gathering hats and coats. He picked up overshoes, grabbed a box of 30-30 cartridges and ran back to the corner where he'd left Bonnie. She and the babies were gone. Quickly tossing his armload over the fence, Monroe stepped on the brace and jumped over. He gathered their belongings and charged toward the pine tree. The dynamite blasts <u>were</u> getting closer.

Monroe found Bonnie safe. "They're blowing the bridge all the way across the canyon, from east to west. Here. Put these clothes on. Kids all right?"

"They're fine. Harold won't stop crying."

"Let him cry, I guess. No one'll hear him with all that dynamite going off." Just then, a quick succession of explosions occurred. "They're beginning on the tipple, now. The sonzabitches! If someone comes over here, I'm going to shoot."

They peeked across the yard while blasts destroyed the tipple and all the surrounding buildings except the house. Monroe watched in surprise, as the destruction did not include the Superintendent's House.

"I wonder why they didn't blow the house, Roe?"

"Harold, I bet. Sam Isgar evidently draws the line at killing his own son."

"Oh, Roe … "

"He doesn't seem to mind killing other peoples kids, though," Monroe added.

Monroe sat silently while listening to the roar and watching the flashes make their way back across the canyon. He thought it strange that they hadn't seen anyone around the mine during the past few days. It was as if the mine structures were destroying themselves. All the trestle piers, the beams, everything, were being blown from the ground. How could so much dynamite have been planted without his knowing it? Sam must have learned some time ago that he and Bonnie were staying there. He must have planted the dynamite at night. "I can't believe they're destroying every log, every board, every plank, every beam … "

"How'll the train get by? Will they blowup the tracks?" Bonnie asked.

"That's a good question. The whole canyon will be full of wood in the morning—if it doesn't burn up first?" said Monroe.

The dynamite continued to explode. Bonnie held Harold's face to her chest and shook him gently. Wade lay unconcerned near the tree.

During a lull in the explosions, Monroe heard what he thought was a car being started. It came from behind him— back down the canyon. He turned quickly, and as he gazed, he saw headlights brighten the road. The car edged forward, heading north out of the canyon. Just then a dynamite blast smothered the sound of the car, but it was obvious that the man, or the men, in the car; were making their get away. Monroe thought about shooting, but he knew he'd miss. "Oh hell, why not." He threw his rifle to his shoulder, aimed at the taillights, and fired.

"Dammit, Roe! I wish you wouldn't do that!" Bonnie laid Harold beside Wade. "You scared me to death. You can't hit anything. It's to dark."

"I know, but I just had to shoot something. Maybe it's about over."

"Oh, Honey! What are we going to do, now?" Bonnie's shoulders began to shake.

He circled her with his arms. "Why, Honey. We're going back in the house and get a good nights sleep." He knew they'd never sleep in that house again, but he couldn't think of anything else to say.

Just as Bonnie's shaking began to subside, Monroe heard the morning train puffing its way up the canyon toward the mine. Oh God! The engineer would have to stop the train, contact a dispatcher in Durango, and there'd be a hundred men climbing all over the rubble in a matter of minutes—sawing—ripping—tearing—and repairing—until the railroad was back in operation. Some of those men would be nosing around the Superintendent's House. Those men would probably include Sheriff Howe.

With the inevitable in mind, Monroe started to move. "We've got to get away from here, as soon as possible. Let's get as much on the truck, as we can, and leave as soon as we can.

"I know," Bonnie agreed, reaching for the bundle of blankets that held Wade. "You bring Harold and I'll start packing."

"Don't pack much. I'll throw two mattresses on the truck—you get the clothes and some dishes." Monroe walked toward the fence.

"Where will we go?"

Monroe put an index finger to his lips. "I'll be right back. I want to be sure we're alone."

"Do you want us to stay put?" asked Bonnie.

"Yes. If you don't hear from me—or hear shooting within five minutes—you can come back to the house with the kids."

Monroe walked cautiously to the fence and began circling the outside of the fence. He glanced in every direction. When he got to the front gate and the truck, he opened the passenger's door and scurried toward the west tunnel. The night air was crisp but not particularly cold.

Hesitating in the dark, he listened for sounds. Nothing. He pulled on the lock at the west tunnel gate and stood listening while glaring into the night. "Where is the damn moon when you need it?"

CHAPTER FIFTEEN

(April and May 1923)

Sam Isgar chuckled and leaned back in his chair. The Evangelical Church on Third Avenue seemed to reverberate with laughter when Earl Mills joined in. "That was the most spectacular thing I've seen in my whole life, thanks to you. Talk about 'The Birth of a Nation' by D. W. Griffith—you should have seen that bridge and trestle go up. If we had taken picture-film, we could make a fortune. I wouldn't have missed it for anything."

Sam smiled when he remembered how he and Earl sat watching the destruction from the car parked about a quarter of a mile down the road. They'd put the last detonations into the hands of a dynamite expert who set the whole thing up, and then, they left the scene before the last explosions started. Sam was pleased with his planning. To Sam's surprise, Earl Mill's deviousness had proven helpful in several ways. In fact, Sam was growing quite fond of the little fellow. It was Earl Mills who had discovered the Morgans living at Porter. It was Earl Mills who had secured the services of the dynamite expert. It was Earl Mills who had helped place the charges. Earl had also fronted the entire episode and faithfully reported the status as the work progressed. Sam had simply shelled out the money. Earl did the rest. Sam didn't need to become personally involved. He just gave Earl five hundred dollars.

Sam sat up in his seat, and with a straight face, looked at Bob Stout sitting in front of him. "Bob, you should have seen it. It would have done your heart good. We must have scared the living shit out of your old friend, Monroe." Bob Stout, Earl Mills and Carméllo Basíllo sat grinning back at Sam. "I hope those baby boys screamed their heads off," said Sam, looking at his watch.

273

It was late in the day. The little church seemed cold and empty. Sam wished he could start a fire, but Reverend Davis had advised against using church coal for Klan meetings—unless the Klan was willing to buy the church two tons of coal. Sam had considered the proposition, but he'd been using the church for Klan meetings since last November, and hadn't bought any coal yet. Reverend Davis wanted him to put the fear of God into the neighboring Mexicans, and he just figured the debt would eventually even out. In the meantime, Sam had his own problems. Personal problems. More and more he thought about getting rid of Bonnie—altogether. If he could make up his mind about what to do with Harold, it would be easier to come to conclusions. Maybe he'd put Harold in an orphanage. "Well, I wish the good Reverend would show himself—he 's always late. And listen fellows: forget about this Monroe Morgan business when the preacher's around—we don't want too many people to know the straight of that story. Hear me?"

All three men nodded. Bob raised his hand. "When I climbed up to the Superintendent's House this morning, they were all gone. Where do you think they went?"

Sam licked his lips. "I don't know—but they can't go to Cascade. They're probably here in town. Anyway, that's your job, Earl. You've been doing a good job so far, so don't let that sonuvabitch make a chump of you."

"I won't. I'll keep an eye on that Laurence fella, too. He's doing legal work for Mrs. Morgan—she says."

Sam exploded. "God dammit! You dumb little shit! Her name's Isgar."

"Sorry, boss. I meant, Mrs. Isgar."

"Use your head, then," admonished Sam.

Sam made an effort to collect himself. "Well, it looks like the Reverend won't be here. I'm going to start the meeting."

Bob Stout put his pocket watch away. "He's about fifteen minutes late."

"Yeah. Well, let's come to order. There are two points I want to make. First, I want to start getting a written report from each of you. The report will be due the first of each month. In that report, I want the names of people you're submitting for membership in the Klan."

"Second, we are going to talk about that whiskey still Carméllo's settin' up on Florida Mesa. It's been two weeks since we've heard anything, Carméllo. You'll recall: we put the still in your cabin to make it easy for you to take care of. We've invested money. Now, tell us what's happening."

Carméllo cleared his throat. "It's comin' along, okay. I've got four gallons of white lightnin' sittin' on the shelf," Carméllo smiled. "We could have a party."

In disgust, Sam gazed out the window. "We're making it to sell, Carméllo."

Carméllo tried to recover lost ground. "Well, we've got to decide how we want it to taste. Right now it tastes like straight alcohol. It's got to have a good flavor," said Carméllo.

"I thought you had a friend in Ignacio who knows all about that?" said Sam.

"I do. But do you want to use whatever blend he comes up with? Maybe you won't like it?"

Sam leaned forward. "Let's just get some booze made and sold. If people complain, we'll change the blend."

"Well. Then, there's something else," said Carméllo.

"What's that?"

"Thieves."

"What do you mean? Your cabin is off the beaten track? Hidden, isn't it?" asked Sam.

"It's off the beaten track, but you can see the cabin from quite a distance—along the road. A lot of people see it and wonder if someone lives there. Sometimes they hike over and look around. If someone finds a still, they might just pick up a jug or a bottle and take it with them. I don't know what you want me to do about that?"

Sam gazed at his group. "What do other people do?" he asked.

"Some spike it with strychnine," said Bob.

"Know where to get strychnine?" asked Sam, looking at Carméllo.

"Maybe, Ignacio. Want me to try?"

Sam nodded his head in affirmation. "Bring me the receipt and I'll reimburse you. Buy plenty. No need buying it every week." Suddenly, Sam saw an opportunity to get some strychnine for his own personal use. An idea was forming.

"I'll try to get some tomorrow," Carméllo said.

"How far is it to Ignacio from here?" asked Sam.

"Depends on which route you take," Bob said.

"I know that," Sam sneered. "Give me a "crow flies" and some miles."

"It's about twenty-five miles by road. Go over to Bayfield, turn right and go nine or ten miles south," Bob said.

"But, if you go to my cabin and 'cross country—it's about nineteen miles."

"How far to your cabin?"

"About eight miles—as the crow flies."

"And your cabin, from Ignacio?"

"Nine or ten miles, I guess. That's my stompin' grounds."

"Oh, yeah. You grew up there, didn't you?" Sam thought he'd taken their minds off his personal interest in the strychnine.

"Yep," Carméllo said. "Born and raised."

"Well, use the strychnine to keep our booze safe. Don't forget which jug you lace with poison." They all laughed. "Now I'm going to ask a question. Give me your opinion. Ready?" All nodded their heads.

"Do you think Sheriff Harvey Howe will join the Klan? You first, Bob."

"Probably not."

"Earl?"

"Nope."

"Carméllo?"

"I don't know."

"Why wont he join?" asked Sam, looking at Bob.

"Too dammed straight laced, I think," Bob said.

"I agree." Earl nodded emphatically.

"I don't know," Carméllo insisted.

"Then, I'm going to give you all an objective—a job—for the future. We're going to get rid of Harvey Howe. I want you to think of things you can use against him—things you can tell people that will destroy his reputation. If you can't find him doing anything wrong, make things up—start rumors. Let people think you're giving them inside stuff. In the next sheriff's election, we'll get our own man elected."

* * *

Early the next day, Carméllo Basíllo entered Ignacio's Mercantile & Trading Post. Being a product of two cultures, his Anglo-Indian ancestry opened doors and made him welcome all over Ignacio. Carméllo, himself, didn't quite understand his own roots because his Indian mother hadn't seen his Italian father since Carméllo was three years old. His mother chose to raise him like an Anglo. He'd received some education and fit well into Ignacio's Indian, Spanish-American, and Anglo community.

"Good morning, Basíllo. How're ya' doin'?" Bill Hillier twisted the tips of an uncontrollable bunch of white hair he called a mustache. Old Hillier had owned the Mercantile for as long as Carméllo could remember.

277

"I'm busy," Carméllo said, gazing into the cracker barrel.

"Doin' what?"

"Trying to fix up my cabin over in Phillips Canyon."

"Gonna try farmin'—ranchin'—Car?"

"Not unless I get rid of the dammed coyotes."

"Hell. They're everywhere. Shoot 'em."

"I do. Every chance I get. But it takes too much time. I want to try poison. Someone said they'll quite coming around if you put out some poison."

"What kind of poison?"

"Strychnine." Carméllo looked at the shelves behind the counter. "Got any?"

"Yeah. But I never heard of givin' it to coyotes. Normally, it's used on rodents. Prairie dogs and such."

"Well, I got some of them, too. How about selling me a bottle, or a can. Whatever it comes in?"

"Comes in a bottle. Not a very big bottle, at that. You mix it. According to the instructions on the bottle. Takes an eye-dropper." Bill Hillier walked to a cabinet, took his keys and unlocked a sliding door. He removed a small bottle from the top shelf and set it on the counter.

"That'll be four dollars. What else?"

"That's it, I guess." Carméllo picked up the bottle and gazed at the label. "You say the instructions are here, huh?"

"Yes, sir. That'll kill a lot of prairie dogs—or whatever."

* * *

Meanwhile, Sam Isgar sat alone in his room overlooking Main Street and watched the people entering or leaving the Strater. He especially liked to watch women—all ages, shapes and sizes. He fantasized about each one. How they looked with their clothes off. How big their feet were? What was real? What was false? Men didn't interest him much—unless they appeared to have money. Then, he'd try to answer questions like: how'd they get their money? How much money did they really have? Did they have more money than he did?

Sam never tired of this activity—no matter how many people came or went. If the traffic slowed down, he waited patiently until someone came along. During lulls, he simply gazed at miscellaneous street happenings and let his observations provide subjects that captured his interest.

Today, as he cogitated, his mind kept coming back to strychnine. Since yesterday, when he told Carméllo to buy strychnine for the still, he'd had flashes of thought about what he, personally, could do with strychnine. And along with the strychnine, his thoughts invariably turned to Bonnie. Nothing precise. He really wanted Bonnie back home in Grand Junction—or out of the way entirely.

To that end, Sam planned to ask Carméllo for some strychnine. He'd tell Carméllo that he had rats in his Grand Junction restaurant, and that he wanted to get rid of them.

But what if Carméllo used all of the strychnine before he could get his hands on it? Well, maybe he'd have to return to his original idea, i.e., make his poison from chokecherry leaves and bark. Maybe that'd work?

* * *

After making a trip to Aztec, New Mexico, Monroe and Bonnie were approaching their homestead on Florida Mesa. Monroe thought they had a good location. Their house would set on a high knoll in the northwest corner of the property. From there, they'd have a spectacular view of the San Juans. They'd look down about seven hundred feet into the Animas River at the bottom of the valley west of the house. Monroe was anxious for Bonnie to see the place. It would be her first look.

As they approached the knoll from the south, Bonnie said, "Oh, Roe, look at those magnificent mountains—still covered with snow! Isn't it beautiful?"

"You're seeing the San Juans in all their splendor. Wait till you see where our house will sit." He grinned. "Of course, you can move it, if you don't like the location."

"I'll like it," promised Bonnie.

"We're going to have to camp out for a while, Honey."

"I don't care," she said.

Monroe cherished Bonnie's never-ending enthusiasm for life and her close attention to the beautiful things she found around her. She seemed to look for and find beauty, everywhere.

After their initial flight from Porter, they'd spent two days moving around Aztec, New Mexico—from one campground to another. And while moving, he and Bonnie had tried to think of reasons for the detonation of Porter. They concluded that it was Sam Isgar's anger about the coming divorce. There seemed to be no other answer.

The boys were taking the moving stress in stride, and now, thank God, they finally had a plan. They would move to Florida Mesa and wait for the divorce to be final.

As Monroe drove across their land, the sun remained high in the sky. The day was warm. The wind was still.

"How much farther, Roe?" Bonnie cradled the boys in her arms, protectively, while the truck wound its way through piñon and pine. Sagebrush scratched the sides of the truck.

"You're here. Right on top of the rise."

"Aren't we getting too close to the canyon edge?"

"It's farther than it looks, Honey." Monroe noted the rather steep stretch of land that preceded the vertical drop.

"Will the boys be safe?" asked Bonnie.

"I'll put up a fence, if I have to."

"Oh Roe! We can see Durango from here. How far is it?"

"About nine miles."

"We could walk it, couldn't we?"

"In three or four hours, maybe."

Monroe drove in circles. "Why are we going around and around?" Bonnie asked.

"I'm trying to find a spot that hides us from that cabin over there. We need a little cover. We want a campsite where we're not easily seen."

Bonnie scanned the countryside. "What cabin?"

"Well. I'm going to stop right here. I'll show you the cabin in a minute."

He stopped the truck behind a thick grove of piñon, pine and sagebrush. "Stay put a minute," he said, exiting the truck and walking directly north to the edge of the grove. He stopped and searched the countryside. Satisfied, he walked to the south edge of the grove and repeated his perusal.

Back at the truck, he stuck his head in the window. "I think this is it. Want to get out and start building your next home, Mrs. Morgan?"

"I love hearing "Mrs. Morgan." Bonnie sat a moment, smiling. "What about the boys?"

"Give Harold to me and leave Wade on the floor. I have something in mind."

"Why not just let Harold run around?"

"Why not? I'll let him play in the good clean dirt." Monroe came around the truck and opened Bonnie's door.

Later, with the children situated, Monroe turned to Bonnie. "Now. Come right over here with me." He led her north to the end of the grove, raised his arm and pointed across the mesa. "See that dark spot—way over there. That's a low-built cabin with its door open. All there is between the cabin and us is sagebrush, so it's hard to see. But, if you look above the black patch, there's a brownish-red streak. That's dirt on the cabin roof. I'm sure we're looking at a cabin—so as we go about our business, here, let's keep our eyes peeled for movement around that cabin."

Bonnie raised her hand to her forehead. Monroe judged her line of sight. "It's on the other side of the road, and it's about three miles away. See it? Someone may live there."

"There's a little hill behind it and there's a row of black trees lining the hill, isn't there?" she said.

"Yep. I think you've got it. Now, keep your eye on it—as we go about our business. And keep looking for people moving about. They could come from any direction. We don't know our neighbors yet, so let's stay alert. If I'm gone and you see someone coming, get yourself within easy reach of the rifle and use it if you feel in danger."

"I don't think anyone will come out here, do you?"

"No, I don't. And I don't want you to be afraid—of anything. But, be aware that there are coyotes—maybe wolves—probably not—but maybe Bobcats, stray cattle, Indians and other people going and coming. We don't know and we don't care, just as long as they leave us alone. Don't be afraid, but do be alert. I'll be here most to the time, but I'll have to go to town, sometime—like tonight."

"I didn't know you were going to town tonight?"

"I think I better. We need to let James and the Laurences know we're here. They probably think we're still in Aztec.

"Maybe James has heard something from Downey," suggested Bonnie.

"Yes. And I'm thinking about bringing Chukaluks out here so we can ride him to town rather than drive the truck. The less the truck is seen in town, the better, don't you think?"

"I agree." Bonnie had mentioned her concern earlier about what would happen if people saw that green Chevrolet truck around Durango. Since it was the only one-ton truck of it's kind in town, she thought it might be too recognizable.

Monroe retrieved a shovel, a grubbing hoe and a double-bladed ax from the truck. "Do you want to do something while I dig sagebrush and clear a place for our camp?"

"Sure, but I think I need to take care of the boys, first."

"Okay, do that, then take a walk back toward the road. Give yourself room to hide if someone comes along. Walk a ways north and look back at our camp and the road, then, walk south a little and see if anyone on the road can spot our camp as they pass. I think we're pretty well hidden, but take a look. Oh yeah! Keep your eye on that cabin."

Bonnie changed the boys and put them on a blanket to play. "Okay. I'm going to see what our camp looks like from the road. Watch the boys."

Monroe ripped sagebrush from the ground and piled the bushes in areas where he thought the trees needed density to hide their camp. When he'd cleared a large space, he surveyed the lay of the land and selected a nearly level spot for their bed. He, then, graded that area and dug a drainage ditch around it to prevent rainwater from running into the bed. In the distance, he could see Bonnie walking and checking views from the road.

He spread a deep layer of pine and cedar boughs for their bed. When the pile of branches was thick enough, he took the large tarpaulin from the truck and fitted it around their mattress, then, he placed the mattress on the fresh bows.

Next, Monroe dug a large, shallow hole in the ground and lined it with various sized rocks. This would be their fireplace, and the fire would breath through the rocks that edged the bowl shaped stove. While cooking their food, the pots and pans in use, could benefit from varying degrees of heat or they could simply sit and wait to be used.

"Is that where we'll cook?" asked Bonnie.

Monroe jumped. He hadn't expected Bonnie to arrive unheralded. "What do you think? Does it look like a stove?"

"Did I sneak up on you?" Bonnie smiled mischievously.

"You must be part Indian?" Monroe gathered her in his arms.

"Nope. Just sneaky Scottish."

Monroe kissed her. "Then, not being Indian, can you cook?"

"I can, if you can." Bonnie laughed as she lifted Wade and placed him on the front seat of the truck.

Monroe grabbed his ax. "I'm going for a big, fat log. Be back in a minute." He walked toward the top of the knoll. On the way, he found what he was looking for: a log thick enough to sit on and long enough to divide into two pieces. When he'd hewn both logs to his specifications, he roped each and dragged them to the fireplace for use as chairs. Anyone sitting on the logs would have his back to the west wind coming into the camp.

"Honey. I'm going to build a rock platform for the chuck box and finish unloading the truck. Then, I want to go to town and see the Laurences, if I can. Where would you like me to set the chuck box?"

"Opposite the logs. That'll keep you out of my kitchen."

After placing the chuck box, Monroe removed everything from the truck except the two twenty-five gallon barrels of water. He rolled the barrel with a bunged spigot to a spot near the edge of the truck bed and arranged the spigot for easy reach. The sun was beginning to swing low in the western sky.

Bonnie, putting the finishing touches on the bed, said, "Honey. I don't want you to go to Durango, tonight."

"How come?'

"I just don't want to be alone with the kids my first night on the mesa. They've been confined to the truck for about three hours, now. I want them out—let them smell the fresh air—eat." Bonnie stepped close to his chest. "When are <u>you</u> going to eat?" She laid her head in the crook of his arm.

"Are you hungry?" Monroe kissed the top of her head.

"Well, we haven't really eaten since breakfast."

Monroe grinned. "And what has that to do with being hungry?"

"The boys need a little freedom."

"Okay. I'll build a fire—and, about the fire—let's only use dry, dead, sagebrush for our fires. It burns with a lot less smoke and, remember, we don't want big fires at night. We'll burn a lot of wood through the day and develop deep beds of live coals for the nighttime. No flame. Okay?"

"Does that mean you won't go to Durango tonight?"

"No. It means that we don't want smoke and fire giving our position away before we're ready."

Monroe watched Bonnie turn away in disappointment. She walked to the truck and looked in. She opened the door, retrieved Harold and carried him to the bed where she deposited him in the middle of a large wool blanket, then, returned for Wade.

"Roe. I wish you wouldn't go tonight. Couldn't you go in the morning? Leave early and take the day?"

"Have I scared you with all my talk about coyotes and wolves?"

"No."

"Well, I told James that I'd keep him informed about our whereabouts and I haven't talked to him since day before yesterday. He doesn't know we're here. No one does. Maybe the Sheriff should know."

"I think the Sheriff should know, alright. He's been up-front with us and I think we should be up-front with him."

"Also, I thought I'd bring Chukaluks back—drive slow, you know. We need both—the car and the horse. Chukaluks to ride into town, and the truck to carry water and provide a permanent bed for the boys."

"Why don't you do it all tomorrow? You can take the whole day, instead of the whole night."

"Okay," Monroe said, reluctantly. "You talked me into it. We'll let James and the Chukaluks go another day."

285

CHAPTER SIXTEEN

(May 1923)

It was late Saturday evening—the sun almost down. Monroe let Chukaluks pick his way through the sagebrush and piñon trees as they made their way back to camp after a day in Durango. Monroe had intended to return earlier, but James had had a series of phone calls from Doug Downey in Grand Junction. It now appeared that the judge handling Bonnie's divorce case would make a decision in Bonnie's favor. If that came about, Downey thought Bonnie could be divorced in short order. Monroe couldn't pass up the opportunity to take such good news home to Bonnie, so he stayed in town longer than he intended. Then, last minute, just before all offices closed and Monroe had given up; the phone rang. Doug related the news that Bonnie's divorce would be final at months end. By Monroe's calculations, Bonnie would be a free woman in a week and five days. If everything went as scheduled, they'd be able to get married on the 16th of June—next month! Since it was Saturday, Monroe wished he'd brought something home with which to celebrate the good news. They'd be able to get married in twenty-eight days … Wow!

All the way from town, Monroe kept out of sight by taking cover from trees and bushes. But as he drew closer to his camp, his attention was drawn to that nearby cabin he and Bonnie had been watching. Was it abandoned? Neither he nor Bonnie had seen anyone moving about. Maybe it was vacant. Maybe they could rent it. It'd be better than living in the open.

But, then again, if they were married, they could rebuild Cascade and live there. They could move into the bunkhouse for now. Maybe they should allow a couple days for Sam to get the word about his divorce and, maybe—just maybe—he'd leave town. He'd talk to Bonnie. See what she thought.

Suddenly, the cabin loomed before him. And, as if by fate, he reined Chukaluks to the left. If the cabin were occupied, he'd introduce himself and get to know the person or persons. If the place were vacant, he'd look around.

Near the cabin, he paid particular attention to Chukaluks. If anyone were in the shack, Chukaluks might give some indication. But when they were within thirty feet, Chukaluks still remained calm.

Stopping beside a piñon tree, Monroe sat silently astride the great stallion. No noise. No movement. He felt the wind against his face. He nudged Chukaluks forward. Chukaluks walked calmly to the door and stopped.

"Hello, the house." Monroe felt impelled to see inside. Why not wait until tomorrow—in the daylight? It was almost dark and getting darker. He turned in his saddle and sat gazing across the distance to his own camp. No sounds came from the cabin.

"Hello, the house." Monroe waited and the silence continued.

Monroe still waited—undecided. Finally, he gripped the saddle horn with both hands and dismounted. Chukaluks grunted and sidestepped to the left as Monroe's foot touched the ground.

"What's your problem, Buster? Behave yourself," Monroe admonished Chukaluks.

Monroe brushed Chukaluks's chin aside and wrapped the reins over a stunted oak beside the door. He entered a pitch-black room. Whipping a match across the seat of his pants and up the side of his leg, he lifted the light high above his head.

At first the place looked empty. But on second sight, he believed the room was larger than he'd imagined.

Paraphernalia seemed widely spaced. Just before the match burned out, he glimpsed three white candles stuck in their own wax and sitting on their respective shelves attached to the east wall. He lit all three candles.

There were bottles and jugs indiscriminately placed on each shelf. Four half-gallon glass bottles and one quart bottle, sealed, on the top shelf. Two one-gallon crock jugs and two quart bottles, sealed, on the middle shelf. A half-gallon jug sat on the bottom shelf, unsealed, and half full—just a cork. The bottles appeared to be clean and recently set. No dust on any of the containers. Turning slowly, he noticed fresh sawdust spread over the packed dirt floor. He saw mud, mixed with twigs, filling the cracks between uneven logs forming the walls. Under a stovepipe, which stuck through the center of the roof, an old Majestic stove supported an oval shaped boiler. The stove and the boiler combined to form the room's centerpiece. Coils of copper tubing and various pieces of glass apparatus lay on a tarpaulin in the northeast corner. A wooden table sat adjacent to the rough shelving. There was no bed or other living accommodations.

"He must bring his water and mash with him." Monroe turned his attention back to the shelves. He heard Chukaluks's snicker.

Reaching for the half-empty jug, he pulled the cork. Raising the booze to his lips, he sipped, paying close attention to the quality of the liquid. Instantly, he recognized whiskey. Passing the jug to his left hand, he set it on the table while he accumulated saliva and swashed the mix around his mouth. He spat the liquor on the floor. Accumulating more saliva, he cleansed his mouth, and spit again. Then he stood back and evaluated the taste in his mouth. There was no bitterness, no burning sensation—just whiskey. Chukaluks was standing with his head inside the doorway.

"What do you think, Chief? Is it okay?"

Monroe gazed through the door into the night while he massaged Chukaluks face. "Think Bonnie'd like a little nip? Think we should surprise her?"

He returned to the shelves and took a sealed half-gallon glass bottle from the top shelf. Then, after he'd blown out the candles and found his way back to Chukaluks, he put the whiskey in a saddlebag, climbed aboard and rode away.

Near their camp, Monroe began to sing. "Buffalo Girls are you coming out tonight? Coming out tonight. Coming out to night. Buffalo Girls are you coming out tonight and dance by the light of the moon." The moon was leaving the horizon in the east—just a small crescent in the sky.

Bonnie sat up in bed and threw a shawl over her shoulders. "Be quiet," she said. "You'll wake the kids."

"Wait until I tell you the news." Monroe jumped down and landed on the bed with both knees.

"What happened? Did Sam fall into a mine shaft?"

"No such luck." Monroe kissed her quietly and returned to Chukaluks. "Let me get this saddle off and hobble old Chuky, then I'll tell you. Oh! I got a present for you." He sat his packages on the table, placed his saddle on the truck bed, picked up the hobbles and hurried Chukaluks down the west hill to a tub of water and a bail of hay.

Back in camp, he dived onto the bed beside Bonnie. "It's here."

"What's here?"

"Oh, Honey. This is too important for guessing games. I'll just tell you."

Bonnie jerked up in anticipation, as Monroe spoke. "You're getting your divorce by the end of this month. We can get married anytime thereafter."

Bonnie sat very still. It had been a long time coming. He tried and failed to see the tears he knew were in her eyes. She raised her hands to her face and wiped her cheeks.

Monroe jumped to his knees, took her to his chest and held her tight for a long time. Finally, he gently tilted her head and kissed her mouth.

"Oh, Honey! Things are really beginning for us. We'll get married, rebuild Cascade, and live happily ever after." Monroe leaped from the bed and piled logs on the fire. The hot coals quickly ignited the dry sage.

"Look what I got for you." He lifted the half-gallon bottle so she could see.

"What is it?"

"Whiskey—your favorite. You won't have to drink my brandy anymore."

"I like your brandy."

"Want to celebrate, now?" he asked.

Bonnie gazed at the moon. "No. I don't think so. I just want you to hold me. I've missed you a lot today."

"Oh, Honey. I'm sorry I'm late, but James started getting phone calls from Douglas Downey about three o'clock and one call led to another. I didn't want to come home without the whole story, you know. I hope it's all right."

"Everything's all right, now that you're home. Come to bed." Bonnie pulled the covers over her shoulders.

"Okay. I'll pee and be right back."

* * *

Monroe got up early the next day. Dawn was just beginning to break. The sun wouldn't be up for an hour or more. But the sky was clear. He looked forward to a beautiful day.

He scooped up an armload of kindling, brushed back the campfire's top coals, stacked the kindling precisely, blew on it, and the fire ignited. Piling on larger pieces of dried sagebrush, he watched the fire grow. He retrieved the coffeepot from the table, walked to the truck cab and peered in. Both boys were asleep. He filled the coffeepot, went to the chuck box, scooped coffee into the percolator filter, and set the pot on two rocks spaced just right for the coffee pot. Next, he filled a bucket half-full of water and placed it on the hearth for heating.

Turning to his tools piled beside the truck, he grabbed his shovel and his grubbing hoe. He walked, almost without thinking, to the spot that had been previously designated for their garden. The garden was to be between their intended cabin site and their current camp. He didn't know whether they'd ever need a garden or not but he wanted something to do. There couldn't be much of a garden, of course, but it seemed a good way to use every bit of the water he'd have to haul from the river. When the bathing, the dishwashing, the clothes washing, and the shaving were over: the used water would go to the garden. "Waste not; want not," his mother always said.

As the bushes fell, daylight intensified. Finally, the first rays of sunlight shot across the Mesa. Bonnie began to stir. Monroe saw her leave the bed and put her dress over her head. Several minutes later, he glanced at the camp. Harold was on the bed with a bottle and playing with his teddy bear. Wade was on the kitchen table; Bonnie was dressing him. He heard Bonnie singing as he continued his work.

* * *

Bonnie evaluated Monroe's activities. She hoped to gage whether he might be able to leave the job and come to breakfast when she had it prepared. It appeared he could, so she made Wade's bottle, took him to the truck, placed him inside the front seat with his bottle, and closed the door.

All the while, she'd been watching the bottle of whisky Monroe had brought home last night. She wondered how it would taste after all the brandy she'd been drinking. After months of brandy, she was anxious to try some whiskey— her preferred drink.

Stepping to the fire, she removed the coffeepot and poured herself a cup of coffee. She reached into the pocket of her dress, pulled forth her pipe, loaded it with tobacco and lit it with a stick from the fire. Finally, Bonnie broke the seal on the whiskey bottle, ladled a tablespoon-full and started to pour it into her coffee. But, wanting a taste, she put the spoon to her lips and took a sip.

Immediately, she sensed something wrong. But, completing the process, she swallowed the booze. The whiskey burned her mouth and throat. It tasted extremely bitter. It had oil in it. Almost instantly, the day began to lose it's light. She stumbled backward, crashing into the truck bed, which extended beyond the chuck box and the table. She extended her arms to grab the truck and grip the table. She shouted, but no sound escaped her throat. Monroe continued his work. Determined to reach him, Bonnie staggered forward; lunging to her right and missing the campfire. She fell into a heap upon the ground while the world whirled around her. Fighting to stand, she stumbled to the truck where she turned and screamed with all her might. Miraculously, Monroe turned and stared. Horror contorted his face as he recognized her pain. He grimaced and grunted while he charged toward her. She wanted to tell him she'd only sipped the whiskey. Just a little. Her hand pointed, but it wouldn't hold directly on the bottle. She felt her heart burst as she watched him agonize over her.

Monroe lifted her from the ground near the truck's front wheel. He carried her to a chair beside the table. As he held her on his lap, she began to convulse. She felt him clinch her head and neck tight in the crook of his right arm while he stretched for the coffeepot with his left. Sweeping the coffee from the table, he dumped the liquid in her face. She gasped and her mouth opened. Coffee grounds fell from the pot. Coffee flooded her mouth and nose. "Drink, sweetheart. Vomit!" His voice was hysterical. He poured again. Convulsions gripped her body. Her feet kicked the table and the ground. She heard him try to pray. She stared at the sky—eyes wide and straining. She sought God's forgiveness. She starred in agony at Monroe. She tried to touch his face. Her hand fell away.

Bonnie felt the pain begin to fade. She saw the fireplace. Tightly, her lover's arms encircled her as her body thrashed, again. She widened her eyes—tried to see. No light anywhere … only darkness … blacker than the blackest night.

* * *

Monroe ducked his head to her breasts. He re-gripped her waist and chest, clutching desperately. She did not move. Her body relaxed. She was dead! He knew it! "God!" he screamed. A flock of blackbirds sprang to the air, their wings reflecting the early light. Chukaluks raised his head high and stared at Monroe. "God! I've killed my only love!" he screamed. Harold screeched as though he'd been slapped.

The flapping wings, the startled stares, all registered in Monroe's memory banks. He gazed long and hard at the blankets … the sagebrush … and Chukaluks. He'd have to move Bonnie to the bed, he thought. He'd check the boy's accommodations in the truck and put Bonnie on the bed before he went to town for help.

Monroe tenderly carried Bonnie from the chair to the bed and sobbed when he gently placed her there. He fell to his knees, straightened her dress, brushed the coffee from her face, and combed his fingers through her sun-filled hair. Kissing her nose, he lifted the blanket and covered her. Blinded by tears, he staggered to the truck for a look at the boys.

"I'm sorry, fellows, I apologize for killing your mother." Instantly, the boys stopped crying and Monroe touched each boy with the fingertips of his left hand.

293

Blindly, he turned toward Durango and without thinking of Chukaluks or the truck; he ran on foot through the sagebrush.

* * *

Monroe: miles from the camp, his legs beginning to cramp, and his chest burning, continued to run. When unconsciousness seemed to consume him, his body began to float and he felt the presence of One-armed Charlie, his old friend. Charlie ran beside him, stride for stride. Like the old days, he and Charlie were racing toward a shared goal. That's right! They were going to town to get help for Bonnie. But why was Charlie here? Monroe turned his head to see his old friend's face and lost sight of the path he'd been following. He staggered, tripped and tumbled down a small cliff. He landed with a thud and passed out. Upon recovering, he found himself wedged between a tree stump and a large rock. He had no idea how long he'd been there, but when he regained his senses, his lungs were on fire and his stomach ached. He wanted to vomit. His legs would not straighten nor would his arms uncurl. He began a struggle to extricate himself from the tree. By rolling sideways he became free. He started rolling again and he continued to roll until he crashed into a huge boulder and wedged between a rock and another tree. Lying still, he thought again of Charlie. Maybe the whole thing was a dream because he knew Charlie was dead. His stomach began to writhe. He gagged and vomited. Only bile—bitter and burning bile came up.

He struggled against his position between the rock and the tree. Where was the truck? Maybe he'd been riding Chukaluks. He had to get to Durango. Oh God yes! Bonnie needed help!

Extricating himself from his confinement, Monroe stood and gazed about. There, below and west of him, ran the Animas River. Durango was on his right. He'd fallen off Florida Mesa at a spot some three miles south of Durango. He hadn't driven the truck. He hadn't ridden Chukaluks. He'd walked or run every step of the way.

He scooted around the great stone and stumbled along the soft shale hillside. At an angle, he leaped and raced down hill. Across Big Canyon Road and on to the gravel pit, he hurried. He had to get to Hood Mortuary on Ninth Street, near Second Avenue.

Monroe found himself staggering into the mortuary staring at his dirty hands. They were scratched and bleeding. His shirt was torn. He'd lost his hat. Maybe he hadn't worn one. He couldn't remember.

Near the entrance to the chapel, Monroe approached a tall, slender man in a black suit. He struggled to appear normal. "Sir. I'm Monroe Morgan. I need your help."

"Of course." The man smiled and extended his hand.

"Are you Mr. Hood?"

"No, sir. My name's James Grable. I work for Mr. Hood."

"Well, Mr. Grable, there's been a terrible accident on the Florida Mesa—on my homestead. My wife is dead and I need your help. Can you come right away?" Monroe felt weak—sweaty.

"Are you all right?" James Grable's large blue eyes squinted into Monroe's face. "You don't look so good."

"I'm fine. Can you come now?"

Grable turned and moved toward the chapel then changed his mind. "No. I better call Mr. Hood. Ask him to cover for me."

James Grable picked up the lobby telephone. Monroe gripped a nearby table and waited. He heard Grable say he'd take the car.

Grable placed the receiver on the hook. "May I make an emergency call?" asked Monroe.

Stepping back, Grable gestured his approval. "I'll get the car keys. Wouldn't you like to wash your hands, Mr. Morgan?"

Monroe could smell his own vomit mixed with the smell of coffee. Mr. Grable must smell it, too. "I'm so sorry, Sir."

"Just step into that room and put on a smock. You can wash a little, if you want to." Embarrassed, Monroe entered the restroom off the lobby, ripped his shirt from his body, quickly washed, dried and slipped into the clean smock. He couldn't have spent more than three minutes.

However, when Monroe returned to the lobby, Mr. Grable was nowhere to be seen. Monroe dialed the Laurences, hoping someone would answer. His anxiety increased with each ring. After the third ring, John Laurence said, "Hello."

Monroe swallowed. Tears ran down his cheeks. "John. This is Monroe."

"Oh good! James just left. Let me try to catch him."

"No. No. That's all right. I'm at Hood Mortuary. Would you and James meet me here in a couple hours?"

"What's the matter, Monroe?"

Monroe hesitated. "I'll explain when I see you. If you'll do me this favor, I'll … I'll … " Monroe couldn't think of anything to say.

"Oh, sure." John faltered. Monroe struggled to talk. "James will be back in a minute. He just went next door—to carry a couch—." The phone fell silent. "Two hours—at the Hood Mortuary, you say. That's on Ninth at Second Avenue, isn't it?"

"Yes. Please wait for us—will you, John?"

"Sure, my boy. Sure."

James Grable returned through the Chapel. Monroe heard John say, "We'll be there." He replaced the receiver.

Monroe started for the front door. Mr. Grable grabbed his arm. "No, no. We have a hearse out back." Then. "You don't have your car, do you?"

"No. Not here."

They walked through the chapel and passed through an outside door. In the driveway, between buildings, a black hearse waited.

"Is this what we're going to take?" asked Monroe.

"Yes. You said she was dead, didn't you?"

"Yes, but ... I'm sorry," said Monroe. "I have two boys."

"They can ride with us," Grable said.

Following the road south of town, Monroe pointed the way through Wilson Gulch, then across Florida Mesa. He remained drenched in his personal guilt and continued to worry about Bonnie lying in the sun. What about hungry animals scavenging the mesa? What about the boys cooped up in the truck? Monroe thought Mr. Grable drove safely, but all too slow.

"How far did you say?" Grable asked.

"We're getting close." Monroe starred at the cabin from which he'd taken the whiskey. "We'll turn off to the right, in a second."

Monroe thought Mr. Gable seemed to be looking for a farmhouse. "We're just camping—on a new homestead," he said. The condition of their lives ... the campsite ... everything in his life seemed unreal now.

"Oh. I was just wondering," said Grable. "It's pretty flat, and I couldn't see any houses—barns—or anything."

"We just moved here."

"Oh, I see," said Grable, still confused.

"Turn off to the right just beyond that clump of scrub oak, Sir. Angle toward that thick grove of pine and cedar near the edge of the canyon." Monroe placed his right hand on the door handle.

"Behind the grove? Back of it." Monroe searched anxiously for the bed, then, everything appeared as he'd left it.

"She's under the cover on the bed," said Monroe.

James Grable drove into the camp and cramped his wheels to steer the hearse into position near the bed. Monroe leaped out while the vehicle was still moving. He rushed to the bed, anxious to see Bonnie. She lay as he had left her, relaxed and radiant. Monroe hurried to the truck and removed the boys. He gave them water, and changed Wade. By the time he'd refreshed the boys and gathered their things, Mr. Grable was ready to return to Durango.

* * *

Back in town, Monroe and Mr. Grable carried the boys and their belongings into the mortuary lobby. James, John Laurence and a graying, professional looking man stood talking. The distinguished man in the dark suit touched his left index finger to the cross bar of his glasses as he extended his right hand directing the group toward the waiting room.

Both John and James Laurence looked worried, but they stepped forward to help Monroe with his awkward burdens. John took Harold and James grabbed the two blankets Monroe had stuffed under his arm. Monroe shifted Wade to his left shoulder. Mr. Grable passed into the small room carrying a large bag of children's clothes and a teddy bear. James and John stepped back as Monroe returned to the lobby. "I'm Andrew Hood," announced the distinguished looking man. "We met when your mother passed away."

"Yes, Sir. I do remember you," answered Monroe.

"Sorry for your loss, Monroe," Mr. Hood said. "We want to help in anyway we can." Andrew Hood glanced over Monroe's shoulder to someone in the chapel. "Excuse me, I'll be right back," he said, and walked past Monroe and turned an ear to James Grable in the chapel.

John looked curiously at the two morticians and addressed Monroe. "Where's Bonnie?"

"Let me get the boys settled, then we'll talk," answered Monroe. "Mr. Grable said I could take the boys to his office and place chairs around them."

Monroe spread blankets on Grable's hardwood floor, turned four straight-backed chairs on their sides, and arranged a cubicle for the boys. When the boys were in their playpen, he gave each boy a toy and turned to the Laurences.

"Okay. Where did Hood go?" Monroe asked, ushering James and John into the lobby.

"I don't know. Grable wanted him to look at something," said James.

Monroe looked at his two friends and felt tears spring to his eyes. He turned away and searched his hip pocket for a handkerchief. "Please, let's sit down."

James and John sat. "Bonnie is dead," Monroe said, simply. Both James and John jumped to their feet.

"Let me tell you the whole story, later. It's very long— very painful. We just brought Bonnie in the ambulance— from our camp on Florida Mesa."

"Your homestead?" James asked, incredulously.

"Yes, James," said Monroe, turning to look deeply into John Laurence's eyes. "John, will you and Mabel be responsible for the boys tonight?"

"Of course. They're no trouble." Monroe saw shock, confusion and disbelief in both friends' faces.

"I know they're a lot of work. I wouldn't blame Mabel if she said 'no,' but … I don't know what else to do?"

Grable entered. "Mr. Morgan. Mr. Hood called the coroner for your wife. He wants you to stay, if you can, until Mr. Denison has seen her?"

Monroe nodded and assumed that it was normal to notify the county coroner when someone died. James said, in a hushed voice, "I'll take Dad and the boys home and come back for you. Okay?"

"I'd appreciate it." Monroe grasped his hand.

The Laurences gathered the boys and their belongings. They replaced the chairs and walked to the front street curb where their car was parked. James Grable followed along, observing the boys transfer from Monroe to the Laurences.

With the car loaded and pulling away, Mr. Grable and Monroe walked back into the lobby.

"Make yourself comfortable, Mr. Morgan. There's coffee and donuts in my office. You must be hungry."

"Thanks." Monroe felt no inclination to eat. He sat staring at the blank wall before him and wrestled with gut-wrenching thoughts that stumbled over each other in his head. He had no idea how much time passed before James came through the door. James seemed aggravated? Irritated? Excited?

Before Monroe could ask his friend to explain his agitation, Sheriff Harvey Howe and his deputy, Bob Stout swung into the lobby. Monroe seemed to notice a smirk on Stout's face as he followed Howe across the lobby. They walked into the Chapel and on into another room. Monroe and James looked quizzically at each other.

Monroe spoke. "What's that all about?"

"I have no idea. Maybe there's something wrong." James left his chair and peaked into the Chapel. "There's a door on the north wall. What's in there?"

"I think they took Bonnie in there," Monroe said.

James looked at Monroe. "Was it an accident?"

"Yes. Strychnine."

"Oh. My God!" James exploded. "What are you saying?"

Monroe felt tears sting his eyes. He stood confused, gazed into his friend's eyes, and then stood helplessly as tears blurred his vision.

"God!" Monroe gasped, wringing his hands. "James, she just drank a tiny bit of that whiskey and died."

Monroe's voice faded away as he heard the scuff of footsteps. When he turned, Sheriff Howe and Deputy Stout towered over him. "I'm going to hold you until we get to the bottom of this," said the Sheriff.

"Stand up," ordered Bob Stout. Monroe jerked to his feet in confusion as shock stunned his brain.

"What … What … " Monroe stammered.

"Turn around," Bob ordered.

Monroe turned. He felt his left hand yanked behind his back and a cold clamp tighten around his wrist. Almost instantly, Bob locked the handcuffs to his other wrist.

"We're taking you down to the station while you tell us how you broke your wife's neck," said the Sheriff.

CHAPTER SEVENTEEN

(May 1923)

Bob Stout felt like a grasshopper jumping from one place to another. His excitement was almost uncontrollable. It was frustrating, too, because he felt the need to be in two places at once. He had to attend the interrogation of Monroe—something he wouldn't miss for the world—but he needed to tell Sam Isgar about Bonnie's death and Monroe's arrest, as well. Isgar had probably already seen the headlines, which read "DEEP MYSTERY SURROUNDS DEATH OF YOUNG WOMAN AFTER DRINKING VERY SMALL PORTION OF POISONED HOOCH."

Locking the bracelets on Monroe Morgan had been a thoroughly pleasurable event for Bob. The Sheriff and Coroner, Donald Denison, were interrogating Morgan, now. Dr. H. D. Bronson would join them after he'd performed his postmortem at the mortuary.

Bob supposed his inclusion into the interrogation process had something to do with the fact that the Sheriff had been keeping him underfoot since the burning of Morgan's barn last fall. The Sheriff probably concluded that his physical size, when compared to Earl Mills, lent credibility to his being involved in the barn burning. And Sam Isgar didn't want him and Earl working together for the same reason. Their differences in bulk made them too easy to spot.

So, when Dr. Bronson showed up with his autopsy report and Earl Mills arrived to begin his shift, Sheriff Howe told Bob he could go home. But before he left, he learned that the Sheriff, along with Coroner Denison, had decided to go out to the Morgan homestead and retrieve the bottle of booze that Grable and Morgan had left.

Since it was getting late in the day, Bob assumed he'd find Sam at the Strater. Acting on his hunch, he made a beeline for the hotel.

Sure enough, when Bob called Sam's room, he found Sam in. He felt like running up the stairs, two steps at a time, but decided against it when he saw the elevator waiting.

Bob knocked at Room 323. The door opened.

Sam Isgar glowered. "I thought I told you not to come here unless you had something that couldn't wait?"

"This can't wait." Bob pushed into the room. "Do you know where I've been?"

Sam was in no mood for games. "Come on. Out with it. What've you got?"

Bob saw the glare in Sam's eyes and felt like cheering. What he had would turn the Klansman's interest into shock and amazement, but he had to deliver the information in just the right way. Should he just blurt out the fact that Bonnie was dead, or filter it out in little bits and dabs? He decided to dribble it out. And, about Monroe being in jail—shouldn't he string that out, as well? He decided to start with something Sam already knew about.

"Well," Bob began, "you know Bonnie and Monroe went somewhere after they left Porter. But you don't know where they went, do you?"

"Where'd they go?" Sam raised his eyes to the ceiling and returned to his chair at the bay window. He began his favorite pastime: watching people enter and leave the Strater.

"They went to Aztec, New Mexico—about thirty miles south." Bob clapped his hands in glee.

"Are they still in Aztec?" Sam was dividing his interest between a party coming into the hotel and the exact location of Bonnie.

"No. They left Aztec last Wednesday and moved to a piece of land on the Florida Mesa. Morgan calls it his 'homestead.'"

Moments passed while Bob waited for Sam to get excited. But Sam only said: "Well. Where is it?"

"My guess is that it's just south of Carméllo's cabin."

Sam sat straight in his chair. His mouth dropped open. "What the hell? Has Carméllo said anything about this? Has Carméllo seen Morgan and that slut?"

"No. Not that I know of. Probably doesn't even know they moved there."

"Probably doesn't know!" Sam exploded. "Probably doesn't know!" Sam jumped from his chair. "Where's his head? Up his ass?"

Bob realized he was losing his audience. "Hold your horses, now. Calm down. There's more." His own excitement restricted the words in his throat. He had Sam upset and he hadn't told any of the good parts. All he'd said was that Morgan and Bonnie had moved to Florida Mesa. "This morning he ran all the way to town. All the way to Hood Mortuary … "

Frustrated, Sam grabbed Bob's arm. "Who ran into town? Carméllo?"

"No. Morgan!"

"Oh shit! Mortuary! What for?" Sam stomped across the room. His eyes were the size of saucers.

Bob couldn't stand it. "Bonnie's dead," he blurted.

"Jesus Christ!" Sam's jaw dropped. He began quick, jerky strides around the room. He banged his fist into the wall. "Who did it? Who did it? Did _he_ kill her? The sonuvabitch!"

"I don't know. No one knows. He says, no. We got him in jail."

"I'm going down there!" Sam reached for his hat.

"Wait a minute! Wait a minute! She left you," Bob pointed out. "She won't be your wife, come the end of the month."

"Who gives a fuck? She's got my kid," Sam roared. "Where _is_ the kid, anyway?"

"I understand John Laurence and his wife are taking the kids. Morgan handed them over this afternoon."

"I want my son. I don't give a shit about that other little bastard. When did you find this out?"

"I've been on the case all afternoon." Bob felt proud. Finally, he was one up on Sam Isgar. He loved the feeling. "There's more, if you want to know what's going on."

"God dammit, man. That's what you're here for, isn't it? What do you want me to do? Kiss your ass?"

Bob decided to change his tactics. He'd be conciliatory, sympathetic. After all he had the great Sam Isgar hanging on his every word.

"Dr. Bronson did an autopsy on Bonnie this afternoon. She died of strychnine poisoning and her neck was broke."

"For Christ sake!"

Bob walked over to the bay window and closed it. "We're only three stories up, Sam. Recommend you control yourself."

"Oh. Fuck you. Fuck 'em all." Sam waved his arms. "I'm gonna kill that goddamned Morgan. The sonuvabitch!"

Bob gazed in mild contempt at the imperturbable Isgar. "I'd worry a little about myself, if I were you."

"What do you mean?" Sam stared at Bob as though anticipating another shock.

"The strychnine may be from Carméllo's still. What if Carméllo tells the Sheriff you told him to buy the strychnine—you told him to poison the booze."

Sam glared. His jaw jerked. Nothing came out. Bob watched Sam devour the full import of his revelation.

Bob continued. "Maybe Morgan broke her neck, but somebody else poured strychnine into the booze that poisoned her. Somebody is guilty of making the poison available for human consumption."

"Well. I'm not guilty of anything. Nobody can prove a shitin' thing. I didn't steal the booze. I didn't give it to her. Maybe Morgan made it. He's a goddamned moon shiner."

"Morgan said he stole it 'from a cabin near by.' He said he wanted it for 'snakebite.' The lying sonuvabitch."

Sam began to pace. "I want Carméllo Basíllo out of the country. But first, I want him to dump that goddamned booze and burn the cabin—before that stupid Sheriff gets out there. I don't care whether Morgan got the booze from our place or not."

"The Sheriff, Morgan and the Coroner are looking around Morgan's camp, right now. The Sheriff wants that bottle of booze. I don't know whether they'll go over to the cabin or not. It's getting pretty late."

"I don't care. Get Carméllo out there." Sam stopped pacing. "Where is he?"

"I don't know. We're supposed to meet tomorrow. He's probably in Ignacio, with his mother."

"Has he got a phone?"

"No. He lives like a goddamned Indian."

Sam clasped his hands behind his back and strolled to the window. The streetlights were on. "I'll take Harold back. See how Morgan likes that."

* * *

Early next morning, James Laurence stood at the jail's booking counter, trying to get Deputy Earl Mills' attention. He noticed the date was May 21, 1923. When Earl left his bunk in the corner, he'd straightened his bed, but not much else. He needed to wash, shave and comb his unruly red hair.

James tried to remain calm while he watched the little deputy, again, pretend he had certain things to do before he could attend to anyone at the counter.

"Sir," James called. "I wonder if I could see my client?"

Deputy Mills continued to peer into one of the back-wall cabinets. He seemed to have lost something.

"Sir," James called again. "May I talk to you?"

"Since I'm the only one here, guess you'll have to—if you talk to anyone." Earl sidled over to the counter. "I've got the night shift. Keeps me pretty busy."

"I want to see my client, Monroe Morgan. Can you let me in?"

"I could if I wanted to, but how do I know Morgan's your client? As a matter of fact, how do I know you're a lawyer? Morgan's held for murder."

"What do I need to do, show you my license?" James took another grip on his patience. "You might ask Mr. Morgan who he has retained as counselor?"

Earl leaned against the counter. "What's your name?"

"James Laurence."

"Never heard of you. And I've lived in Durango all my life." Earl reached for a stack of papers in a file basket.

"Well. I've heard of you, Deputy Mills. You're a pretty famous fellow." Earl stopped shuffling and looked up. "All the time I was in school at Boulder, my folks wrote about the police work you were doing here in Durango."

"Really." Earl turned his complete attention to James. "What's your dad's name?"

"John. John Laurence." James paused, hoping Earl would know the name.

"John Laurence," Earl repeated. "Did he use to work on the railroad? Was he an engineer?"

"That's him. He's retired, now. Likes to keep an eye on who's on the police force, and such."

"Oh yeah, I think I know him. Pretty good guy. Sent you to Boulder to become a lawyer, huh?"

"Yep. I'm opening an office."

"Well. You're a little older than me. Probably why I don't remember you."

"I'm kinda working out of my home."

"Well. Never let it be said that Earl Mills stood in the way of a good old Durango boy. We fella's gotta stick together, don't we?"

"That's for sure," James said. "That's for darn sure."

"We'll have to talk over old times sometime, but come on back here. We'll see if Morgan's up. It's about breakfast time."

Earl opened the flap in the counter top and led the way through the green metal door into a large room divided into four cells. Monroe was in #3, the only cell occupied. Monroe lay on his bunk with his arms across his face.

James sized up the place. "I thought you had a bigger jail."

"Oh, we do. There's eight more cells downstairs. These are holding cells for interrogation and stuff like that. Here's your man."

"Thank you. Thank you very much."

"Mr. O'Riley wants to question him sometime today, probably this morning."

"Joseph H. O'Riley, the Assistant District Attorney?"

"Yep."

"Well, Earl, I appreciate you letting me talk to him."

By this time, Monroe was on his feet and standing at the front bars. All the light had gone from his eyes. The whites were red and sunken. But his hair was neatly combed. He had shaved and his boots were cleaned and shined.

James reached through the bars and took Monroe's hand. "Hi. How're you doing?"

"Fine, I guess. I'm glad to see you."

Mills came back with a chair. "The Sheriff should be here about ten o'clock."

"Thanks. Thanks, a lot."

When Earl closed the green door, James turned to Monroe. "I'm going to start introducing myself as your attorney today. I understand the Assistant District Attorney,

Joe O'Riley, is going to start his investigation by questioning you this morning. And you shouldn't talk to anyone without me present. Do you understand?"

Monroe stood gazing at the floor. "Oh, I don't care, James. I just don't give a damn about anything."

"Come on, now! It's your constitutional right to have a lawyer present when you're being questioned and you don't need to say anything without your lawyer. Don't incriminate yourself just because you don't give a damn, right now. Think of the boys. What's going to become of them? These guys are looking for a murderer. You know you're not a murderer, and so do I."

"I can't think of anyone but Bonnie." Monroe's eyes filled with tears. His hands gripped the bars.

James placed his hands over Monroe's. "I know. I know. We've got to work our way through this. And we will, believe me. But now, you've got to tell me everything you can about what happened after you left our house and went to your homestead. I mean the whole story—at the homestead—the mortuary—the jail—everything."

While Monroe talked, James questioned and made notes. Finally, James felt he understood everything except Charlie's appearance while Monroe ran to town.

James folded his note pad. "Dad and I will get your things from the mesa, the furniture, the truck and Chukaluks. We'll take all your belongings to Cascade, store them and see that they're protected from the weather. Don't worry about the kids. Don't worry about the stock. Don't worry about anything. You haven't done anything wrong except steal some poisoned whiskey."

"And kill the only woman I'll ever loved. Oh God!" Monroe clutched his head.

James rushed to change the subject. "Did the rocks and bushes cause those scratches and bruises? What I'm getting at is: the police haven't hurt you, have they?"

"No. No one's hurt me. I wish they had." Monroe gripped the bars.

"And you went back out there, with the Sheriff and the Coroner, after they questioned you here yesterday?" asked James. "Is that right?" Monroe nodded.

"That's when they brought the liquor back? You and Grable didn't bring it in—is that right?" asked James.

"Yes."

"And that was after Bronson had completed his postmortem and come over here to question you at the jail. Is that right?"

"Yes."

"And what did Charlie look like, when you saw him?"

"Well, I didn't look directly at him on the trail, but I thought we were young again and he was running along side of me with his shirt off—braids flying."

The green door opened and Assistant District Attorney, Joseph O' Riley, walked in. Following O'Riley was Sheriff Harvey Howe and Earl Mills. The tall, slender district attorney strode directly to the jail cell and confronted Monroe by placing his face within six inches of Monroe's face. He stared directly into Monroe's eyes. His blonde hair parted in the middle and lay in waves on either side of his head. His long face seemed particularly grave when taken with the black suit and white shirt. Sheriff Howe appeared business-like and determined. Earl Mills just looked curious.

"Earl, you cover the front office until Bob gets here, then go on home." Sheriff Howe held the door open while Earl left, and then introduced the District Attorney. He established the fact that the District Attorney was on a fact-finding mission and would be asking Monroe some questions.

James watched Monroe while the Sheriff made his speech. He could see the frustration, the pain, and the exhaustion Monroe felt when he learned that he would have to tell his devastating story again. Monroe dropped his hands from the cell bars and began to pace like a caged animal.

"Gentlemen," James said. "Mr. Morgan has already told his story on several different occasions. It is a particularly devastating story for him personally. He wants to cooperate in every way, and he will, but we ask for your understanding."

The Assistant District Attorney nodded his head. "We understand. But, I'm afraid he's going to have to answer my questions today, and then tell his story as many time as is required. We must get to the bottom of what appears to be something more than an accidental death by poison."

"We understand, and we'll continue to cooperate in every way."

"You should counsel your client that there will be several opportunities to repeat his story, beginning tomorrow when I convene an inquest into this matter. He'll be requested, at that time, to tell his story to a number of Durango citizens who make up a jury."

"Mr. Morgan will continue to answer questions truthfully, no matter how painful it may be," said James.

* * *

It was close to 1 P.M. before Joe O'Riley finished his questioning, then, he and James left for lunch together. The smell of food coming from the jail below caught Monroe's attention. These last three or four days, he'd eaten what they'd placed before him, and he hadn't cared whether he ate or not. Now, he actually looked forward to eating something—ham hocks and beans, he thought.

Monroe sopped the last bite of biscuit in the last bit of bean juice and the green door opened again. It was Deputy Bob Stout and Sam Isgar. They walked to his cell.

"Morgan. Here's someone to see you." That's all Bob said before he turned on his heel and left, closing the door behind him.

Monroe gazed at his guest. Among his emotions, surprisingly, he felt sorrow. Sorrow for Harold who had had more than a year of uncertainty, and sorrow for Sam who must have experienced great pain as a result of loosing Bonnie.

Sam walked right up, grabbed a handful of bars, and leaned his face part way into the cell. Monroe remained seated on his bunk.

"You sonuvabitch! You dirty sonuvabitch," Sam hissed.

That remark brought Monroe back to reality. He began to experience some of the anger that had lain just under the surface. Moments ago, while he watched Sam approach his cell, he'd been ready to blame himself for all their problems, but now, after just a few words, Monroe began to believe that Sam Isgar's attitude and moral principles were liable to some blame. In any event, he wasn't willing to take any guff without giving something in return. He thought immediately of Harold. This man was Harold's father.

Monroe stood. "If you want to talk, keep a civil tongue in your head."

Sam's words continued to hiss through his teeth. "Let me put it like this, you sonuvabitch. I'm going to kill you. You'll never be rid of me—not until you're dead."

Monroe sneered and stepped closer. "I take it your friend disarmed you before you came in or you'd be shooting up the jail by now."

"I didn't bring a gun, but you can plan on one when you're out, if you ever get out. You deserve all you're getting, and if I can help give you more, I'll do it."

"I don't think you can kill me. After all, you missed when you blew up my house—when you threw dynamite at my truck over by Moab, and—when you destroyed Porter trestle."

Sam backed away from the bars. He wiped saliva from his lips.

Monroe glared from his cell. They were at an impasse. "Just what did I do that hurt you the most? It wasn't taking your wife and child, because you didn't really care for either of them."

"You embarrassed me, you sonuvabitch! You embarrassed me," Sam shouted, almost out of control. "Nobody embarrasses Sam Isgar and gets away with it."

"You mean you embarrassed your self by having to admit your wife left you. You didn't want people to know what a sonuvabitch you really are."

"I wouldn't have married her, if I hadn't needed her."

"But you often beat her, didn't you?"

"Only when she didn't do as I said."

"Like you telling her to stay away from church?"

"She didn't need to go to church."

"You forbid her to have lady friends, didn't you? Didn't she need lady friends?"

"She had me and Harold. That was enough." Sam grabbed the bars and shook them. "You killed her, you sonuvabitch, and you're going to pay." Sam strode toward the green door, and then turned as if he'd remembered something. "I want my son."

Now it was clear to Monroe why Sam had come. Sam wanted to bully, to threaten, and to hurt. As terrible as Sam was, Monroe couldn't think of a way to keep Harold from him—especially, if Sam really wanted the boy. After all, Sam <u>was</u> Harold's father.

Monroe pleaded with Sam. "You wouldn't want to separate Harold from his brother, would you?"

"I wouldn't have my son within a mile of that other little bastard. I don't want my boy to associate with that little bastard a minute longer than he has to."

"What would you do with Harold if you had him—train him to be a Ku Klux Klansman?"

"Don't get so high and mighty, asshole," Sam said. "We're getting stronger than you fuckin' Catholics think. If you weren't a jailbird, you'd see a big parade of Klansmen right down the middle of Main Avenue pretty soon."

"When?"

"Next Saturday," Sam bragged. "In four years, we'll have the whole western slope organized and I'll be in the Governor's chair. Don't worry about Harold."

Monroe tried to be more conciliatory. "What would you do with Harold?" Considering the past activities he'd attributed to Sam, he felt he had to protect the Laurences and their home from whatever danger Sam might cook up. What if Sam's anger turned against John and Mabel? Wouldn't the Laurences and both boys suffer?

"I'd take him back to Grand Junction where he belongs. I'd probably arrange a foster home for him. He'd never want for anything. He'd be my only heir."

Monroe remembered Sam's considerable wealth. "Sam. I don't want to be unfair—about your son. I believe a boy should be with his father. Let me talk to my lawyer and see if we can't settle this question amicably. Could you come back on Wednesday? I should have an answer by that time."

Sam seemed to calm down. "Well. If you'll be halfway decent about this, I'll wait until Wednesday. But I'm telling you: I'll get him. Hell and all your twisting won't stop me. And another thing, this doesn't let you off the hook. You're still a sonuvabitch."

"And you get this straight, Isgar. I don't like you any more than you like me. So, when I get out, we'll settle it—one way or the other. I'll be looking for you. Is that understood?"

"You goddamned right." Sam turned and stomped toward the green door, which wouldn't open.

Monroe smiled at Sam's frustration with the door. "Don't forget Wednesday."

314

CHAPTER EIGHTEEN

(May 1923)

When James entered the Denison-Amory Mortuary and sized-up the Chapel, he contemplated the chair arrangement for the 2 P.M. inquest. He wanted to know where the jury was going to be located in relation to the audience. Who was going to sit where? Next, he strolled around the lobby, looking for Monroe and the Sheriff. Nope. Considering the stir Bonnie's death had caused in the community, he thought citizens would be lined up trying to get in by 1:30 P.M. That's why he was early. He strolled back to the chapel.

The chapel was filled with folding chairs. That fact caused James to suspect the Coroner looked for a big crowd, too. There were six upholstered chairs grouped in the right-front corner of the room. Those chairs were, undoubtedly, for the six jurymen he'd heard about. Directly opposite, on the left, were four straight-backed chairs—probably for Monroe, the Sheriff, and any deputies the Sheriff might bring along. In the front middle, and angled slightly toward the jury, was the witness chair. James visualized Monroe in that chair. All of the other chairs were obviously for other attendees: he, the press, other witnesses and the general public.

He heard voices out front—on the walkway. Turning, he saw, coming to the door, Sheriff Harvey Howe, Deputy Bob Stout and Monroe. He moved to a position near the center of the lobby. The Sheriff walked in front, Monroe followed the Sheriff, and Bob brought up the rear. Monroe was handcuffed.

Sheriff Howe pushed the door open and strode directly to a small conference room on his right. James gazed at Monroe. Monroe returned the look with a nod and an expression of sheepishness. Monroe and Bob followed the Sheriff into the room.

James arrived at the door just as Sheriff Howe directed Monroe and Bob to sit in chairs that had been placed around a small table in the middle of the room.

"Good afternoon, gentlemen," James said. "Has Mr. Morgan been behaving himself?" As the men seated themselves, James stepped inside the room.

"No complaints," the Sheriff answered, taking off his hat and hanging it on a rack. Bob removed his hat and placed it on the floor beside his chair. Monroe remained bareheaded. That fact was notable because Monroe Morgan had never been seen in public without his hat.

"Where's your hat, Roe?" James asked.

"Lost it on the trail, I guess."

James leaned against the jam. "Is it absolutely necessary for Monroe to ware handcuffs, Sheriff? He hasn't been found guilty of anything, and he's been a model prisoner."

The Sheriff stared back at James, then turned to Monroe and removed his cuffs. "Don't give me cause to put these back on," the Sheriff advised, as he stuffed the manacles into his hip pocket.

Monroe massaged his wrists. "Have no fear, Sheriff. I'm anxious to get this over with. I want the mysteries surrounding Bonnie's death cleared up, and I'm willing to do anything to give assistance."

"It's going to take some time, because we've had to send the contents of her stomach and a large sample of the booze to Boulder for analysis. We can't expect to clear things up until we get a report back."

"How about Bonnie's funeral, James?" Monroe looked wistfully at James. "Can't we bury her?"

The Sheriff thought a moment. "We can talk to the Coroner, but don't forget—she's not your wife. She's Mrs. Sam Isgar."

"Until the end of the month, when the divorce is final," James said.

"I want to bury her as soon as possible. Let her rest in peace," said Monroe.

"How about Isgar? What does he say?" The Sheriff looked first at Monroe and then at James.

"He told me, in the office this morning, that he don't care what happens to her, any more," Bob said. "He just wants the boy."

"Well. It's up to you, then," said the Sheriff, glancing at Monroe.

"I want her to rest right next to my mother in our Greenmount Cemetery family plot." Monroe clinched his hands and placed them in the middle of the table. "Would you please coordinate that, James?"

"Sure. I'll talk to the coroner today—after the inquest."

"I want Hood to bury her, James."

"Okay. I'll talk to Mr. Hood, then."

James heard people walking through the lobby on their way to the chapel.

"Sheriff," Monroe said, "has anyone found the man who poisoned the whiskey? Are you looking for him?"

"Are you getting ready to criticize my actions, Morgan? You're not in a position to criticize."

"I'm sorry, Sheriff. I don't mean to criticize, but it just seems to me someone out there has some explaining to do—as well as me."

"Yes. I am looking for him. I know who owns the place. He lives in Ignacio. But the fellow who owns the property may not be the fellow that poisoned the whiskey. No one lives in the cabin."

James leaned over and laid his hand on Monroe's shoulder. "Did you fellows see in the paper yesterday that the state of Ohio has a law that deals with people who poison hooch?"

"Yes. I read that," Sheriff Howe said. "But we don't have any such law on the books in the State of Colorado.

317

We're bound by federal law which don't say anything about people who have stills and poison their liquor to protect the still."

James continued. "If an Ohio man did what this fellow has done, he would be charged with second degree murder. Plus, an Ohio man could go to prison for operating an illegal still, and, he could be fined $2,000 for trying to sell booze— if proved. In Ohio, if a person is convicted, the trial Judge is prohibited from modifying fines or suspending sentences."

"Well. Right now, I don't know what charges we might make," said the Sheriff. "That'll be up to the District Attorney. This inquest is just the beginning. There'll be other hearings. I'm sure the jury will want to hear testimony from the cabin owner <u>and</u> Morgan, here. The still, the cabin, and the booze, are objects of suspicion in this case. That's why we'll have to have the test results we've asked Boulder for."

Donald Denison, the Coroner, appeared at the door. "Most everyone's here. If you boys will come in, we'll get started."

* * *

The Coroner ushered the Sheriff, Bob Stout and Monroe to the four chairs located front and left. James counted fourteen people seated in the main audience. There were no women. A blond young-man, in a blue business suit and wearing brown oxfords, sat on James right. The fellow held a note pad and pencil. The overhead lights were bright.

After Coroner Denison seated Monroe and the two police officers, he walked back to the lobby. Moments later, he returned with a file of six men who were shown to the upholstered chairs on the right. All jurors wore suits and ties. A black haired man, in the far chair, wore a red and yellow tie. He appeared to be the foreman. He looked like a barber, but James couldn't remember having seen him around town. The fellow next to the black haired man had on a black suit, white shirt, black oxfords and red tie. James thought one of the other men might be a minister or a grocer. The young man sitting in the chair beside James began taking notes.

James leaned slightly to his right and whispered, "Do you know those fellows?"

"Most of 'em," the young man confided, "I'll get their names from the Coroner."

"You with the <u>Evening Herald</u>—covering the case?" asked James.

The young fellow nodded affirmatively and immediately turned his attention center stage. James followed the reporter's gaze and watched the Coroner position himself directly in front of the witness chair facing the audience.

"Gentlemen," said Mr. Denison, "I'm going to convene this hearing today, the 22nd day of May, 1923, not because I think we can conclude all of the business required, but because we must get started with our work. Today will lay a foundation for future meetings." Mr. Denison turned slightly to his left and addressed the jury more directly. "You will hear from several witnesses today—some of whom will testify only once—but, in order to give you a chronology of the case, you'll need to hear from everybody having a role in the development of the case. We plan to present each witness in the order of his participation. You will hear from Mr. Morgan last because he is central to the entire matter—from beginning to end.

"District Attorney, Joseph O'Riley, will call the witnesses and ask the questions. If you members of the jury have questions, you may hand your questions to Mr. O'Riley, through the clerk, and those questions will be answered in subsequent hearings.

"All information gathered here, will be accumulated in the form of a report. That report may be used by a Grand

Jury as a basis for a murder indictment. Even though the State of Colorado has not, as yet, passed laws that specifically deal with persons who make and/or sell poisoned hooch, there may be players in this case who have broken laws that <u>are</u> on the books. This inquest is convened for the purpose of discovering whether anyone has broken laws that do exist. If so, those persons will be indicted.

"I will turn the investigation over to District Attorney, Joseph O'Riley. Mr. O'Riley will call his first witness."

James noted that Coroner Denison took the seat left vacant beside the Sheriff. Joseph O'Riley walked to center stage.

"I call, as my first witness, Mr. Jesse H. Grable."

James watched Mr. Grable step forward and take the witness chair as indicated by Mr. O'Riley. "Where are you employed, Mr. Grable?"

Mr. Grable revealed how Monroe Morgan had contacted him, at the Hood Mortuary, on Sunday morning the 20th of May. He told of Mrs. Morgan's body being retrieved from Florida Mesa and the poisoning as reported to him by Monroe Morgan. He told of his aroused suspicions when he lifted Mrs. Morgan and her head hung limp in an abnormal manner.

Mr. Andrew Hood, owner of Hood Mortuary, testified next. He disclosed that Bonnie's broken neck made him decide to call Coroner, Donald Denison.

Mr. Denison took the chair and said that after examining the deceased and finding evidence of poison and a broken neck, he called Sheriff Howe and Dr. Howard D. Bronson.

The Sheriff testified that it was his decision to confine Mr. Morgan until the authorities found answers to their questions and until Dr. Bronson had performed a postmortem.

Dr. Bronson's confirmed previous testimony and brought to light the fact that there were no marks of violence, whatsoever, on Mrs. Morgan's body, but that her stomach contained vast quantities of fusel oil, as well as strychnine.

Mr. Denison then returned to the chair and said that he had sent the contents of Mrs. Morgan's stomach, plus a large sample of the bottled liquor, to the State Chemist at Boulder, for analysis and report. He said authorities were waiting for that report.

James paid particular attention to Monroe's declarations. In addition to Monroe's corroboration of all the previous testimony, he made public the fact that Bonnie was married to Sam Isgar and that Sam Isgar lived in Grand Junction. He said that Sam Isgar had fathered a child and that that child was presently living in Durango with friends. He continued, saying: that he, personally, knew little of Bonnie Morgan's husband, but that Bonnie had said the child's name was Harold Isgar.

Monroe stated that Sam Isgar had visited in jail and expressed a wish to recover his son and take him back to Grand Junction. Monroe said, further, that since he had no legal control over the boy, he made the decision to turn the boy over to Mr. Isgar on Monday, the 28th of May. He said it was his understanding that Mr. Isgar would be ready to leave Durango for Grand Junction on that date.

Monroe also added the fact that Bonnie was a native of Kentucky. He said that in her younger days, Bonnie had won three beauty contests and that she had had a successful stage career as a singer and dancer in traveling Chautauquas.

Upon hearing that testimony, James realized that even he hadn't known quite everything about Bonnie. But he didn't have time to reflect on that fact, because as soon as Monroe finished testifying, Coroner Donald Denison announced that the inquest would be reconvened when he received the State's Chemical Report.

James turned, immediately, to the blond reporter next to him. He introduced himself by saying: "My name's James Laurence, Attorney at Law. I'd like to trade business cards with you. I have a feeling we might be of assistance to each other in the future."

The reporter responded by reaching in his wallet, retrieving a small white card, and handing it to James. "My name's Steve Sawyer, Evening Herald. I've heard your name mentioned in this case. You're with Mr. Morgan, I believe."

"That's correct, and I intend to open a new law office next month in one of the buildings down town. Are you new to Durango?"

"Got here from Kansas City right after Christmas. Don't know why the Herald hired me—just because I applied, I guess."

"Well, I've lived here all my life and can't think of a place I'd rather be. Let's keep in touch."

"Good," said Steve. "I'm trying to meet as many people as possible. I appreciate your card. Stop by the office anytime." They shook hands.

James had been watching, a conversation that had erupted at the front of the room. The Sheriff, Monroe and Andrew Hood were deeply engaged. The discussions continued while the jury and the audience filed out.

When James approached the group, Monroe turned to him and said, "I'll get James to handle that."

"I saw the discussion. Couldn't imagine what was being said," James remarked.

Monroe turned to James. "Mr. Hood, knows I want him to bury Bonnie, but he doesn't want the responsibility without some agreement from Sam Isgar. The burial could take place before the 31st, but Isgar needs to wave his rights."

"So, you want me to get Isgar to signed a waiver and present it to Mr. Hood. Right?"

"Yes. Will you?"

"Of course," promised James.

* * *

When James approached the Strater desk and asked for Sam Isgar, the clerk paged Sam's room and James climbed the stairs as the sun slipped behind the western mountains and a cold wind smashed against the north side of the hotel. James intended to get Sam's waver.

For some reason, James enjoyed all his meetings with Sam. Maybe he liked the challenge. It had been a pleasure when he negotiated Harold's transfer from Monroe to his biological father. The battle of wits wasn't easy, but it was fun. Now he looked forward to another opportunity.

James knocked at Room 323. The door opened.

"What is it this time?" Sam rolled his eyes to the ceiling and sounded bored.

James adopted a wait-and-see attitude. "May I come in?"

"Yes, Yes. I'm pretty busy." Sam stood aside.

James walked in and closed the door. He moved straight to a chair in the corner. "We need your signature." He laid a "To Whom It May Concern" waiver on the table.

"What's this?" Sam strode across the room.

"Better read it," advised James.

"You damned right I will." Sam yanked the paper nearer the light.

After reading the release, Sam said, "So. He wants my permission to bury the adulteress, does he? Well. I don't care what happens to her. The sooner she's out of my life—and my son's life—the better." He took a fountain pen from his shirt pocket, scribbled his name on the document, and pushed it toward James. "But you can tell your friend for me, that this in no way squares things between us. In fact, it only makes things worse. He owes me a favor, now, and I'm going to take it out of his hide." Sam stepped to the door and opened it. "Now, get the hell out of here and make sure my boy is ready to travel on Monday the 26th."

"You mean the 28th, don't you?" James asked, smiling.

"Oh shit! I was thinking of the parade."

"Gotta keep your dates straight, Sam. You're such a busy man."

Sam nodded toward the hallway. "Get going," he said, quietly.

"Thank you very much, Mr. Isgar. We'll have little Harold ready. Know what time you'll be by?"

"I'll call an hour before I get there." Sam slammed the door.

CHAPTER NINETEEN

(May & June 1923)

A harsh wind shook the branches of the huge cottonwood tree outside Monroe's cell. Scraping sounds emanated from the wall. But the harsh sounds were only a minor irritant compared to the scenes tumbling through Monroe's mind. In each instance, Bonnie repeated a joy, a sorrow, a hope or a fear. Tears kept forming in Monroe's eyes—rolling down his cheeks—soaking his pillow.

He kept telling himself that his weeping would stop. But it didn't. He'd catch another glimpse of Bonnie in his mind's eye, and off he'd go again. Try as he did, Monroe couldn't remember pain like this. Now, when alone, he blubbered all the time. "Oh well," he despaired. "It'll be daylight soon."

On this particular morning, as he sorrowed over and over, another presence caught Monroe's attention. Instantly alert, but without opening his eyes, he gave the intruder his full attention. He tried to recall whether the Sheriff had put someone in an adjacent cell yesterday … last night. Couldn't remember. The premonition remained strong. His eyes popped open. He glanced around in the dim light. Without moving, he rotated his eyes to every accessible part of the room. No one. The presence remained … however.

Monroe leapt from his bunk, and whirled toward the outside window … there stood One-armed Charlie. There was no mistaking—Charlie. But, my God! … how much he'd changed. The face, the braids, the eyes, and the mouth … everything about him looked younger … smaller. His left arm extended down from his shoulder and finished with a perfectly good hand. Of course, Monroe couldn't see the actual hand because it was covered with a pure white glove. The glove rested on the silver handle of an ebony cane.

As Monroe slowly moved his eyes, from the gloved hand, to the rest of Charlie's body; he saw a man about three foot tall and beautifully dressed. He looked like Prince Albert's pictured on the tobacco cans. Spats, striped pants, frock coat with satin piping on the lapel, a cravat and a boutonniere. Charlie stood lightly on his right foot with his left leg bent slightly at the knee to point his left toe and touch the floor across his right leg. Monroe could remember Charlie standing like that, but never with such elegance.

"Charlie! Is it really you?" Monroe asked, agape.

Charlie smiled the old Charlie smile. Monroe relaxed a little. Then, Charlie's right arm bent at the elbow and began to rise. When his gloved right hand reached waist high, his thumb jumped up in the universal sign of approval and hope.

Earl Mills crashed through the green door grabbing Monroe's attention. In a loud voice, Earl started blabbing. "It's five-thirty and I couldn't sleep. Thought I'd check on you. We've got a big day, today, you know."

Monroe glanced first to Earl then back to Charlie. Charlie was gone.

Earl kept right on talking. "I don't blame you, Morgan. I'd be disappointed too, if I couldn't go to my own wife's funeral. Well, she's really not your wife. That may ease your suffering. Might as well get ready for breakfast, though."

Earl headed for the green door. When the door closed, Monroe stood motionless for a long minute. Finally, he reached for his pipe and his can of Prince Albert pipe tobacco. He moved closer to the cellblock light and peered at the picture on the can. "I'll be damned," he said, aloud.

* * *

When additional time had passed, Monroe became aware of the fact that the gray dawn had turned to distinct daylight, and as he liked to do, Monroe wanted to go downstairs, get washed, shaved, and combed before the other prisoners woke up. He quickly dressed, rattled his tin cup on the cell bars and hoped that Earl would hear his signal because he was ready to go. It crossed his mind that this was the sixth day of his incarceration, and he'd established an amiable relationship with Mills. They'd arranged a deal whereby Monroe would rattle his cup on the bars when he needed something. In exchange, Monroe would keep Earl awake so he could avoid the taunts and admonitions handed out by Sheriff Howe or Bob Stout when they found him sleeping in the office.

On this particular morning, Monroe had meticulously groomed himself and was prepared to wait for the funeral to take place at 2 P.M. He hoped he might get to go.

But, after breakfast, when Monroe approached the Sheriff again about the funeral, nothing had changed. He would miss the funeral. He'd have to wait for James' report—after the fact.

At about 4 P.M., James walked into the cellblock with a pleasant look on his face. "I've got news for you, Roe, and I don't think it's all bad. You decide."

Monroe came to the bars. "I need some good news."

"Then, first off, we'll talk about Bonnie's funeral. Mr. Hood thought Bonnie deserved special attention, so he dressed the team with plumes and Conchos attached to their harnesses. He used a wagon instead of a car to transport her to Greenmount." James removed his hat. "We all liked the idea. Thought the wagon more fitting than a car. Then came the big surprise."

Monroe had watched James' enthusiasm build as he talked. "You're going to tell me they've paved Main Street— just for the occasion?" said Monroe.

"Are you kidding?" said James. "Guess again!"

"I can't imagine. Just tell me." Monroe was happy Bonnie had received special treatment.

327

"Father O'Malley did a brief ceremony at the mortuary and we all left for Greenmount. My folks were with me. The Jacksons and their boys were in their car. The Jackson's had another couple with them—I don't know who they were. Anyway, we had our car and the Jacksons had theirs, but the couple I didn't know, rode horses. We all got together in the street outside the mortuary and when we left the corner of Second and Ninth Avenue, people started coming from everywhere." James eyes moistened. "We were crossing Main Avenue on our way to the Ninth Street Bridge when it seemed everybody was going to join our procession. In all, I bet seventy-five people walked to the cemetery." Monroe felt the tears well in his own eyes. He tried to stop the tears, but they just rolled down both his cheeks. He wiped his hands across his eyes and turned away.

"It's all right, my friend," James said. "I was proud, too. But, let me tell you everything."

"Did Father O'Malley say a few words at the cemetery?" Monroe asked, while he struggled to stop the tears.

"Yes, and do you know who was there—waiting at the grave site—when we got there?"

"Can't imagine."

"Mr. and Mrs. Eagle!"

"Oh, my God! Charlie's mother and father? They must've heard. Wished I'd seen them."

"Okay—you can," James said, enthusiastically. "I'll grant that wish."

James turned on his heel and literally ran to the green door. A moment later, Mother Eagle, her youngest son and her husband approached Monroe's cell.

The whole family was beautifully dressed. Huge buckles, massive bracelets, heavy rings and hefty pins— all turquoise and set in shinning silver. Massive silver heishis mixed with brilliant turquoise necklaces and draped themselves across Mrs. Eagle's blood-red blouse and hid under her purple jacket—all velvet. A strikingly beautiful eagle feather sprang from each hatband on the Stetson hats worn by father and by son.

Monroe felt his heart pound. His last memory of the Eagles involved a gorgeous Navajo blanket in which Charlie's body was moved from Mercy Hospital.

"Mother Eagle! Joseph! Theodore!" Monroe reached through the cell bars for Joseph's hand and Mary's waist. Joseph grabbed the outstretched hand and shook it eagerly. "Thank you, Theodore!" Monroe reached for Charlie's younger brother and finally shook his strong hand. "Thank you all, for coming. You're a wonderful surprise."

"We didn't know we could see you, my son," Mrs. Eagle said, hugging Monroe through the bars.

"Ya 'at eeh!" Joseph said, using his own language to say: "Hello, it is good to see you."

Monroe addressed the whole family. "You should have known Bonnie."

"She is my daughter," Mary Eagle said, proudly. "She had a big crowd."

Monroe smiled. "That's what James said, just before you came in."

Joseph stepped forward nodding up and down. "You come see us, in Window Rock—when you get out. You—rest up."

"I'll go see Bonnie, first," Monroe responded, and then hesitated … <u>What if he never left jail?</u> The thought was too horrible to contemplate. He shook his head. "I'll visit you sometime, Joseph. And you folks are welcome at Cascade, anytime."

"We have to go, now," Mary said. "It's getting dark—and cold."

Monroe reached for Mary. "Where will you stay the night?"

"At Breen. My brother's ranch." Monroe recalled the older brother's point of land along the La Plata River just north of the Breen Store. The Eagle family had farmed that place before Monroe was born.

Mary extended an arm through the bars and hugged Monroe. "We want you to come to Window Rock. Bring your boy." Monroe remembered Wade, and the tears came again.

Monroe watched the Eagles go. The green door closed and opened again. This time it was Sheriff Howe. Monroe turned to the small stand beside his bunk and retrieved his pipe. He began to fill the pipe with Prince Albert pipe tobacco while he thought of Charlie's ghost.

"Monroe," the Sheriff said. "A High School chemistry instructor named Clifton did a preliminary test of that poisoned hooch this afternoon. He found strychnine, as well as, a large quantity of fusel oil. He gave a few drops of the stuff to a frog and the frog died instantly." The Sheriff paused a moment. "We're still waiting for official word from the state chemist, but I thought you'd like to know about the local test. I'm going to try to keep you posted on the progress we're making as the case goes along. We've visited the cabin on Florida Mesa—O'Riley and me—to investigate. We found a piece of poisoned meat. In addition, we found a little bottle with some strychnine remaining in it—from Ignacio Mercantile. We also found part of a distilling outfit." The Sheriff paused as though he were waiting for Monroe to say something. "Did you see anything like that?"

"No."

"A fellow by the name of Carméllo Basíllo bought that bottle of strychnine on the 28th day of April, this year. We checked at the Trading Post. And we've located Mr. Basíllo. I'll pick him up tomorrow."

The Sheriff started to walk away and stopped. "I'm sorry about your wife. Sorry you couldn't be there." The Sheriff turned away again.

"Sheriff," Monroe said. "What's fusel oil? They mentioned it at the inquest."

The Sheriff leaned a hand against a cell bar. "They tell me, it's an oily acid you get in organic material if you haven't completed a distilling cycle. One thing's for sure: it's poisonous as hell. In this case, it looks like your wife got poisoned by hooch that wasn't completely distilled, and then somebody added strychnine. But, we'll have to wait for the official report."

Monroe pressed. "You say his name is Carméllo Basíllo?"

"Yes. You know him?"

"I think he's the man I saw with Sam Isgar behind the Mason and Ambold Grocery, the night Isgar and I had our fight."

"What would he be doing with Sam Isgar?"

"I'm sure in my own mind that a Ku Klux Klan meeting was just breaking up." Monroe leaned forward toward the bars.

"And—was anyone else there who can corroborate your story?"

"Bob Stout and Earl Mills. I saw them come out and go down the alley before Sam appeared. Carméllo's the fellow who helped Isgar back to the hotel after the fight."

"I suppose you have someone to swear you're telling the truth?"

"Well. I had Charlie Eagle until they burned him to death on a cross in my front yard. But, if Charlie were here, I'm sure he'd tell you Carméllo Basíllo is the same man. That _is_ your man's name, isn't it?"

"Yes. But your friend's dead." Sheriff Howe shook his head thoughtfully.

"And if all of them—Sam, Carméllo, Bob and Earl— deny it, then I'm a liar because I haven't anyone to verify my story. Is that right?"

The Sheriff gazed at Monroe with a thoughtful stare. "I'll keep your story in mind." The Sheriff walked to the green door. "So far, Carméllo hasn't satisfactorily explained what happened to the strychnine he purchased in April.

* * *

331

At 10 A.M. Monday, May the 28th, Monroe looked up to see James hurry into the cellblock. Before James said anything, Monroe knew Sam had taken Harold. He knew today was the day. He knew it would bother him when it happened. He knew Bonnie would have fought the transfer to the very last. But what he didn't know was how much it would hurt when it actually happened. The only thing that helped was the fact that Harold was really Sam's son.

James was hesitant. "Harold is gone to Grand Junction with his father."

"James. Do you think Sam is really taking Harold to Grand Junction?"

"Yes. I do. He doesn't know anyone around here. He was alone in the car when he drove up, and he was alone when he drove away. He seemed to be dressed for a trip. He had his suitcases, and he headed for Graden's Bridge."

"What car does he drive?"

"Buick."

"Enclosed?" asked Monroe.

"Yep."

"Where did he put Harold?" asked Monroe.

"What do you mean?"

"Well. Did he put him on a seat or tie him in or did he put him in the back seat and lock the doors, or what?" asked Monroe, urgently.

"Oh. I think he plans to take care of him, if that's what you're asking. He put him in a large basket sitting on the floor, between the gearshift and the passenger's door. When he locked the door, Harold couldn't go anywhere. He could just move around or sleep—whatever. Sam could keep and eye on him at all times." James paused. "It looked pretty good to me, and my Mom didn't say anything."

"How's Wade taking it?"

"All right, I guess." James scratched his head. "He's only eight months old, ya' know."

"Yeah. But I thought he might cry or something," said Monroe.

"No. He's acting okay."

Monroe remained quiet while he felt the pain of separating "his" boys. He wondered if they'd ever get together again. Maybe when they grew up. He hoped so.

"No problems, then," Monroe said.

"No problems. Well, not really."

"What happened, James? Tell me." Monroe was anxious, again.

"Well. When Sam got in his car and Mom had gone into the house, Sam leaned out his window and said 'you can tell your asshole friend that I'm coming back for him—if he ever gets out of jail. He hasn't seen the last of me.'" James smiled a wry smile. "That's a quote."

Monroe tossed his head. "I'm not going to worry too much about it. I've got to testify at tomorrows inquest."

"What's that all about? Did the Sheriff say?"

"He didn't say, but they've arrested Carméllo Basíllo and they probably want to question him with me present. Carméllo is in a cell downstairs. Don't want us in the same part of the jail, I guess." Monroe gazed at James. "Anyway, I told the Sheriff that Carméllo was in the alley when Sam and I fought last January. I also told him: Bob and Earl were there."

"You can't prove that, you know" James admonished. "It'll be your word against theirs."

"Yeah," said Monroe. "But I know the truth. And it lends credence to our KKK theory."

"I know, but it's three against one."

"They have a reason for lying, I don't," Monroe reminded James.

"You need to have the story on the record, anyway. So you just tell the truth and keep on telling the truth. The truth will set you free."

333

"That's all I can hope for. Frankly, I don't care. If it weren't for Wade, I'd just as soon die."

"Baloney! Focus on positive things, Roe. Quit talking nonsense." James turned toward the door. "I'll be there tomorrow. What time?"

"2 o'clock," Monroe answered.

* * *

James arrived late for the second inquest. All attendees were seated in the mortuary and the proceedings had started. Coroner Donald Denison sat in the front row with Assistant District Attorney Joseph O'Riley. They had their heads together. Seemed to be discussing a significant point. The smell of formaldehyde filled the air. Either an embalming had just taken place or someone had spilled a bottle on the floor.

The seating arrangements for this session remained the same except there were eight chairs for officials at the left front of the room instead of the four chairs previously used. In the front row, James recognized Deputies Bob Stout and Earl Mills, but he didn't recognize the man sitting between them. Probably Carméllo Basíllo. Even though Monroe had described the man, James wasn't quite prepared for his appearance. The beady eyes, broad forehead, stringy beard, protruding nose, and dirty face—all looked disgusting. Monroe hadn't mentioned that Basíllo resembled a rat.

James found himself staring at Carméllo's thin lips— his large rectangular mouth that never closed. Inside the gaping mouth were long, heavy, tarter-coated teeth, that peaked through the sparse whiskers on his distorted chin. There were wide gaps between each tooth. His neck and his sloping shoulders became a coiled snake as he hunkered down in his seat. He looked like a demented animal trying to hide in a pile of dirty clothes.

Coroner Denison took a position in front of the witness chair. The second session of Bonnie Morgan's inquest began. James observed some noticeable differences between the two sessions, however. While the same men were in the jury box, the overall crowd was smaller than the first meeting. Sheriff Harvey Howe and Monroe sat alone behind the Deputies and Carméllo. Monroe looked more like a guest than a witness. Steve Sawyer, the Evening Herald reporter, sat on the front row. Carméllo Basíllo sat handcuffed and braced by his deputy friends.

Carméllo was called to the witness chair. He received O'Riley's first questions and denied everything except his ownership of the cabin. He knew nothing of the poisoned meat … nothing of the distilling outfit … nothing of the small strychnine bottle. He had no idea how any of the exhibits got into his cabin. He had no explanation for what happened to the whiskey Monroe saw on the shelves.

When Monroe took the chair, he could not shed light on where the whiskey had gone after he left the cabin, he did emphatically swear that the booze had been there. He clearly remembered the shelves, the stove, the bottles—everything. No. He hadn't seen the little strychnine bottle or the distilling outfit. Other than the candles he'd lit to view the shelves, the cabin had no light. When asked about a possible relationship between himself and Carméllo, Monroe reiterated what had occurred behind Mason and Ambold's Grocery last January. He readily made public his fistfight with Sam Isgar. He told how Mr. Basíllo helped Mr. Isgar back to his hotel, and he spoke of his suspicions regarding the men and their affiliation with the Ku Klux Klan.

But when Bill Hillier, owner of the Ignacio Mercantile and Trading Post, came forward from the audience and testified that Carméllo had purchased strychnine in April and that the small bottle in evidence was the same bottle that had been purchased by Carméllo: Carméllo became unduly excited and had to be subdued. Evidently, Dr. Bronson thought he might be having a stroke because he asked the deputies to take him into an adjourning room where the good doctor could sedate him.

James watched the confusion with interest. He tried to stand within earshot of conversations held by the Coroner, the Sheriff and the District Attorney. The gist of each conversation seemed to revolve around questions associated with the possibility of there being two separate cases co-mingled here. They seemed to think that one case involved the making and selling of illegal booze, and the other case dealt with the accidental death of Bonnie Morgan. The two cases were being mixed because Monroe had stolen some of the illegal booze. In addition, James had the distinct impression that Carméllo may have involved Sam Isgar and the Ku Klux Klan in illegal activities such as burning barns and killing people.

It soon became evident to James that the officials were changing their mind about Monroe. They were beginning to feel a need for additional time to reconnoiter and think the matter through. They saw Bonnie Morgan's death as an accident. The broken neck resulted from Monroe's attempt to save her life—not take it. Carméllo's illegal, poisoned booze was one concern; Monroe's thievery was another.

The questioning of witnesses halted. The meeting adjourned. Coroner Denison announced that the inquest would be continued at a later date.

James sought out the officials, over the next several days, and tried to discuss the subjects he thought might be confounding each official. On Saturday, June the 2nd, they released Monroe and kept Carméllo for further investigation. The inquest took a different direction, but the authorities still waited for a report from the state chemist at Boulder.

* * *

When James, with Sheriff Harvey Howe, came for Monroe on Saturday, June 2ⁿᵈ, the sun was setting. Long shadows stretched across Monroe's cell and flattened themselves against the wall opposite his bunk. Sheriff Howe unlocked Monroe's cell door. "We're going to let you go home, Morgan. Still don't have the report from Boulder, but based on the tests here in Durango, we think the state chemist isn't going to add much. Every last thing you've told us has proven true. You've created a lot of doubt about your guilt. We think we've gone far enough."

Monroe felt guilty while the authorities felt he was innocent! It seemed reasonable to him that he should be punished. But when James moved to take him home to Wade and the Laurences, he put his foot down. "No. I'm going to the cemetery. I want to see Bonnie."

"We can go to the cemetery tomorrow," James argued. "It's getting dark—colder. You're not wearing a warm jacket."

"I'm not going to eat, or anything else, until I've spent time with Bonnie."

"You mean: see Bonnie's grave, don't you?"

"I mean I'm going where Bonnie is." Monroe put his hands in his pockets. "Gonna take me or am I gonna walk?"

James hesitated. "I'll take you, of course. It's just that Mom and Dad are waiting for you. I called them, right away, when I learned you were getting out."

"I want to spend some time with Bonnie. Then, I'll come home." Monroe knew his debt to these people, but he wanted to be near Bonnie.

John Laurence's Model-T was parked directly in front of the courthouse. James drove across the Ninth Street Bridge and into Greenmount Cemetery. When they arrived at the bull elk statue, James turned down the road to the right. He stopped almost immediately. Monroe had been staring into the darkness with his hand on the door latch.

As the car stopped, Monroe leaped out. "You can come back for me in the morning."

"Don't be stupid, Roe. You need warmer clothes."

"Don't worry about me. Go home and get some dinner. Tell the folks I'm not hungry."

"I'll be back in less than hour. If you stay all night, you'll need warm clothes." The car lurched away.

CHAPTER TWENTY

(June 1923)

On through the night, Monroe prayed to God and talked with Bonnie. The giant ponderosa pine near Bonnie's grave towered over the two lovers and remained silent. The grazing elk herd relieved Monroe's loneliness, but nothing disturbed his visit. Before James left the warm clothing, the cold penetrated and dug at Monroe's bones, but he stayed on his knees. He left the grave only once to relieve himself. Twice he lay on the cold ground trying to huddle close to his darling. He couldn't swear he hadn't napped. But lighting a match and looking at his watch seemed to shift him from raw emotion to real thought. It was 4:35 A.M.

As soon as the match went out, he glimpsed an undersized figure beside the tree. Instantly, he recognized his friend, One-armed Charlie. The white gloves still covered both hands. He was still wearing the Prince Albert clothing he'd worn in the jail cell. Monroe stood up and fumbled for another match.

"We can talk without a light, Roe."

"Is it you, Charlie?"

"Who else?" Charlie answered.

Monroe ceased his search for a match and considered how the Laurences might view his behavior. In fact, he thought anyone learning of his night in the cemetery, might consider his behavior bazaar, if not down right crazy. Now, if he told them that Charlie Eagle was standing among the headstones, they'd surely question his sanity. He looked for the moon. There was none. He dropped to his knees, again. Perhaps, he thought, through God, he might regain his sanity and let Bonnie know how much he loved her.

"Don't ignore me, Roe. I'm here to help."

"I know, Charlie. But how?"

"We'll find a way, Roe. Don't give up."

Monroe closed his eyes and prayed. Sometime later, he peeked toward the giant pine tree. Charlie was gone. Monroe continued to pray, and finally an automobile engine purred up the hill. James? Turning his eyes toward the east gate, Monroe recognized Laurence's Ford making its way into the burial ground. True to his word, James was arriving and daylight was at hand. Immediately, Monroe's thoughts turned to his son, Wade. His heart leapt.

"Good morning," James said, stopping the car near Bonnie's grave.

"Good morning yourself." Monroe rounded the car and climbed into the passengers seat. "Take me home, my friend."

"Are you ready?"

"Yes." Then nodding toward the grave, Monroe said, "We never really said 'goodbye', you know."

James glanced at the tip of sun rising and released the emergency brake. The car jumped forward. "The folks will be glad to see you." He shifted from low to second stomping the clutch pedal.

"I'm anxious to see them. How's my boy?"

"He's fine. Trying to walk."

Monroe gazed at James. "Really! I guess that proves he's a Morgan."

The automobile bounced over the dirt road, turned east at the great elk statue and headed for the Laurences. "I'm going to build Bonnie a headstone," Monroe said, firmly.

"Why don't you let Vanarsdal do it? Dad says he does fine work."

"I can do 'fine work' myself. It might take a while—but I'll do it."

* * *

340

John and Mabel rushed from the house to greet him when the car pulled into the driveway. He felt the warmth of their welcome and saw the happiness in their faces.

"Oh, Roe!" Mabel said. "You're home. We're so glad. Come in and have some breakfast."

John reached for Monroe's hand, saying, "Let's go in where you can get warm, my boy."

Monroe kissed Mabel on the cheek while he hugged them both. "Thank you. Thank you both for all you've done."

Mabel took Monroe's hand and literally dragged him up the steps. "Come see Wade," she said. And in the middle of the living room floor, on his hands and knees: Wade. His large, brown eyes and cowlicky hair stared up at his Daddy. Monroe gazed into the brown eyes that said Morgan, but the face screamed: Bonnie! Monroe knew right then that he'd never see the child again without seeing Bonnie, as well.

Monroe stooped, lifted Wade high in the air, turned round and round trying to control his tears. "You look like your mother, young man." He folded the baby in his arms and hugged him as tight as he dared. "Have you been a good boy?"

"Oh, he has. He's been a joy," Mabel gushed.

"I bet. I just bet." Monroe grinned at Mabel.

"Bring him to the table while we eat," John said. "He's got his own high-chair."

When the family had settled at the table, Monroe spoke at length about his gratitude for the Laurences support over the months and especially during these last weeks. He tried to tell them that he was finding it difficult to carry on without Bonnie.

"Last night I prayed a lot," Monroe said. "I tried to develop a plan for going forward with Wade. But, I'm afraid all I really accomplished was a realization that I still need your help. I decided sometime around four this morning that I would ask for your advice. You've been so good, and

I've imposed so heavily, already; I'm ashamed to ask. But for the sake of Bonnie and Wade, I gladly humble myself by begging for your continued assistance. I have no place to turn."

John cleared his throat. "Roe. We understand. We'd be disappointed if we couldn't continue to help. We know it won't be forever. Don't give it another thought. We'll work through this, together."

"You'll never know how much all that means to me."

"We loved Bonnie, too," Mabel said.

John stood and placed his hands on the back of his chair. "What do you have in mind, Roe?"

"Well, I can't ask you to keep Wade indefinitely, and I'm certainly in no position to do it myself, so I thought I'd try to find a foster home for him until I can get Cascade put back together. Then, maybe I could hire someone to live out there with us."

"Well, if you want some advise about that, you're going to get it," Mabel said. "You'd be a damn fool to take him away from me. As a matter of fact, I won't stand for it. Not while I have a breath." Mabel stopped talking with her chin jutting out a mile. "I mean, unless you have a better place to put him." Tears sprang to her eyes.

Monroe leapt from his place at the table and knelt beside Mabel's chair. "Oh, Mabel. There's no better place for him." He placed his arm around Mabel's shoulders. "You're, by far, the very best I could hope for, but I must quit burdening you, eventually."

Mabel lifted her apron to her eyes. "I don't think I could sleep, if I didn't know he was all right."

Monroe searched for words. "I'll be proud and grateful to leave him with you." Then he added: "But I want to pay his way—and mine too. I figure I owe you a lot for all of us: Harold, Wade, Bonnie, and I."

"We'll work that out—in a way that's satisfactory to everyone," John said. "But, how do you plan to go on with your life?"

"Well. I've got to rebuild Cascade—the house and the barn. That'll take a lot of work and plenty of money. That means I'll have to earn money while I'm spending. I figure I can only accomplish both things by moving to Cascade and continuing my whiskey business. I figure I can live in the bunkhouse while I rebuild the place. If I work the house during the day and work the business at night, I might be able to get out of the whiskey business in a year. What do you think, John?"

"I think you've cut a huge chunk of work for yourself. How do you feel, James?"

"I've been thinking about the illegalities of the booze business." "Colorado doesn't have the laws today it may have tomorrow. If we're going to make prohibition meaningful in Colorado—like I assume they have in Ohio, for example— we'll have laws on the books that make moon-shining a very risky business."

"I've been thinking about that, too," Monroe said. "That's one reason I want to get out after a year—or sooner—if I can. And, too, I don't need more jail time to explain to my son when he's older. I'm not sure I can ever explain, now."

"Think you'll have Cascade free and clear in a year?" John asked.

"I could take everything I've got in the bank and pay Cascade off now, but I've already paid the interest, in advance, for a year. I worked that deal with McGovern after Mother died. If I let the deal ride and try to rebuild the place, maybe I can start fresh around this time next year."

James scratched his head. "Does that mean you intend to leave your still in the mine at Porter and travel between Cascade and Porter during the coming year?"

343

"Yes. Oh, I could move everything into the hills behind Cascade—or the gold mine, maybe—but the mine's too hard to get to, and why move anyway. My still's all set up."

"Sheriff Howe would have a harder time finding your mine," James pointed out.

"Yeah, but why would he think I'm using Porter, again?"

James looked out the window. "Maybe the Sheriff or Bob or Earl will keep an eye on you for curiosity sake?"

"Do you think I shouldn't take the chance?"

"No, not really," said James. "There's not much the Sheriff could do, even if he found you with the still. The District Attorney is worrying over that question right now. Wondering how it applies to Carméllo Basíllo. We've got Federal Law declaring Prohibition and establishing some jurisdiction, but to arrest and imprison citizens for making booze—well—it'll probably take a Colorado state law. And, in Carméllo's case, even if there was a law against having a still, they can't prove the still you took the whiskey from belonged to Carméllo. He admits the cabin is his, but he says he don't know anything about a still—whiskey—or poison. And as far as the strychnine bottle, it's Carméllo's word against the storeowner in Ignacio. That's all the law has."

"I think I'll take a chance, for a year. What do you think?" Monroe looked for assurance from all the Laurences.

John smiled. "We're always here, if you get caught."

James put out a hand and touched Monroe's arm. "I'll keep on top of the law."

Mabel lifted Wade from his highchair. "I think our boy wants to get cleaned up. I'll put him down and be right back."

John retrieved the coffeepot and poured another cup. "What else do we need to decide?"

Monroe gazed at John and thought a moment. "Since I've decided to make a headstone for Bonnie, could I get you to vouch for me with Vanarsdal?"

John looked surprised. "<u>You're</u> going to cut it, yourself?"
"Yes."

"Out of stone? Granite?"

"I think so. I'm not sure. I'll try granite first."

James looked quizzically at Monroe, then at his father. "Ever carve granite, Roe?"

"No. But I can learn,"

"From Vanarsdal?"

"I guess so. He'd the only one in town, isn't he? I thought I'd buy a headstone for mother and talk about a headstone for Bonnie."

Mabel came into the kitchen. "Did I hear you right? You want to buy a headstone for your Mother and make one for Bonnie?"

"That's what I'm planning." Monroe looked at his benefactors. "Something wrong?"

"No-o-o-o," John said. "But with everything else you have to do … well, I don't think you become a stonecutter overnight."

"I know. Maybe I can't make her a <u>proper</u> headstone <u>right away</u>. But I'm going to make it as soon as possible. I want her to have something special. You think I'm crazy?" Monroe turned to John. "John?" "James?" "Mabel?"

With tears in her eyes, Mabel bent and kissed the top of Monroe's head. "I think you're wonderful."

* * *

Two weeks later, Monroe stopped by the cemetery to visit Bonnie. He was on his way to Porter mine. It was his practice, now days, to call on Bonnie every day whether he went to Porter or not.

Today, inside the cemetery gate, the grounds were silent except for the Blue Jay's scolding each other as they flitted from tree to tree. Often, in the past, deer or elk grazed quietly while he prayed or whispered softly to Bonnie. Now, the wildlife seemed to know him and they seemed to understand his great sorrow.

Strange that he should remember it now, but Bonnie crossed herself just before she died. <u>Why hadn't he thought of it before?</u> He raised his eyes to heaven. Scanned the sky for an answer. <u>Bonnie had died without unction of any kind!</u> His mind kept repeating the condemnation.

Finally, he resolved to ask Father O'Malley whether Bonnie could have some kind of anointing ceremony after being buried. Then, he began to worry about the day he might be forced to miss a visit. Surely it could happen. Surely, missing a visit would happen. The idea shocked him. He'd have to do something about that.

The graveyard was like a park to him. It was gorgeous at twilight. The oak trees, the pines, the grass, the box elders, the lilac bushes, the piñons and the junipers; all things growing and changing through time, as life moved on, providing a beautiful place for his darling. Even Charlie appeared, from time to time, as if waiting for Monroe to tell him what to do.

After each visit, Monroe practiced special precautions for leaving the grounds. If he were going to Cascade, he watched at every downtown corner to see if someone might be tailing him. If he were going to Porter, he varied his paths through town and watched for potential followers. From time to time he felt foolish, but regardless, he continued his watchfulness.

On this particular evening, on his way to Porter, Monroe drove his truck down the hill, crossed the Ninth Street Bridge, headed east into town and stopped at the corner of Ninth Street and Main Avenue. He purposely parked near the First National Bank, got out and walked around the corner to the bank's front door. He knew the bank wasn't open, but he cupped his hands against the windowpane as though he expected to see someone inside. Shaking his head to indicate that he'd failed his expectation, he walked to the middle of the sidewalk and gazed up and down Main Avenue. His actions would indicate that whomever he'd planned to see, might be late. This time, nothing out of the ordinary caught his eye, so he went to his truck and drove north, pretending to go home. However, at Twelfth Street, he turned east to Third Avenue, then turned south to Sixth Street and went west out of town toward Porter. Throughout the entire maneuver, Monroe saw nothing suspicious.

He always drove into Porter just after dusk. If any one were there, he reasoned, they would surely have their lights on—either in a house or on the road. He was particularly watchful for wagons, buggies and saddle horses because he knew lights would not be used. When he saw neither people nor lights, he'd park his truck in the lean-to near the entrance to the mine. The truck would remain hidden from anyone who might be traveling the road below.

When he was confident he'd not been seen, either going to or stopping at Porter, he began his circuitous climb to the slope tunnel he had used when he and Bonnie lived in the superintendent's house over a month ago.

On this particular evening, Monroe entered the tunnel, found his lantern hung on the iron pipe he'd placed there for that very purpose, lit the lantern and made his way down the slope to the large room where he kept his still. Once in the room, he continued with his security procedures by checking the floor surface for strange footprints. He thoroughly investigated the three different drifts that radiated from the central room. Also, he checked the dust on the old boards that covered a shaft that had been used during an exploratory dig for another vein of coal thought to be below the main stratum. He even checked the dust on the winch handle. Thus, he was assured that no one had raised or lowered the lift since he last visited.

Satisfied that no one had been near his still, Monroe lit three additional lanterns and hung them on spikes he'd driven into eight-by-eight stanchions. All stanchions worked together with numerous other supports to buttress the room's ceiling. Next, he extinguished the lantern he'd brought down the slope tunnel and set it aside. He didn't want to waste kerosene.

He gave the still a cursory investigation. Everything was normal. The last of some peach mash was distilling. So, while the fermented wine completed the process, he decided to begin filling quart bottles with some of the brandy he'd brought from Grand Junction.

He hadn't completed filling the fifth bottle when he heard a voice reverberate through the room. "Don't make a move, you sonuvabitch, or you're a dead man."

Intuitively, Monroe knew the voice came from Sam Isgar. He hadn't heard Sam's voice all that much, but who else could it be.

"Turn around, slowly," growled the voice.

Monroe turned to face Sam. "Where are your friends, Sam? Not the one already in jail, but the other two that should be."

Monroe knew he must keep talking calmly and not give in to the fear sticking in his throat. His tongue dried. "Been following me, huh? Like to sneak up behind people, don't you?"

"Turn around and back-up against that stanchion there." Sam nodded to the nearest wooden ceiling support. One of Monroe's lanterns hung overhead.

"Move!" Sam grunted, while waving his chrome-plated revolver in the direction he expected Monroe to step. The gun looked like a forty-four. The black hole at the end of the muzzle yawned wide.

"Put your arms behind your back. Reach around the post."

Monroe did as he was told. His mind raced as he tried to develop a plan before his wrists were tied. Sam moved behind the post and Monroe felt a handcuff clamp tight on his right wrist.

"Stay steady, you sonuvabitch, or I'll blast you. Push that left hand back here."

Monroe felt the cuff clasp tight over his left wrist. A sharp pain shot through his shoulders as he allowed his body to ease away from the big stanchion. To clear the pain, he leaned back and placed the small of his back tight against the buttress.

"Now. Let's talk, asshole," Sam said moving around front and stepping back a pace while placing his gun in his shoulder holster.

"Where are your friends?"

"Why in the hell are you so concerned about my friends, asshole?"

"Because you've always had somebody to front for you. I'm not aware that you've ever done anything in your life when you didn't have someone front for you. Someone to hide behind."

"Well. You're in for a surprise, then," said Sam. "I've never killed anyone with a crowd watching. And this time, you've been a lot of help to me because you've selected a perfect place. No one around. No one to see. No one to hear. I doubt they'll ever find you." It seemed Sam had a second thought. "Oh, maybe your friend James … James Laurence isn't it? I think, so. Maybe he'll find you."

"Okay, Isgar." Monroe was anxious to know what Sam's next move would be. "I take it you want to kill me, but not right away. Correct?"

Sam stuck his face within inches of Monroe face and stared deep into Monroe's eyes. His face twisted into a sneer, then, he tried to grin. "God damn you, Morgan. I hate you so much I can barely look at you without vomiting."

Monroe gazed at the ceiling. "You probably won't believe this, Sam, but I feel much the same way about you. Why don't you get on with it?"

"When I planned this, you asshole, I thought I'd just kill you and leave you to rot. But, the more I thought about it, the more I realized that that would let you off the hook."

Sam turned and walked a few steps away. He stopped. Turned around. Then, slowly and insidiously, he removed a sheaf of papers from his breast pocket.

"What Bonnie saw in you, I'll never know," said Sam.

"Ditto," replied Monroe.

"I have a contract here, you asshole. You're going to sign it or I'm going to kill you without a second thought."

Confusion crowded Monroe's mind. Sam had a contract … a proposition of some kind. Monroe didn't care one way or the other about dying, but he didn't want to enter into a contract with Sam Isgar, either. In fact, just a few weeks ago he'd thought death was appropriate for himself. He had reasoned then, that Wade would get all his worldly possessions and the Laurences would raise Wade a lot better than he would. James, being a lawyer, would probably benefit Wade a lot. He reasoned, if he had any brains, at all, Bonnie would still be alive and life would be worth living. So, even now, who cared?

"Go ahead, shoot." Monroe's voice echoed down the mine tunnels.

Sam looked up in surprise. "Hey! You dumb sonuvabitch. You don't know my proposition yet. Don't be so eager to die. Do you <u>want</u> to die?

Monroe gazed into the black tunnel on his right. "Don't bore me," he said.

"You wanna take the easy way out, don't you? You want somebody else to pick up after you, don't you?"

Sam's words startled Monroe. He'd never thought about in just that way—somebody picking up after him. Suddenly he realized that Sam might be right. Dying would be a coward's way out. Dying would be sweet compared to living without Bonnie. Even Sam had a higher opinion of himself than he did.

The thought rankled Monroe. "What's your proposition?"

"Now. That's better, Morgan. Do you hold life dear? Want to live?"

"Why?" asked Monroe.

"Because you may have someone depending on you—some one needing you. You don't want to let anyone down, do you? If I shoot you, it'd be like committing suicide, wouldn't it? And being a good Catholic, suicide would be a sin, wouldn't it?"

"You're just full of good arguments, Sam. What's your proposition?"

Sam continued. "This contract is legal and, when you sign it, it's binding. If you signed it, I'd consider your debt to me paid and I'd live up to my end of the deal. Signing it would mean you could start over again."

"So what's your proposition?"

"You give me Cascade and any other property you have—you give me this still—for example—although it's not mentioned in this contract. We'll just let that be a little understanding between gentlemen. You give me Wade and let him grow up with his brother, Harold. You simply take your truck and all the money you have in the bank and leave Colorado. You never return under any circumstances."

"And, why should I do this?" Monroe couldn't believe he was hearing Sam correctly.

"You should do this to make restitution for stealing my wife. You should do this to get from under a tremendous burden you've created for yourself. You should do this in order to save your own fucking life." Sam's voice pitched higher and higher as he spoke.

"Sam. How do I know you wouldn't shoot me as soon as I signed the paper?"

"You can trust me, Morgan. My word is my bond. All I want is payment for the pain and suffering you've heaped on me. I want to know that you suffer every day of your life—one way or another—without that little bastard you and Bonnie brought into the world. To the good: you can satisfy your religion by refusing to commit suicide and you can rest assured that the bastard will have a good life— probably better than he'd get with you—as long as he pleases my boy, Harold."

Monroe recognized a plan forming. "Well, you're probably right, but, if I do as you ask and clear out forever, would you mind satisfying some of my questions? I have questions that would haunt me for the rest of my life if I didn't ask them now. Questions only you can answer. I won't be able to do anything about the answers, even if I know the truth because I have no proof. It might even make you happier to know that I know the truth and can't do anything about it."

"Ask your questions. If I can answer them, I will," promised Sam.

"You'll tell me the truth, then. Is that right?" asked Monroe.

"Yep."

"Who burned my barn, hurt my mother and shot Charlie Eagle?" asked Monroe.

Sam remained silent while he casually gazed about the mine. "Bob Stout and Earl Mills. They were carrying out a mission for the Ku Klux Klan. I ordered the mission."

Monroe swallowed hard. "You ordered the burning of Charlie on the cross in my front yard when you blew up my house, too, I suppose?"

"Yep. Well. I wasn't there, but I ordered the house blown up and the boys thought it better to kill Charlie than to deal with him later. He knew everybody there."

"And you blew up the trestle across this valley just to give Bonnie and me a hard time, is that right?"

"We'd have killed you both, if I could have thought of a sure way to keep Harold safe while we blasted the rest of you." Sam spoke matter-of-factly.

"Were you with the men who dynamited our truck as Bonnie and I drove back from Grand Junction?"

"I wasn't with them, but they were carrying out my orders. We had you under surveillance all the while you were in Grand Junction." Sam seemed to be enjoying himself.

"Who did Charlie recognize, that night at Cascade?"

Sam smiled. "He recognized Carméllo and Bob. Carméllo said Charlie would be a dangerous man to leave alive. They also thought it'd be a good lesson, if you lost a friend."

"Did Carméllo put the strychnine in the hooch I took from his cabin?"

"Yes," Sam admitted.

"Did Carméllo do the distillation job that allowed fusel oil to remain in the hooch?"

"We didn't know anything about fusel oil until they broke the news during the inquest," said Sam. Then, Sam elaborated: "I made Carméllo get rid of the stuff. He carried it miles away and dumped it on the ground."

"The still belonged to the Klan, right?"

"Of course." Sam folded the papers he held in his hand and put them back into his pocket. "Any more questions you can't prove."

Monroe felt sick, but shook his head from side to side. He knew he had to get out of those handcuffs. He had to overcome Sam and get his big gun, even if he died in the attempt. "Can I read the contract?"

"There's no need. It explains that you're of sound mind and not under duress. In fact, it explains that I'm doing you a big favor by relieving you of so many heavy burdens." Sam pushed his face close to Monroe. "You say that you realize that you did a very bad thing when you interfered with me, my wife, and my child. You're sorry. You want to make amends. This contract is restitution for your wantonness."

Monroe twisted and tensed himself against the timber. "I can't sign anything cuffed to this roof support."

"Okay. I'm going to unlock the cuffs, but I'll have my gun on you with the hammer cocked. If you make a false move, I'll shoot you, at close range. And I won't shoot just one shot. I'll unload three or four in your gut. That way, you'll die slow and painful as your blood seeps out on the cold floor." Sam grinned. "Do you want that? It'd be better if you go down the road and hide for the rest of your life. If they find you dead, they'll think you died protecting your booze: the stuff you and Bonnie loved more than life itself." Sam laughed a low chuckle.

Monroe breathed deeply. "You win, Sam. Let's get it over with."

Sam pulled his gun, cocked it, and moved the gun to his left hand. He dug into his pocket, retrieved keys and walked behind the stanchion. Monroe heard a key slip into the lock. He felt one cuff drop from his right wrist. He continued to hold the left wrist as though he expected to have that cuff removed also. Sure enough, Sam complied.

Just at that moment a loud hissing ensued from the boiler on the stove. The distilling process had completed its cycle.

"Can I set that boiler off the stove? It's dry and the residue will burn. Makes an awful mess."

"Remember, any false move gets you plugged."

"I won't try anything."

Monroe tried to calm himself as he walked to the stove massaging his wrists. He lifted the boiler from the stove. Sam stayed some ten feet away.

"I'll just set it over here," Monroe said, indicating a table with a barrel sitting on it. "There's water in that barrel, and I need some in here. This stuff won't come out, if I don't."

Sam stood his ground. Monroe had to get closer.

Monroe splashed the boiler. "Want me to put a lantern on the table, so I can sign?"

"Put the lantern on that table over there and take that chair." Sam waved his gun indicating where he wanted things placed.

With the lantern on the table and the chair sitting by, Monroe waited. Sam moved two steps closer, and then stopped cautiously.

"Sit down," Sam ordered.

"I don't have a pen," Monroe pointed out.

"Don't worry. I do. I'm going to uncap it and clip it to the contract. I'll lay the contract on the table with my left hand and keep you covered with my right—so don't get any funny ideas."

Monroe tried to smile. "Sam. You seem a little jumpy. Don't get nervous and fire that dammed thing before you're ready." Monroe turned slightly to his left and raised his right arm to clear the table for Sam.

As Sam extended his left hand to lay the paper on the table, Monroe gripped the pen in his right hand and without stopping the movement, swung the pen in a blurred arc that sent the pen stabbing into the flesh on the back of Sam's gun hand. The gun roared. The bullet zipped across Monroe's chest and tugged at his jacket as he continued to move in Sam's direction. Out of the chair, like a cat, Monroe sent his left fist crashing into Sam's jaw. Sam screamed with pain and dropped the gun. Stumbling backward, Sam tried to regain his balance. Monroe was on him, grappling to find a hold that would subdue Sam. He finally had Sam by the neck. But Sam was bigger and stronger than he'd remembered.

Neither man uttered a word. It was a death struggle. Sam tried to pull Monroe's arm from around his neck and Monroe felt slick, warm blood slide across his jaw while Sam's torn hand gushed red. Monroe decided to lift Sam bodily and smash him into one of the stanchions—hopefully, breaking his back or one of his limbs. The maneuver failed. Sam wriggled away.

Sam reached for a quart bottle. Monroe, discerning Sam's objective, grabbed him just before he reached the weapon. They whirled each other around, circle after circle, gasping for air in the heavy dust that was kicked up by their feet. Finally, they bumped into the platform winch, which was secured to the edge of the covered shaft. They punched and scratched desperately.

Sam seemed to be getting the upper hand. Monroe found himself in a hammerlock with Sam on his back squeezing his windpipe with a forearm. Monroe struggled to break the hold. It was do or die. He whipped his body forward in a quick jackknife maneuver that threw Sam off the ground and onto the dusty boards that covered the shaft. Sam scrambled to his feet. The boards cracked. Sam's expression registered surprise—then shock. He couldn't move, if he expected the old boards to remain intact.

Regardless of his attempt to put off the inevitable, the brittle covering beneath his feet held for only a moment, and then gave way altogether. Sam disappeared from view. Dust rose above the shaft. Sam was gone, but he found his tongue when he landed on a platform about twenty-five feet below the winch.

"You sonuvabitch! You dirty sonuvabitch," Sam shrieked from the shaft.

Monroe ran for the gun. He found the weapon in the dirt beneath the table. Grabbing the gun, he blew debris from its cylinders, gripped the butt in his right hand and hurried back to the shaft.

Sam was struggling to balance himself on the lift platform. Monroe shoved the revolver into his waistband and rushed to lower the lift a few feet deeper into the shaft. He wanted to make it more difficult for Sam to climb out. He fumbled with the latch that locked the winch handle in place. A spring fell out in his hand and the latch came off. The drum, which held the lifting rope, began to unwind. The drum spun and the platform fell bouncing into the sides of the shaft. The winch handle began to whirl at a rate that made it impossible for Monroe to stop the action. Shortly, the drum was completely unwound.

Sam had screamed his way deep into the dark and forbidding hole. Monroe stood in shocked surprise. No one could have foreseen the accident.

Monroe cautiously approached the shaft. Peered into darkness. He could hear Sam far below. "Help! Help!" Sam pleaded.

Monroe fixed a fascinated gaze on the triple circle of binders' twine that attached the rope to the drum.

His first thought was simply—cut the twine. Let the rope fall. Be rid of Sam forever. Then, he changed his mind. If Sam pulled heavily on the rope, the twine would eventually break or come undone. He—Monroe wouldn't have to kill him—Sam would kill himself. While he contemplated the turn of events, he thought he'd continue with the work he'd planned for the evening. He'd think about cutting the twine and replacing the boards. He felt compelled to finish the work that needed done.

But just as he turned away, he spied Charlie standing cross-legged with the toe of his right shoe pointing to the cement slab that secured the winch. Charlie leaned his left elbow lightly on the drum, straightened his right arm before him and let his thumb extend stiff above his hand.

CHAPTER TWENTY-ONE

(June 1923)

Sam Isgar found himself skinned, bruised, and bleeding at the bottom of the mineshaft. He couldn't see the blood, but he was well aware of the battering his body had taken when the platform kept wedging itself against the sides of the shaft and stopping abruptly for a moment before it continued to fall. Finally, he and the platform had hit the bottom of the shaft. None of his bones were broken. His eyes were okay. He had all his teeth and he still had the use of both hands, both arms and both legs—well, the right hand hurt like hell. The pen must have torn some muscles—badly. The damage to his ego was immeasurable. The darkness confounded him beyond comprehension. Total blackness everywhere. That he couldn't tolerate. He began to panic.

When he grabbed the ropes that canopied above the lift, he found himself looking straight up. He thought he saw a dim light, but he couldn't be sure. Maybe it was light from one of the lanterns Monroe had hung on a stanchion! Maybe the lantern hung near the pit entrance into which he had fallen.

That dammed lift had crashed into the sides of the shaft over and over again. But thank God, the bumping—while extremely rough—had slowed the thing down as it hurtled through the blackness. That bumping and slowing may have saved his life. It seemed a miracle that the platform hadn't shattered into a million pieces—so violent was the contact with the sidewalls. The level at which he stood, must be, conservatively, a hundred-fifty feet below the room above.

After he'd yelled, "Help" and had time to think about it, he was sorry he'd yelled. Sorry he'd given Morgan any idea that he'd ask him for help. After all, the rope was still attached to something up there at the top. All was not lost.

He grabbed the rope and tried to scale the wall by placing his feet tight against the sandstone pit walls. He found that he was not tall enough to span the distance created between the wall and the rope. Next, he thought he'd just travel up the rope—hand-over-hand. But, as he struggled on the rope, his wounded right hand began to ache severely. Nevertheless, he continued his climb and finally reached a point some fifteen feet off the floor. There, he learned that his strength wouldn't allow him to go farther, and he realized that he didn't have the strength to ease himself back down the rope, either. What if he should fall? What if he should fall and land awkwardly—perhaps twist an ankle or break a leg? What if, in the darkness, he should straddle one of the ropes still attached to the lift—that could do some real damage to his genitals? Oh God! What could he do! Wouldn't he burn his bare hands by <u>sliding</u> down the rope? Panic returned again.

Quickly grabbing handfuls of his coat tails and wedging the tails between the rope and his hands, he slid carefully back to the platform. Still resisting a call for help, he sat quietly in the dark, fighting panic. God, he wished he hadn't decided to attack Monroe at all!

He stood and extended his hands to the wall directly in front of him. Touching the wall, he stepped sideways and continued to sidestep until he had some idea of the size and shape of his prison. The hole was basically round. The platform, on which he'd stood, was basically square. That gave the impression that the shaft itself was intended to be square. But the condition that made his situation impossible was the fact that the circumference of the hole was so big. Too big and too deep to climb out of—even with the help of a rope. When that fact dawned on him, his hair began to creep. Chill-bumps popped out all over his skin. He felt dizzy. The blackness thickened. He thought he'd faint!

Sam clutched the rope and screamed, "AARROOOUUU!" He felt hot. "Get me out of here, you sonuvabitch!" He blindly searched for a rope attached to the lift, and when he found one, he shook it, reached for another and tugged both, all in a mad frenzy. He screamed, cried, yelled. After about five minutes, his throat ached. His voice began to squeak. More air than sound emitted from his throat. He began to fear he'd destroyed his voice. Oh, my God! What could he do? Nothing? No! He rejected that idea, out of hand. But still—what could he do? He could do nothing! The idea was so bitter—so sickening—he began to vomit.

"Hey, down there," shouted Monroe. "How do you like having your own little world? Can I get you something? A drink of water, perhaps? You've been yelling a lot, and I don't know what's happening to you, but generally speaking, yelling like that makes me thirsty. Now, don't get the idea that I mind your screaming, because I don't. You're so far away the noise doesn't bother me. In fact, I hardly hear you."

Monroe stopped talking. Sam listened in silence. He felt exhausted. His mind was numb.

"Well. I'm going home now," Monroe shouted. "First, I'm going to visit Bonnie's grave. I'll tell her where you are. You better pray nothing happens to me between now and the time I get back. I'm your best hope of survival. Think about it."

Sam gripped the lift's central rope. Shook it. The rope vibrated through the air. It reminded him of the jerking sensation he felt when he hooked a large fish. But before he could analyze the feeling further, the rope came plummeting down the shaft, draping itself over his head and shoulders, and forming coils about his feet at the bottom of the pit. The sonuvabitch had detached the rope!

* * *

Shortly after leaving Sam in the mineshaft, Monroe drove into Greenmount Cemetery and parked in the roadway beside Bonnie's grave. After he'd turned the engine and the headlights off, he found himself surrounded by moonlight and silence. He stepped quietly from his truck, eased the door shut and paused beside the truck. He wanted to make sure he didn't disturb the deer, not fifty feet away.

Impressed again with the beauty of the place, Monroe allowed his eyes to move slowly into every visible space. He walked lightly to a spot beside Bonnie's grave, knelt and removed his hat. "Honey," he said. "I've got a lot to report tonight. I need to tell you what's happened today." He glanced toward the deer herd when he heard them jump to attention. Seeing nothing, he assumed a coyote or a mountain lion might be prowling. "Okay. Its plain Sam Isgar has been following me, because tonight he came into the mine and surprised me. He's still trying to punish me for taking you away from him. I know you'll argue that you made the decision yourself. But, anyway, he had some cockeyed scheme whereby he thought I'd give him Cascade and Wade. Well, to make a long story short, I threw him down that old mine shaft in the big room where I'm distilling brandy. It was an accident, but I feel like leaving him there and just covering the shaft over. Thought I'd talk to you first." Monroe glanced again at the deer. They were grazing contentedly. "What do you think?"

At that moment, Monroe became aware of Charlie, partly shaded by moonlit shadows near the big pine above Bonnie's grave. Charlie's presence did not deter Monroe.

Waiting for Bonnie's reply and getting none, Monroe said, "I know you're concerned about the church. I know you'll think that if I leave him down the shaft, and get away with it, I'll still be a murderer." Monroe reached for a small, dead branch that had fallen from the giant pine. He snapped the twig and stuck a piece in his mouth. "You'll probably ask how I'd explain all this to Wade … if events demand it … about killing the father of his half-brother, and all. You're probably wondering how I'd explain … or get around explaining … Sam's death to the Laurences and the Jacksons. You're probably wondering why I don't think of some other way to rid us of Sam Isgar."

Monroe turned away, searching for the moon. The orb was big and very bright—quite a lovely sight. "Honey, I think I'll sit on your other side. I'm blocking your view of the moon."

After he'd re-arranged himself, he waited, quietly watching the deer and glancing toward Charlie. Suddenly, an idea came. "You know, Honey—what I ought to do? I ought to do to him what he tried to do to me. He got real confidential this evening and admitted burning the barn, destroying the house, killing Charlie and everything else. I could write all that down and get him to sign it. Then release him from the shaft. If he doesn't take care of Harold or if he continues to bother Wade and me, I could give the signed confession to the law and let them prosecute. What do you think?" His eyes wandered to Charlie. Charlie raised his right hand, signaled thumbs-up, and faded away.

The longer he concentrated on the idea, the better he liked it. He had truly damaged Sam, and possibly Harold, too, when he interfered with the marriage.

"Of course," Monroe continued. "Sam may have told someone he was going to Porter this evening, but I doubt it. He indicated that he liked to be very secretive when he killed someone—and he intended to kill me. If I had signed his contract, he'd have the best of both worlds. He'd have my property, my son, and no worry about me changing my mind in the future."

Monroe stood. "Honey, I'm going to spend some time with Vanarsdal learning to cut stone. I've promised to work for him one day a week, if he'll teach me how to carve granite. As soon as I'm able, I'll start your headstone. Maybe I'll start with wood. It'd be faster."

"Back to Isgar," Monroe said. "I know James will say Sam's confession would be obtained under duress and that such a confession wouldn't hold up in a court of law, but I think it might work for us, because it involves the Ku Klux Klan and Sam's political ambitions as well as his murderous intent and property damage. The whole story in the Evening Herald might prove very embarrassing to Mr. Isgar, whether or not it held up in court. Sam's fear of publicity might keep him off our backs forever. I'm going to try it. If he don't bite, I'll seriously consider leaving him there and condemn my own soul to hell, in the process."

Monroe knelt, brushed debris from the grave, stared at the moon for a moment, and then said: "God bless you, my darling. I'll see you tomorrow." He rose and walked to the truck. The engine broke the silence. Deer raised their heads and watched as the truck slowly pulled away.

* * *

Monroe arrived at Porter the following afternoon. He was anxious to check on Sam. He'd gotten James concurrence about his idea and they had worked hard on the confession. They felt everything had been covered.

He brought a wicker basket with a lid, a new ball of binder twine, a fountain pen, and the confession he and James had written and re-written. In addition, he had two big ham sandwiches for Sam—just in case the man cooperated.

When Monroe entered the underground room, he did so in a particularly quiet mode. Continuing his silent alertness, he lit three lanterns and hung them on his respective pegs. He picked up a clean jar, filled it with drinking water from a twenty-five-gallon barrel and grabbed a jug. Using a funnel, he poured the jar of water into the jug.

Taking a handsaw, he searched for a one by six-inch board. He measured off three feet, marked it, and sawed the board in two. Next, he picked up the three-foot board and carried it with him to the winch platform. He loosely fit a ball of binder's twine over the winches' handle, using the center hole in the ball of twine. With the twine positioned, he tied the twine's loose end to the jugs finger loop. Retrieving his spare lanterns, he shook each in search of the one that had the least amount of kerosene. One was nearly dry. He took that lantern, tied a loop in the string some ten to twelve feet back from the water jug, then looped the string over the lantern's bail and tied it tight. He lit the lantern and set it aside.

"Isgar," Monroe shouted. No response. "Isgar. Answer me." Silence prevailed while Monroe paused to listen. "Now, don't act like you don't hear me. Playing games today won't buy you anything. I've got water for you. If you play your cards right, I've got food, also."

Monroe waited quietly. He thought he heard a movement at the bottom of the pit. He couldn't be sure.

Monroe leaned far over the edge. "Speak up, Isgar. Want a drink? Can't live without water, you know."

"Give me the water," Sam growled. "You're a sonuvabitch, you know?"

"Yeah. I know," Monroe agreed. "But I'm going to send the water on a piece of string, anyway. The string has a lantern tied about ten feet above the water. Don't fuck with the string—for any reason—or any of the items I've tied onto it. Got that? There's only one way you're going to win today and that's if you do exactly as I say." Monroe paused. "Say you hear me,"

"I hear you," Sam said, grudgingly.

"Say you understand," Monroe pressed.

"Okay, for Christ's sake!"

"All right. Here comes the water and the lantern."

Monroe put on his gloves, wrapped the twine around his left hand and threaded the water jug over the side until the line had fed past the lantern and beyond. He looked for a way to fasten the string to the winch after he'd lowered the lantern to a position where he could see Sam at the bottom of the pit. "Can you reach the jug now?"

"No. Ten more feet."

"Okay. Here it comes."

Monroe paid out a good ten foot of line. He watched Sam catch the jug and drink greedily.

"You're sure as hell stingy with your water. I'm still thirsty."

"I bet you are. Well, there's more water up here, but you'll have to return the jug to get it. And—oh—I almost forgot. There's not much kerosene in that lantern, so we don't have a lot of time to talk—or argue, whichever."

"Talk about what?"

"I'll show you next time around, Sam. I'm going to bring the jug back. You ready?"

"I guess. Who's the one with games now?" asked Sam, grudgingly.

Monroe looped the binder's twine and tied two knots in the string as a signal to when he'd released the same amount of string again. That would be Sam's depth inside the pit. With his knots marking the depth of the shaft, he lifted the twine constructing a loose pile, which lay in circles at his feet. When the lantern came up, he set it on the winch platform and retrieved the jug.

"Get me out of here, Morgan. We can settle things when you get me up there. I won't be hard to deal with. I promise."

"Just a minute," Monroe shouted back. "I've got something for you to read."

Monroe brought his three-foot board over to the twine he'd circled on the ground. He began to wind the string, end for end, around the board. He counted the loops as he worked.

"One, two, three ..." he counted under his breath. All told, there were twenty-seven wraps. "Let's see, 27 times 6—is 162 feet. That's what I thought. He's about one-hundred-sixty-two feet down."

365

He retrieved the wicker basket from the table, opened the basket to assure that he'd placed the three-page, hand-written document inside, taped the basket closed, and carried it to the winch platform. There, he cut the twine at a point approximately six feet beyond the one-hundred-sixty-two-foot mark, wound the added six-foot length around the winch drum and tied it securely. He replaced the broken latch on the winch and tested it. The winch seemed to work properly.

"Okay, Sam," Monroe shouted. "I'm going to send down a wicker basket. In the basket, you'll find a fountain pen and a document for you to sign. You are not to harm, destroy or in anyway damage this document. It is the one thing in the entire world that can guarantee your continued life. If you sign it, I will lift you to the surface. If you do not maintain the document in good condition—if you do not properly sign the document—or if you do not return the document to me in good condition: I will leave you where you are for the rest of time. It's your choice. Do you understand?"

"I thought you said you brought some food, Morgan."

"We'll get to that. Do you understand what I've just said to you?"

"Yes," Sam screamed. "Get the God Dammed paper down here!"

Monroe attached the wicker basket to the end of the line and began lowering it. Next he placed the lantern on the line and let both the basket and the lantern swing free. When he had the basket close over Sam's head, he held the twine secure in his left hand while he cranked the winch to take up the slack at his end of the twine. Next, he released the left handhold and let the basket and the lantern float in the air. He checked to assure that his rigging was correct. He unlatched the winch, applied the brake and practiced controlling the load. Soon the basket was within Sam's reach. "Now take the basket and remove the pen and paper.

I'll lower the lantern when you get the basket open. Save the tape so you can secure the basket lid after you sign and date the papers."

Sam opened the basket and removed the articles. As he read, Monroe could hear him grumble. Finally, he said: "You sonuvabitch! You sonuvabitch! You've tricked me."

"Whatever do you mean, Sam?" asked Monroe, innocently.

"I shouldn't have admitted anything."

"Why not, Sam? Confession is good for the soul."

"What will you do with it, if I sign it?" Sam wanted to know.

"I'll arrange for the authorities, here and in Grand Junction, to get it, if and when, you don't live up to the agreement."

"What if I don't sign?" asked Sam.

"Then, I'll leave you down there where you are— forever—in the dark—with no food or water."

"That'd put Harold in desperate straights, wouldn't it? Bonnie'd roll over in her grave, if anything ever happened to Harold, you know."

"I don't know, Sam. Harold would inherit your entire estate. The Courts would probably continue to pay the folks you've hired to raise him. Maybe I could get him back with me and Wade. He'd probably get your money when he's of age—if there is any. He might get along better without you. Anyway, I'm not going to worry too much about Harold, right now. I'll look in on him, whether you're alive or not."

Monroe waited in silence while Sam thought it over. Again, he searched his mind for details he might have overlooked.

"I guess I have to sign—if I want to live." Sam was speaking more to himself than to Monroe.

"Are you going to sign, Sam?"

"Yes." Sam's destruction was at hand.

"Then be sure you sign your correct and legal signature, Sam—and date it."

"Fuck you! You wouldn't know my <u>legal</u> signature if it jumped up and bit you."

"Don't be a fool, Sam," Monroe admonished. "Bonnie has your signature on several things, all legal documents signed the same way. Trust me. I <u>know</u> your correct and legal signature. If I don't see that signature when I pull the basket up—I'll exercise my options." Monroe waited for sounds at the bottom of the pit. "Come on, Sam. Get it over with."

"Okay. Okay."

Monroe thought he saw Sam dust a spot on the platform, lay the papers on the boards and take the pen in his right hand. Sam recoiled as though he'd experienced a sharp pain. "I don't think I <u>can</u> sign. You ruined my writing hand with that dammed fountain pen."

"Come on, Sam. I know you're left handed. Get on with it."

Sam shifted the pen to his left hand, but stopped again before he signed. "How many people will see this signature while you're 'arranging for the authorities' to see this document—when and if I don't hold up my end of the bargain?"

"Just James Laurence and me. He's my attorney. He'll help me set up a foolproof system for processing this document under any of several eventualities, here and in Grand Junction. You should never test the system we set up. It will be designed to blowup in your face."

Sam bent over the papers. "Don't forget the initial 'H' in your signature," Monroe reminded.

"Shit. You don't even know what the 'H' is for."

"It's for your middle name, Sam."

"Yeah, yeah. You're probably right, but what's my middle name, Asshole?"

"Harold, Sam. Harold's your middle name. Now, can we get the signing done? Or, are you getting so you like it down there."

Sam signed, put the papers and the pen in the basket, taped the lid and tied the basket to the binder's twine. He stepped back and said: "How're you going to get me up?"

"I'll let you know that when I've looked at the paper."

Monroe cranked the winch and the lantern came up first. Monroe set it aside. He grabbed the string and hauled the basket up. He ripped the tape off the wicker. The signature was dated. The signature was authentic.

"Okay. When do I get out?" Sam shouted.

"Tomorrow," Monroe answered.

"You sonuvabitch. You sonuvabitch. You said 'today', you bastard."

"Sam. Let's quit arguing. I'm going to send food and water, and then I'm going to leave. I'll be back tomorrow."

"No. Goddammit! Let me out."

"Look at it this way, Sam. You're going to stay where you are—unless you told someone where you were going when you came here. Did you?"

"Did I what?"

"Did you tell anyone you were coming out here yesterday?" answered Monroe, a little impatiently.

"No. I didn't."

"Then, no one's coming for you, Sam. Just take this food and water and wait for me until tomorrow."

"Why can't you let me out now? I signed the papers," argued Sam, dejectedly.

"I know, and I appreciate it, but I want to take the papers to James and give him twenty-four hours to make the proper arrangements. You see how important that is, don't you. We're going to make it impossible for you to wriggle out from under your responsibilities to Harold without the authorities and the news papers knowing about your confessions and the real objectives of the Ku Klux Klan in Colorado."

"Give me the food," said a resigned Sam.

Monroe sent down the ham sandwiches and a full gallon of water, as well as a lantern full of kerosene.

"Sam. I'm leaving now. Have you got matches?"

"So, what?"

"I thought you might want to turn the lantern out when you sleep. If you don't, I'm not sure how long the kerosene will last."

"Don't worry about me, Asshole."

"Okay. But be careful with that platform rope. Don't burn it up. I'll need it to lift you out of there next time I come."

* * *

Just after 4 P.M. the following day, Monroe returned to Porter. He had turned the confession and the agreement over to James. James had gone active to establish a system of checks and balances for the safety of Harold, as well as peace and security for Wade and Monroe. Monroe felt good about the arrangements. He was anxious to turn Sam loose. He wanted to urge Sam to return to Harold and be a good father.

When Monroe approached the deep shaft and peered into the darkness, he could see a lit lantern and a man sitting motionless with his back against the wall. Sam turned his face upward and squinted quizzically. "Sam. I'm back. Are you ready to come up."

"You know damn well, I am. What do you want me to do?"

"I'll thread the twine down to you. You tie it to the end of the lift rope. I'll pull the rope up. When I get the rope attached to the winch, I'll crank you up.

Monroe worked carefully and when he finally believed he was ready to lift the platform from the bottom of the pit, he shouted, "Get on the lift, Sam. I'll bring you up a little, and stop. You check everything over. If you find anything wrong, let me know."

"What'll I look for?"

"Well. The platform should be fairly level. Make sure the ropes are in good repair—not tangled or torn so they might break. See that there isn't anything protruding from the sides of the platform—to get caught on the sides of the shaft. Stuff like that."

Moments later, Monroe heard Sam say, "Everything looks okay to me. Haul me up."

As Sam's head cleared the surface, Monroe stopped the winch and watched Sam carefully. "Haven't got another gun have you, Sam?" Believing Sam was clean, he latched the drum into a locked position and stepped back. He pulled Sam's revolver from his belt and said: "All right, Sam. Head for the slope tunnel."

Monroe followed Sam until they were outside the mine. "Now, I'm going to put you in your car and let you leave."

Sam hiked silently up the tunnel and down the hillside to the thick clump of oak bushes where he'd hidden his car. Monroe followed observing every move. At the car, Monroe said, "I know you've got a room at the Strater. And I can see no reason for you to be in town tomorrow. You may have some loose ends to take care of—like seeing Bob, talking on the telephone—the business you just have to get done. The only thing is: I don't want to learn that you've over stayed your welcome. Rest assured, my spies will be watching."

"What about my gun? Are you going to steal it?"

"I'll send it to you. Now, get out of here. Remember we have a bargain. Take good care of Harold and leave Wade and me in peace. If you don't, I assure you the newspapers and the authorities will learn that the great social leader and politician on Colorado's Western Slope is actually a bigot, a murder and a charlatan. All the people named in the confession will owe you their thanks for the trouble you've caused them."

Monroe watched the car find the road to Durango and turn right toward town. Instead of joy, he felt an unspeakable sorrow. A gripping hurt for all that had gone before. All his losses came tumbling in. First he experienced the loss of his mother, then the loss of Charlie, next his boyhood home, and then Bonnie. Oh God! How could he survive?

The moment of sorrow was almost too much for Monroe to bear. He sank to his knees, there in Wildcat Canyon, and prayed for strength. He closed his eyes to pray for himself, for Harold, for Wade, for Bonnie, and then, he felt the presence of Charlie nearby. Opening his eyes he stared into the deep black eyes of Charlie Eagle. The black Prince Albert coat, the striped pants, the spats, all seemed a part of Charlie now. Charlie's closeness startled him. Charlie seemed to be trying to tell him something. Though Charlie did not speak, he shook his finger from side to side, as if to say, "Don't feel sorry for yourself." and then he moved away. Monroe's thoughts turned in a different direction. He couldn't help wondering about Harold's future? Wade's? His own? And he realized that he couldn't stay in Wildcat Canyon forever. He must go to Bonnie. He must let her know that Sam had been dealt with.

Monroe turned back toward the mine. Retracing his steps up the hill, he angled toward the superintendent's house. On the other side of the house, he went directly to the shed and his truck. He jumped in the truck, started the engine and headed for Greenmount Cemetery.

CHAPTER TWENTY-TWO

(July 1923)

In Greenmount Cemetery, Monroe parked his truck near Bonnie's grave. The overwhelming grief he'd experienced when Sam drove away, was still with him. Charlie's chiding about self-pity had helped, and now, he thought he'd feel better when Sam actually left Durango.

Remembering the conditions in the graveyard last night, Monroe hoped to give Bonnie an unobstructed view of the brilliant moon, so he sank to his knees on Bonnie's right. He peered in all directions, hoping to see deer or elk, but none appeared. Maybe later.

Monroe brushed a sharp pebble from beneath his right knee as though it were somehow related to Sam's final irritation. He began his chat with Bonnie by explaining that Sam would be gone tomorrow. Next came a revelation of his confusion, his pain, and his exhaustion. He talked constantly—even if he didn't make sense. "Honey, I've been wondering where I'm going from here—without you? If we were together now, we could get married. You're legally divorced, you know—single."

He stared at the moon, hoping his mind would stop wandering. In the night's silence, the smoke from the smelter furnaces entered his nostrils. Something kept nagging—scratching at his soul. It wasn't Sam. Somehow, he'd moved beyond Sam. But what was it? Nothing really mattered since Bonnie left. And yet, from time to time, he seemed to strike an impediment, a jog in his line of thinking. He took the deviation casually at first. But soon he began to expect the interruption to repeat itself. With that, he became more attentive to his thinking. Then, deliberately, he began to concentrate, deeply. He analyzed the confusing thoughts and sensations. Lo and behold! The answer struck him like a stick of exploding dynamite. It was Wade struggling for a place in his thinking! And now, quite suddenly, Wade was everything. His <u>direction</u> reappeared. He had a reason for <u>living</u>!

Monroe placed his hands on the grassy mound before him. "Honey, I've been a nearsighted fool! There <u>is</u> something to live for. There's someone we <u>both</u> love. Someone for me to work for. Someone to struggle for. It's <u>Wade</u>, Honey! It's <u>Wade</u>!" Monroe rose to his feet, raised his arms to the moon, and quietly gave thanks to God.

As he continued to pray, several elk cautiously entered the grassy glade. They moved haltingly, at first, as though they'd traveled far and feared a penalty for being late. Finally, they confidently entered from all sides.

Almost giddy with joy, Monroe knelt again. "I'm going to mark your grave with something special, my darling. No one will touch the monument but me. I'll start with wood. Granite takes too long. You need a headstone, now. I'll glue hardwood together—carve it. Wood won't last long, but I'll make something better!"

The moon was nearly overhead. "Honey. I'm going to take Wade to Cascade as soon as possible. I'll rebuild our house. We'll live in it. Maybe, I'll hire people to help." Then a disturbing thought crowded in. "And Honey, one day—I know it'll happen—I'll fail to visit. I worry about it—and I don't know what to do about it. I just want you to know that when it happens, you shouldn't think I love you any the less. I'll simply be out of town or something like that—maybe going to Grand Junction for peach juice or something. Who knows what could intervene."

Monroe gazed into the dark. "Guess that's about it for today, Honey. Just wanted to keep you posted. I'll love and adore you forever, my darling. Things will be all right.

Don't worry." He heard the snort of a bull elk nearby. "This is such a beautiful place, sweetheart. I'll be glad to join you, when I've raised our son."

* * *

Monroe was exhausted as he drove from Greenmount toward the Laurences, but his head was consumed with plans. He now had confidence that the minutes, the hours and the days ahead would help him recover from these past dreary weeks. He was buoyed by the need to raise his son. He didn't have that objective when he knelt earlier at Bonnie's grave. Maybe he could take Wade to Cascade with him—now—while he was living in the bunkhouse and making repairs. But who would care for Wade while he ran to the still, sold whiskey, bought material and worked on the house. A nanny! That's what he needed! A full time someone for Wade. A mature, responsible, educated someone.

He'd talk to Mabel. She might be able to recommend a proper person. He'd certainly ask her advice regarding whomever he hired. Maybe John could recommend a good carpenter to reconstruct the house. The Jackson boys might help rebuild the water system.

Too many jobs working at once might be a mistake. He'd slow down and plan wisely. Replace the barn next summer.

As he drove through town, he turned toward the Strater Hotel. Sam's car might be parked there. If he found no car, Sam might be gone. He hoped Sam would see him checking. He wanted Sam to know how serious he was.

Monroe drove slowly past the front of the hotel. There was no light in Room 323. It was almost eleven P.M. He drove completely around the hotel. As he came east on Sixth Street, he saw Sam's car. Sam was probably asleep—getting ready for an early start to Grand Junction. He'd go into the hotel and ask for Isgar, tomorrow. If Sam were still there, he'd look him up.

Suddenly, Monroe experienced a wave of euphoria. Now, Sam was the hunted.

* * *

When Monroe pulled into the Laurence driveway, Mabel came to the living room window and observed his arrival. The front door opened as he stepped onto the stoop.

Mabel said, "Come on in. We've been waiting."

Monroe smiled. "Okay. What've I done now?"

Both John and James appeared as Monroe entered. They turned back to the living room.

Mabel closed the door. "You look like something the cat dragged in."

"It's been a heckuva day. But I think I got rid of Sam Isgar."

James said, "I went to the Evening Herald and made copies of the confession. The original is in my new safe. A copy is in your safe-deposit box at the First National Bank. A third is in the hands of our district attorney and he has another copy for the district attorney in Grand Junction. Each envelope bears the same message: "Open in the event of a special message from James Laurence or Monroe Morgan, and/or upon mysterious circumstances occurring with the death of Monroe Morgan."

"Thanks, my friend. Send me a bill," Monroe grinned. Then, seeing a slight smile on James face, he said: "I'm serious."

"I know. I know," James said, waving him off.

Monroe expressed his desire to rebuild Cascade and raise Wade at the ranch. Mabel couldn't recommend anyone for Wade's nanny. She did suggest that Monroe put an ad in the Herald, use the Laurence's phone for respondents and let her do the interviewing. She thought her home would provide an accessible place for applicants and free Monroe for other things.

"I agree with all of your suggestions, folks," Monroe said. "I'll never be able to thank you properly."

"And I'll scout around for a good carpenter," John said.

"I thought I'd try to hire the Jackson boys to help me rebuild the water system. I want to get the house and the water system done this summer—try to rebuild the barn next year."

"Good plan," John said.

"Leave Wade here, until you get a housekeeper," Mabel said.

With that, Monroe left for Cascade and his bunkhouse: a tired man, but a lifted man.

* * *

In the following days, Monroe made sure Sam Isgar had left Durango. He hired the Jackson boys, and with John's help, acquired a carpenter who would assume full responsibility for rebuilding the house. Still, after advertising for two weeks in the Durango Herald, Mabel had discarded, out of hand, all applicants seeking to care for Wade. Perhaps more disconcerting, Monroe hadn't finished a marker for Bonnie's grave.

However, at the beginning of the third week, Monroe decided to take Wade with him while he shopped for groceries and run errands in town. He felt the need to have his son with him whenever possible.

In town, Monroe found the Mason & Ambold Grocery a busy place, and there among the vegetables, he chanced to meet Charlie's parents as they moved to leave the store.

"Well, I didn't know you were in town," Monroe said, shaking Joseph's hand.

"We've been helping my brother at Breen. My other son, Theodore, is a good shearer." Mary hugged Monroe.

"A little late for shearing sheep, isn't it?" asked Monroe.

"Depends on the wool. Late spring or early summer is okay," Mary said. "How are you, my son?"

"Pretty good, Mother Eagle. Just trying to get lined out."

"We heard you got out of jail," Mary said.

"Yes, Mother Eagle. I've been out for a while, but I've been wondering about something. I meant to ask you when you visited me in jail. Where is my brother, Charlie?"

"He is with the spirits, my son." Mary seemed to think he should know that.

"I know, but where?"

"Oh. He's on a high mountain in Arizona. He sleeps in his own window. Looks out for you every day," Joseph said.

Mary's expression changed to sadness. "When you come visit us, we'll take you there. He would like to see you."

Monroe fell silent and starred at his feet while thinking of Charlie.

"You are changed, my son," Mary said.

"How so, Mother Eagle?"

"Your eyes are empty. They see too far away."

"I'm sorry," Mother Eagle.

"Yes, my son—too sorry." Mary grasped Monroe's hand. "You have too much sorrow."

Monroe looked away to the colorful labels marking cans of food on a shelf. He had nothing to say.

Joseph interrupted. "You working on your house—rebuilding?"

"Yes. Among other things." Monroe dabbed a tear with the back of his hand.

"Take Theodore for your house. He's a good worker. Needs a job when he's through shearing."

"Well, Joseph, that's probably a good idea. But, what I need is a woman to care for my son. Wade needs a mother. I want Wade with me, but I need a woman who can stay there and help my boy grow up."

"Take Rachel."

Monroe stared at Mary. "Your sister? The one who went to school at Fort Lewis—then got married?"

"Yes. She's smart—and lonesome. She needs a baby boy."

Monroe looked eagerly at Mary. "Didn't she have a boy?"

"The flu took him. Four years ago," said Mary.

"I'm sorry. I didn't know. Maybe Charlie said something. I don't remember. Where's her husband?"

"He died, too. Same flu—remember?"

"Oh. I remember the epidemic, all right." Monroe was awe struck. "People were dying everywhere. Hundreds died here in Durango. 1918 and 1919. No one can forget. Did she lose her husband and her child at the same time?"

"No. Her boy died in 1918. Her husband died in 1919. Rachel would be a good mother for your boy." Joseph nodded his head.

"Where is Rachel? Window Rock?" asked Monroe.

"No. She's here. She's cooking for the men who shear the sheep."

"How old is she, Mother?"

"Forty."

"I'll get a newspaper and show you the ad I'm running." Monroe stepped to the front of the store. When he returned, he said, "I've been letting Mrs. Laurence—James' mother— do the interviewing. Do you think Rachel would like to answer the ad?"

"Why not. She's not Indian anymore. Since school, she's white-eye."

"She sounds great to me, Mother Eagle. How long did she attend Fort Lewis?"

"Six years. She studied reading, writing and arithmetic every morning. Cooking, sewing and cleaning in the afternoons. She lived at the school.

"The school was a little before my time, but if she's interested, have her call this number and make an appointment with Mrs. Laurence. I'll tell Mrs. Laurence to let me know if Rachel comes in, then, I'll be sure to be there for the interview. Okay? And, if you'll tell Theodore to come see me, maybe we can get together on something after he's through with the sheep. I've got to get back to the truck and check on Wade. Then, as a second thought: "Oh. What's Rachel's last name?"

"Velarde. Rachel Velarde." Mary and Joseph moved toward the truck with Monroe. "Is your boy with you in the car?"

"Yes. Want to see him?"

"I want to see my grandson," Mary said, eagerly.

Mary and Joseph followed Monroe to the truck where Wade played in a bushel basket situated on the front floorboards. Mary's "ohs" and "ahs" drowned Wade's "oo's" and "goo's," and Monroe thought he'd be lucky if Mary didn't eat the child. Finally, Mary backed away and Monroe moved to toward the grocery store. The Eagles waved goodbye and Monroe went in the store.

* * *

When Monroe took Wade back to the Laurences, he told Mabel of his meeting with the Eagles. Mabel said she'd keep him informed, and he turned to chat with James.

"I talked to District Attorney, Joe O'Riley today," James said. "He thinks they'll turn Carméllo Basíllo loose. Don't have enough evidence to hold him. They believe he poisoned the hooch, but can't prove it. In fact, there's no way to prove he broke any laws."

Disappointed, Monroe turned the full blame for Bonnie's death on himself. Why did he let his curiosity steer him to that cabin? Why did he steal the whiskey?

"Stop it!" James snapped. "You're starting to blame yourself again. We've been over that a hundred times. You've got a boy to raise."

True, Monroe thought. Maybe he'd never stop blaming himself. Maybe he'd never cease hurting deep inside. Maybe this was his punishment. "You're right," he said. "But who else is there to blame."

"Performing your responsibilities to Wade maybe all God expects, right now," said James.

Monroe placed a hand on James shoulder. "James, try to figure how much I owe you. I'm sure I'll never be able to pay, no matter what."

"I'm keeping good records, so save your money," advised James.

"Don't forget to add the bill for doctoring."

"That's the most expensive part of my work," James said. "Are you going to see Bonnie before you go home tonight?"

"Yes. But, I want to work on her headstone, too. Maybe I can install it tomorrow.

* * *

The next day dawned gray and full of mist. Monroe finished the chores and hurried back to the bunkhouse. In addition to putting the marker on Bonnie's grave, he wanted to spend time working the still at Porter. Also, he thought he'd shop for things he hadn't picked up yesterday. Perhaps, he'd go see Sheriff Howe. Certainly, the men working at Cascade could do without him for another day.

After he'd washed, shaved, and eaten a hearty breakfast, he felt good. His liquor sales were up and he'd been contemplating another trip to Grand Junction. He really needed more fermented peach juice.

He loaded the gravesite marker onto the truck. Then, he tossed in a pick, a shovel, and a bag of cement mix. He wasn't happy with the marker. It wasn't big enough, it wasn't the right color, it didn't have quite the right words on it, and the wood wasn't the right wood. Nothing was right. But, he would set the dammed thing up, anyway. At least, it wouldn't fall down anytime soon. He'd start another marker. He'd try wrought iron next time. Iron would certainly last longer than wood. He really wanted granite—maybe?

After positioning the memorial in the graveyard, he embedded it in cement, then, loaded his tools and the remaining material onto the truck, and headed for Porter. But, just as he turned toward Greenmount's main gate, he recognized a Duesenberg pulling up the hill. It looked like the same car he'd dragged away from the revetment at Junction Creek. Could it be Fletch Farmer? He kept an eye on the driver and as they passed each other, they both waved excitedly. They both slammed on the brakes and backed up.

"Hello," said the man in the Duesenberg. "Don't I know you?"

"I think so," Monroe said. "I seem to recognize your car as the one I pulled away from a culvert last year."

"Fletch Farmer," the man identified himself, climbing from his car. "And you're Monroe Morgan. How could I forget you? You did me a big favor."

"Well. It's a pleasure seeing you again," Monroe said, getting out and shaking Fletch's out-stretched hand. "I've got that sample from my mine and I've been intending to send it to you. Just haven't found the time."

"I'll take it with me when I go back. I guess we're both busy."

"You still in Denver? Still doing assays?" asked Monroe.

"Yes, but why don't we meet for supper tonight? You bring your sample and I'll take it back with me. We can eat and talk."

"That's fine," Monroe said. "How about the Strater at seven o'clock?"

"Great," Fletch said. "I'm just visiting the grave of a family friend, and then I'm going to the smelter. So, I'll see you tonight."

"Look forward to it." They shook hands and drove away.

* * *

Monroe turned south on Roosa Avenue and headed toward the burned-out shack where Wade was born. When he approached Wade's birthplace, his heart ached with memories. He gazed at the ashes where the bedbug-ridden house had stood. Near the corral and behind the tack room, he was surprised to see two horsemen sitting astride their mounts. They seemed to be staring across the river at Durango. Bob Stout and Earl Mills!

Monroe turned in. He couldn't resist the urge to stop and engage the deputies in conversation.

Bob and Earl turned in their saddles as he approached. He slid to a stop near their horses while maintaining a smile on his face.

"Well, imagine me finding you two here," Monroe said, turning his engine off. "Do you remember what happened here last September? Remember our conversation?"

"Yeah," Bob said. "We were just talking about that. You said Mrs. Isgar wasn't here—but she was."

"Well. You boys and your friend, Sam Isgar, gave Bonnie and me a lot of trouble after that. Your support of Sam sure off-sets any lying I may have done—don't you think." Monroe felt his temper smoldering.

"Now, wait a minute, Morgan. Don't start getting all tightened up. There's been plenty changes," Bob said. "We were both just saying how sorry we are for our part in your difficulties. And we want to tell you that we know you've

383

got us over a barrel. We talked to Sam before he left town. He didn't say much, but he asked us to change our attitude. Said you could make big trouble for us. So, we're willing to tell you that we're sorry and that we're going to try to forget the past."

"We're sorry for your loss—your wife, I mean—which we had nothing to do with," Earl said.

"You're members of the Klan, and I expect you'll be doing your duty to that organization, won't you?" asked Monroe.

"We think the Klan's dying. Sam's turned everything over to Reverend Davis. He's not the go-getter Sam was."

"Doesn't Sam plan to come back to Durango?" asked Monroe, as a feeler.

"Don't think so," Earl said. "And from what we hear, the Klan's fading in Grand Junction, too."

"Well," Monroe said, "there's nothing here but ashes, so, if it's all the same to you boys, I'm willing to let the past remain—ashes. I've got a boy to raise. If you stay out of my business, I'll stay out of yours."

Monroe started his engine, put the truck in gear, and headed for Porter. He looked at his watch. It was late. He'd have to hurry if he took care of Porter and got back to Cascade for his ore sample before he met Fletch at seven o'clock.

* * *

Monroe enjoyed dinner and his visit with Fletch. He was glad to turn the ore sample over for assessment, but after the dinner was over and the ore sample transferred, Monroe was anxious to go home. He was tired and it was 10:15. As he approached the bunkhouse, he heard the house phone ringing off the hook. He hurried across the separator porch, grabbed the receiver and said: "Hello." The line was dead.

He wracked his brain for a logical caller. Maybe James had a thought that couldn't wait until tomorrow. Maybe something was wrong? Maybe Wade was sick?

He rang Central to get the Laurences.

"Hello."

"I hope I didn't disturb you, James, but when I started for the bunkhouse, I heard the phone. Thought it might be you."

"Yeah. Mother got a call from Rachel Velarde. I was trying every five minutes. Rachel will be here at 3 tomorrow. Can you make it?"

"Sure. I'll be there. I really want to meet her. Thanks for the call. Anything else?"

"Well. I talked with Sheriff Howe this afternoon. He said they let Carméllo Basíllo go."

Monroe felt disappointment. "I guess we knew that was going to happen."

"I suppose," agreed James.

Sucking in a deep breath, Monroe said, "See you tomorrow, if you're around when Rachel shows up."

* * *

About 2:45 P.M. the next day, Monroe parked in the Laurence driveway leaving space for Rachel. He wondered if she'd be alone.

He hadn't been in the house five minutes when he saw a white horse pulling a black, canopied buggy toward the Laurences. On the seat sat a tall, straight and slender woman with a long whip in her hand. She appeared to be all business. The buggy slowed to a walk just before it reached the driveway. There was no hesitation or guessing about where this woman was going.

Monroe shouted over his shoulder. "I think Rachel's here, Mabel."

Mabel came from the kitchen carrying Wade's highchair. She peeked around the draped window and raised an eyebrow. "Good looking woman." She placed the highchair at a focal point in the room. "Clean and well dressed. You get Wade. I'll open the door."

Monroe re-entered the room carrying Wade. He saw, through the window, a tall, handsome Indian woman; impeccably dressed. She wore a black suit, white blouse, black cloche hat and gloves to match. Her shiny black hair was bobbed in the style of the day. Her smooth dark skin fit snuggly over an artistically structured face. This physically strong woman was obviously not a field hand—nor simply a cook.

Mabel opened the door. "How do you do. Mrs. Velarde?"

"Yes. Mrs. Laurence?" questioned Rachel.

"Yes. Please come in," Mabel invited. "Mr. Morgan is with us today. He wanted to meet you."

Rachel entered the living room and smiled upon seeing Monroe standing near Wade. "Wonderful. I've been looking forward to meeting Mr. Morgan and the baby."

"Well. This is Wade Morgan," Mabel said, gesturing to the dark-haired boy in a blue jumpsuit, "and this is his father, Mr. Monroe Morgan." Mabel's hand pointed to Monroe.

"I'm pleased to meet you, Mr. Morgan. I've heard so much about you from my nephew Charlie. May God rest his soul?"

"And I'm glad to meet you, Rachel. Please call me 'Monroe. I think it's strange we've never met."

"I think so, too."

"Please, have a seat over here, Mrs. Velarde." Mabel touched a straight-backed chair. "I'm going to place Wade next to you. After all, he's the reason we're interviewing. We're looking for a lady to take complete charge—within certain guidelines, of course. Monroe and I will sit here." Mabel pointed to chairs arranged for a relaxed but discerning interview.

Rachel took the chair indicated and continued her pervious thought. "I'm a little older than you are—Monroe. I probably finished my schooling and got married before you completed High School."

When all were seated, Mabel asked: "How old are you, Rachel? Well ..." Mabel interrupted herself. "Why don't you just tell us a little about yourself? That might be best."

"Of course." Rachel removed her gloves and laid them over a medium-sized black and white purse, which she'd placed in her lap. She looked at ease with her legs crossed at the ankles, her back straight and her black shoes with two-inch heels placed comfortably in front of her chair. "I'm forty years old. I graduated from Fort Lewis Indian School in 1904 after six years of study. We were not allowed to speak our native tongue nor were we allowed to wear our native dress. Dr. Breen was very strict about that. Dr. Breen found it difficult to pronounce our Indian names so we all took names from the bible or from public life. "Rachel," as you know, is biblical, and Theodore, Charlie's brother, is after Theodore Roosevelt." She smiled. "We girls studied reading, writing and arithmetic each morning. In the afternoons: cooking, laundry, cleaning and sewing. We lived at the school. Everyday, except Sunday, was the same. Sunday was the day we studied Christianity.

"I married George Velarde in 1905. We had a boy, Harry, in 1907. Harry would have been fifteen, now. My son died in 1918—during the flu epidemic. My husband died in 1919—also a flu victim. I've been alone since that time. I want to help with Wade."

Monroe cleared his throat. He gazed at Mabel. Mabel fidgeted with her handkerchief and studied Wade.

"I'm going to pour tea," Mabel said, rising. "Would you care for tea or coffee, Rachel? I have both."

Rachel's dark eyes followed Mabel. "That would be very nice. I'll have tea, please." She glanced at Monroe.

"And you," Mabel asked, looking at Monroe.

"Could I have coffee, please?"

Monroe turned his attention to Rachel. He saw a very special lady. He wanted her for Wade's nanny. She seemed ideal, but he'd wait for Mabel. "Where were you born?"

"Window Rock—our ranch, there. I'm Navajo. I'm sorry. I should have mentioned that in answer to Mrs. Laurence's question. I was among the first Navajos to attend Fort Lewis. My mother and father wanted all their children to cope."

Monroe smiled. "It seems to me you've done very well."

Mabel entered with a large tray furnished with tea and coffee. She poured from the teapot and served Rachel. She handed Monroe his coffee.

Mabel took her tea and asked, "Would you be able to move to Cascade, Mrs. Velarde?"

"Oh yes." Rachel answered without hesitation. "It would be my life. I have nothing, now. I have no place on the reservation."

Mabel reflected a moment. "And what recompense would you expect?"

"That would be up to Mr. Morgan—Monroe."

"You realize that the position would make you responsible for Wade and the entire house. You'd have the cleaning, the laundry, the cooking—everything."

"Of course."

"And, if hired, when would you be available?"

"I'm available immediately. But I will make myself open to your offer whenever it's convenient for you."

"Do you know where the Morgan's ranch is—where you'd be working?"

"I know it's in Animas Valley—east of the river, I think, and about nine miles out. I don't know exactly."

"The house has been damaged—extensively, and even though it's being repaired, it may be sometime before the house is livable. Would it be inconvenient for you to live and work in a house where construction is in progress? Would it be a hindrance of any kind?"

Rachel picked up her gloves. "Not in the least."

"Is there a phone where we could reach you—or an address? I think it's just a matter of determining a point in time when you can start. As I see it, the house should be livable, but not necessarily finished. Is that right, Monroe?"

Monroe shifted happily in his chair. "Yes. And I think the house will be livable in about two weeks, if everything goes as planned. We may have to carry water or cook among litter for a short time—four to six weeks—but no longer. Let's plan on two weeks and if something unforeseen happens, we can work around it."

"Let me call you every three days, beginning next Monday," Rachel said. "If things change significantly, we can move my starting date up or slide it back. How would that be?"

Mabel seemed pleased. "That would be wonderful, Rachel. How do you feel, Monroe?"

"Sounds great to me. And you notice Wade hasn't cried once."

Rachel stood and reached for Wades hands. "I'm anxious to know him."

* * *

For Monroe, the two weeks seemed to drag, but true to her word, Rachel called every three days. She was proving to be "a real jewel", Monroe thought.

Finally, the big day arrived. Rachel and her bags appeared at Cascade. She drove into the yard with her white horse prancing and the wheels of her black buggy spinning. She explained that Theodore would come on horseback and take the buggy back.

It was a bright and warm July day, so Rachel traveled bareheaded and let her bobbed hair fly while her full skirt billowed. The blue blouse, the tan skirt, the black oxfords and the white horse with the black buggy blended nicely into the green countryside.

"Welcome to Cascade," Monroe greeted her. "Let me show you your room, then we can go for Wade." He felt as though an old friend were arriving for a long stay.

"I've been so excited since Mrs. Laurence set the day," said Rachel, setting her reins aside and climbed from the buggy. Monroe tied the horse to the hitching rail.

"We'll just take your things inside," he said.

"This is all I own, so you can see I've come to stay."

"We're all extremely happy about that," said Monroe. "I want you to be comfortable. I'm going to do my best to see that you are."

Monroe removed a trunk and set it by the screen door. Returning, he reached two large bags sitting on the buggy's floor. Rachel gathered her purse, a hatbox and a smaller bag. She held the screen door for Monroe when he passed through with the trunk.

"We'll go right ahead to your room, if you don't mind," Monroe said, indicating the kitchen door.

They crowded across the separator porch and Rachel held the kitchen door while Monroe sidestepped and angled into the kitchen. He led the way through the living room, past the stairs, and down the hall to a large corner bedroom that looked out over the lush green valley. A small herd of white-faced cattle grazed near the river. The western red rock mountains jutted into the sky.

"Oh, what a beautiful room!" Rachel gushed. "The view is breath-taking."

"This part of the house wasn't damaged. And, I want you to notice, right across the hall is a smaller room. I thought that room might be a good place for Wade, but if you want to change things around, you can."

"Perfect," Rachel said, placing her belongings on the double bed.

Monroe placed the trunk on a bench at the foot of the bed and said, "Fine then. I'll bring the suit cases, put up your rig, and you can go with me into town."

"Take your truck?"

"Yes. If you don't mind?"

"Not at all. I like cars, but I haven't ridden in many."

* * *

When they returned to Cascade with Wade, Monroe noticed his stuffed mailbox at the edge of the road. He helped Rachel into the house, and then, lifted Wade to his shoulders and walked to the mailbox. Rachel began her job of unpacking.

Rummaging through the mail, Monroe found a letter from Fletch Farmer. He quickly deposited Wade on a grassy spot beside the mailbox and surrounded him with envelopes to keep his attention. Monroe, then, ripped the flap from Farmer's message. It was his assay report. The information indicated that the sample he'd submitted was significantly heavy in carnotite—mostly carnotite, in fact.

Monroe gazed at the paper in disbelief. He had assumed that the ore would assay heavy in gold—perhaps some vanadium. At least that's what his father had predicted. Now he had tons of carnotite and he didn't even know what it was. Thank God for the personal note, handwritten by Fletch.

Eagerly he read: "I remember you said this ore is quite a distance back in the mountains and that it would be difficult to retrieve. You were also thinking of gold. Sorry. There is some gold here, but it probably wouldn't pay to dig or haul it out. However, as you can see, your sample is heavy in carnotite. Carnotite is a complex compound of uranium.

Your carnotite is mixed with vanadium, potassium, and oxygen. There doesn't seem to be a great urgency to mine the stuff, right now, but who knows what the future may bring. Don't sell this claim, my friend, and look me up, if you ever come to Denver. Fletch Farmer."

Monroe leaned an elbow on the mailbox. He gazed over the burnt-out barn, beyond the river of lost souls flowing through the lush valley below. He looked into the magnificent San Juan Mountains, and then, past the brilliant white clouds that floated in the sparkling sky. He wished he could tell Bonnie about the note. But when he knelt to gather his son and the remaining mail, the corner of his eye caught the figure of a small man in a black Prince Albert suit. The fellow was walking slowly away up the road. Charlie was leaving! Monroe watched until his friend turned and waved, then, he lifted his own arm and moved his fingers hesitantly. Charlie was gone.

Bending to Wade, again, Monroe said: "Do you have any idea how much you look like your mother?" Wade gurgled and swung an arm at the descending face.

"No? Well, big boy, then listen to this: my father gave me a gold mine when he left and I'm going to give you a uranium mine when I pass on. What do you think of that?"

THE END

ABOUT THE AUTHOR

The author was born on the west bank of the Animas River (dubbed: El Rio de las Animas Perdidas, and translated: The River of Lost Souls) near downtown Durango, Colorado, on September 5, 1922. The following day his determined grandmother burned the shack while killing bedbugs. With that inauspicious beginning, the author continued his education on the western slopes of Colorado. After completing high school in Beaver City, Oklahoma, he started college at the University of Southern California and finished with a Bachelor of Science Degree in Great Falls, Montana when he was fifty-six years old. He served in the United States Navy during World War II, was a contract player for Metro-Goldwyn-Mayer, did night club stints as a singer-master-of-ceremonies, worked in construction and finished his career as an Industrial Engineer for the United States Air Force Procurement Division in Albuquerque, New Mexico.

Printed in the United States
79785LV00001B/19-21